GW00391104

The SQL Server 6.5 Performance Optimization and Tuning Handbook

The SQL Server 6.5 Performance Optimization and Tuning Handbook

Ken England

Digital Press
Boston • Oxford • Johannesburg • Melbourne • New Delhi • Singapore

Butterworth–Heinemann supports the efforts of American Forests and the Global ReLeaf program in its campaign for the betterment of trees, forests, and our environment.

Library of Congress Cataloging-in-Publication Data

England, Ken, 1955–
    The SQL server 6.5 performance optimization and tuning handbook /
  Ken England.
        p.   cm.
        Includes index.
        ISBN 1-55558-180-3 (pbk. : alk. paper)
        1. Client / server computing.   2. SQL server.   3. Database design.
I. Title.
QA76.9.C55E64   1997
005.75'85—dc21   97-10627
                                                                                  CIP

British Library Cataloguing-in-Publication Data

A catalogue record for this book is available from the British Library.

The publisher offers special discounts on bulk orders of this book.
For information, please contact:
Manager of Special Sales
Butterworth–Heinemann
225 Wildwood Avenue
Woburn, MA 01801-2041
Tel: 617-928-2500
Fax: 617-928-2620

For information on all Digital Press publications available, contact our World Wide Web home page at: http://www.bh.com/digitalpress

Order number: EY-W086E-DP

10   9   8   7   6   5   4   3   2   1

Printed in the United States of America

Dedication

To Margaret, Michael and Katy,

Together again at last.

Contents

Preface

There is no doubt that the combination of Windows NT and SQL Server is proving to be extremely popular. Many companies are using these and other Microsoft products to build their next generation of applications.

There are many reasons for this. The Windows NT and SQL Server combination offers excellent price performance in an area of software development that has been traditionally very expensive. The integration of SQL Server with other products such as Microsoft Access, Visual Basic, SMS and, of course, Microsoft's Internet product suite have made it the obvious choice for many new developments and have guaranteed Microsoft SQL Server a place in many companies' database shortlist.

As the demands on SQL Server grow, because companies want larger and faster databases supporting hundreds of users instead of just a handful, so does the requirement for SQL Server performance tuning and optimization. The more data in a database the more important it is to ensure that appropriate indexes are created to support complex queries and the more users accessing a database the more important it is to be able to avoid lock contention.

This book is about such topics, from the initial physical design to the ongoing monitoring and tuning of SQL Server and Windows NT. The chapters are written to follow one another in a logical fashion, building on some of the topics introduced in previous chapters. The structure of the chapters is as follows:

- ▶ Chapter 1 introduces the goals of performance tuning and the elements of the physical database design process including data volume analysis and transaction analysis. It also introduces the example *Banking* database.

- ▶ Chapter 2 describes the SQL Server storage structures including database devices, databases, database pages, extents, allocation units, and data rows.

▶ Chapter 3 introduces clustered indexes and nonclustered indexes, how data is inserted and retrieved, and choosing the appropriate index for a given situation.

▶ Chapter 4 introduces the query optimizer and steps in the query optimization process. This chapter also discusses the different types of update performed by SQL Server and the special approach to query optimization used by stored procedures.

▶ Chapter 5 looks at the interaction between SQL Server and Windows NT in the areas of CPU, memory, and disk I/O. How to track down bottlenecks and remove them is explored.

▶ Chapter 6 introduces SQL Server locking mechanisms and strategies and the methods and tools available for monitoring locks.

▶ Chapter 7 looks at performance monitoring and the tools available to assist the database administrator.

▶ Chapter 8 provides a performance tuning checklist.

I really enjoy tuning databases and making them run fast. Even more, I really enjoy taking an elusive performance problem, tracking it down, and fixing it. I hope you too find the same level of enjoyment that I do and that this book kick-starts your interest in performance tuning SQL Server.

Acknowledgments

Most of all, I would like to thank Margaret, Michael, and Katy England for their long suffering while I was locked in my study writing this text. Writing about databases is, unfortunately, not an activity in which most of the family can join. Because of this, writing and being sociable are usually mutually exclusive!

Margaret had to spend many a weekend anchored to the house. Michael missed out on computer game time, kicking a ball around, and tinkering with our old Series II Land Rover. He was very patient while his dad kept disappearing in front of a PC for protracted periods of time! Katy missed out on company while she watched cartoons.

As well as the friends and colleagues who encouraged me with the book, I would like to give an extra special thanks to the following people:

A very special thank you to Keith Burns who always has a bubbling enthusiasm for SQL Server. Nigel Stanley and the folk at ICS Solutions for helping to put SQL Server on the map. Dave Gay from Microsoft (UK), an old friend, who stimulates my grey matter through many deep discussions. Steve

Riley from Microsoft (UK) who gave me the opportunity to give query optimizer and locking presentations at European TechEd. Karen Green from Microsoft (UK) for supporting me on the SQL Server beta programs. Doctor Lilian Hobbs, a database comrade-in-arms. Doctor Jeff Middleton for debating many SQL Server and related topics while on 20 mile hikes!

I would also like to thank Karl Dehmer, Lori Oviatt, and Adam Shapiro from Microsoft Training Development who came all the way over to the U.K. to teach an absolutely superb SQL Server 6.5 Performance Tuning and Optimization course. Their enthusiasm for SQL Server performance tuning rubbed off on me which gave me a much needed boost to complete this book. Another special thanks goes to Mike Cash and Liz McCarthy at Butterworth–Heinemann. Many thanks to our other friends at Microsoft, without whose skill and hard work SQL Server 6.5 would not be the excellent product it is today.

Ken England

February 1997

Introducing Performance Tuning and Physical Database Design

1.1 What Is Performance Tuning?

What is the goal of tuning an SQL Server database? The goal is to improve performance until acceptable levels are reached. Acceptable levels can be defined in a number of ways. For a large online transaction processing (OLTP) application the performance goal might be to provide sub-second response time for critical transactions and to provide a response time of less than 2 seconds for 95% of the other main transactions. For some systems, typically batch systems, acceptable performance might be measured in throughput. For example, a settlement system may define acceptable performance in terms of the number of trades settled per hour. For an overnight batch suite acceptable performance might be that it must finish before the business day starts.

Whatever the system, designing for performance should start early in the design process and continue after the application has gone live. Performance tuning is not an one-off process but an iterative process during which response time is measured, tuning performed and response time measured again.

There is no right way to design a database as there are likely to be a number of possible approaches and all these may be perfectly valid. It is sometimes said that performance tuning is an art not a science. This may be true but it is important to undertake performance tuning experiments under the same kind of rigorous controlled conditions in which scientific experiments are performed. Measurements should be taken before and after any modification and these should be made one at a time so it can be established which modification, if any, resulted in an improvement or degradation.

What areas should the database designer concentrate on? The simple answer to this question is that the database designer should concentrate on those areas that will return the most benefit. In my experience, for most database designs I have worked with, large gains are typically made in the area of query and index design. As we shall see later in this book, inappropriate indexes and badly written queries as well as some other contributing factors can negatively influence the query optimizer such that it chooses an inefficient strategy.

To give you some idea of the gains to be made in this area, I once was asked to look at a query that joined a number of large tables together. The query was abandoned after it had not completed within 12 hours. The addition of an index in conjunction with a modification to the query meant the query now completed in less than 8 minutes! This magnitude of gain cannot be achieved just by purchasing more hardware or by twiddling with some arcane SQL Server configuration option. A database designer or administrator's time is always limited so make best use of it! The other main area where gains can be dramatic is lock contention. Removing lock bottlenecks in a system with a large number of users can have a huge impact on response times.

Now, some words of caution when chasing performance problems. If users phone to tell you that they are getting poor response times do not immediately jump to conclusions about what is causing the problem. Circle at a high altitude first. Having made sure that you are about to monitor the correct server and that disk counters are turned on, use the Performance Monitor to look at the CPU, disk subsystem and memory usage. Are there any obvious bottlenecks? If there are then look for the culprit. Everyone blames the database but it could just as easily be someone running their favorite game! If there are no obvious bottlenecks and the CPU, disk and memory counters in the Performance Monitor are lower than usual, then that might tell you something. Perhaps the network is sluggish or there is lock contention. Also beware of the fact that some bottlenecks hide others. A memory bottleneck often manifests itself as a disk bottleneck.

There is no substitute for knowing your own server and knowing the normal range of Performance Monitor counters. Establish trends. Measure a set of counters regularly and then when someone comments that the system is slow you can wave a graph in front of them showing them it isn't!

So when do we start to worry about performance? As soon as possible, of course! We want to take the logical design and start to look at how we should transform it into an efficient physical design.

1.2 The Physical Database Design Process

Once the database logical design has been satisfactorily completed it can be turned into a database physical design. In the physical design process the database designer will be considering such issues as the placement of data and the choice of indexes and, as such, the resulting physical design will be crucial to good database performance. Two important points should be made here:

▶ A bad logical design means that a good physical design cannot be performed. Good logical design is crucial to good database performance and a bad logical design will result in a physical design that attempts to cover up the weaknesses in it. A bad logical design is hard to change and once the system is implemented it will be almost impossible to do so.

▶ The physical design process is a key phase in the overall design process. It is too often ignored until the last minute in the vain hope that performance will be satisfactory. Without a good physical design, performance is rarely satisfactory and throwing hardware at the problem is rarely completely effective. There is no substitute for a good physical design and the time and effort spent in the physical design process will be rewarded with an efficient and well tuned database, not to mention happy users!

Before embarking on the physical design of the database it is worth stepping back and considering a number of points:

▶ What kind of system are we trying to design? Is it a fast *Online Transaction Processing (OLTP)* system perhaps comprising hundreds of users with a throughput of hundreds of transactions per second (TPS) with an average transaction response time that must not exceed two seconds? Is it a multi-gigabyte *data warehouse* that must support few online users but must be able to process very complex ad hoc queries in a reasonable time or is it a combination of the two?

The type of system will strongly influence the physical database design decisions that must be made. If the system is to support OLTP and complex decision support then maybe more than one database should be considered, for example, one for the operational OLTP system and one, fed by extracts from the operational OLTP system, to support complex decision support.

▶ What are our hardware and budget constraints? The most efficient physical database design will still have a maximum performance capability on any given hardware platform. It is no use spending weeks trying to squeeze the last few CPU cycles out of a CPU bound database when, for a small outlay, another processor can be purchased. Similarly, there is little point purchasing another CPU for a system that is disk I/O bound.

▶ Has the database design been approached from a textbook normalization standpoint? Normalizing the database design is the correct approach and has many benefits but there may be areas where some denormalization might be a good idea. This might upset a few purists but if a very short response time is needed for a specific query it might be the best approach. This is not an excuse for not creating a normalized design. A normalized design should be the starting point for any effort made at denormalization.

▶ How important is data consistency? For example, is it important that if a query re-reads a piece of data within a transaction it is guaranteed that it will not have changed? Data consistency and performance are enemies of one another and therefore, if consistency requirements can be relaxed, performance may be increased.

How does a database designer move from the logical design phase to a good physical database design? There is no single correct method. However, certain information should be captured and used as input to the physical design process. Such information includes data volumes, data growth and transaction profiles.

1.2.1 Data Volume Analysis

It is very important to capture information on current data volumes and expected data volumes. Without this information it is not even possible to estimate the number and size of the disk devices that will be required by the database. Recording the information is often a case of using a simple spreadsheet as shown in Table 1.1.

This may appear a trivial operation but it is surprising how few database designers do it and it is also interesting to find the different views from the business users on what the figures should be! Another column that could be added might represent how volatile the data in a particular table is. The percentage annual growth of a table might be zero but this may be because a large amount of data is continually being removed as well as being added.

Table 1.1 *Capturing Simple Data Volume Information*

Table Name	# of Rows	Row Size	Space Needed	% Annual Growth	Space Needed in 12 Months
Accounts	25,000	100	2,500,000	10	2,750,000
Branches	100	200	20,000	5	21,000
Customers	10,000	200	2,000,000	20	2,400,000
Transactions	400,000	50	20,000,000	25	25,000,000

Simple addition of these figures gives the data size requirements but this is only part of the calculation. The database designer must take into account the space required by indexes, the transaction log, the dump devices and no experienced database designer would ask for the disk space that came out of the sum from Figure 2.1. They would, of course, add a percentage on for safety. Users typically do not phone you to complain that you oversized the database by 20%, however, they do phone you to complain that the system just stopped because the database was full!

So how is the size of indexes calculated? The *Microsoft SQL Server Administrator's Companion (Appendix B)* gives sample calculations to assist in the sizing of clustered and non-clustered indexes for tables with both fixed and variable length columns. It is highly recommended that these calculations are performed and it is worth using a spreadsheet such as Microsoft Excel to perform the calculations to save time and effort. There are also stored procedures in circulation that do these calculations.

A rule of thumb is to double the size of the user data to estimate the size of the database. Crude though this appears, by the time indexes have been added and some space for expansion, double the size is not far off!

What about the size of the transaction log? This is difficult to size as it depends on the write activity to the database, frequency of transaction dumps and transaction profiles. Microsoft suggests that about 10% to 25% of the database size should be chosen. This is not a bad start but once the system testing phase of the development has started the database designer can start monitoring the space usage in the transaction log with *dbcc (checktable)* and *dbcc sqlperf (logspace)*. The transaction log space is a critical resource and running out of it should be avoided.

Unfortunately, many factors contribute to transaction log growth. These include the rate per second of transactions that change database data and the amount of data these transactions change. Remember that, in an operational system, if a transaction log dump fails for some reason the transaction log will continue to fill until the next successful transaction log dump. It may be desirable to have a transaction log large enough such that it can accommodate the failure of one transaction log dump. Replication failures will impact the effectiveness of transaction log dumps and, of course, there is always the user who runs a job that updates a million row table without warning you.

For all these reasons, do not be tight with transaction log space. With the price of disk space as it is, a transaction log can be created with a large amount of contingency space.

Lastly, do not forget that, as a database designer/administrator, you will need lots of disk space to hold at least one copy of the production database for performance tuning testing. Not having a copy of the production database can really hinder you.

So we now have documented information on data volumes and growth. This in itself will determine a minimum disk configuration, however, it is only a minimum as transaction analysis may determine that the minimum disk configuration will not provide enough disk I/O bandwidth. If data volume analysis is concerned with the amount of data in the database and the space it needs, transaction analysis is concerned with the way in which that data is manipulated and at what frequency.

1.2.2 Transaction Analysis

The data in the database may be manipulated by code such as Visual Basic or a tool such as Microsoft Access or a third party product accessing SQL Server though Microsoft ODBC. Whichever way the data is accessed, it will presumably be as a result of a business transaction of some kind. Transaction analysis is about capturing information on these business transactions and investigating how they access data in the database and in which mode. For example, Table 1.2 shows some attributes of a business transaction it might be useful to record.

Clearly, by their very nature, it is not possible to capture the above information for ad hoc transactions nor is it practical to capture this information for every business transaction in anything other than a very simple system. However, this information should be captured for at least the *most important* business transactions. By most important we mean those transactions that

Table 1.2 *Capturing Transaction Attributes*

Attribute	Explanation
Name	a name assigned to the transaction
Average frequency	average number of times executed per hour
Peak frequency	peak number of times executed per hour
Priority	a relative priority assigned to each transaction
Mode	whether the transaction only reads the database or writes to it also
Tables accessed	tables accessed by the transaction and in which mode
Table keys	keys used to access the table

must provide the fastest response times and/or are frequently executed. A business transaction that runs every three months and can be run on a weekend is unlikely to appear in the list of most important transactions!

It is important to prioritize transactions as it is virtually impossible to be able to optimize every transaction in the system. Indexes that will speed up queries will almost certainly slow down inserts.

An example of the attributes captured for a transaction are shown in Table 1.3.

There are various ways to document the transaction analysis process and some modeling tools will automate some of this documentation. The secret is to document the important transactions and their attributes so that the database designer can decide which indexes should be defined on which tables.

Again, it is often a case of using simple spreadsheets as shown in Table 1.4.

The first spreadsheet maps the transactions to the mode in which they access tables with the modes being 'I' for insert, 'R' for read, 'U' for update and 'D' for delete. The second spreadsheet maps the transactions to the key with which they access tables. Again, there is nothing complex about this but it really pays to do it. Depending on how the system has been implemented a business transaction may be modeled as a number of stored procedures and, if desired, one may wish to use these instead of transaction names.

It is also important when considering the key business transactions not to forget triggers. The trigger accesses tables in various modes just as the application code does.

Table 1.3 *Example Transaction Attributes*

Attribute	Value
Name	Order Creation
Average frequency	10,000 per hour
Peak frequency	15,000 per hour
Priority	1 (high)
Mode	Write
Tables accessed	Orders (w), Order Items (w), Customers (r), Parts (r)
Table keys	Orders (order_number), Order Items (order_number), Customers (cust_number), Parts (parts_number)

Table 1.4 *Capturing Simple Transaction Analysis Information*

Transactions / Tables	Orders	Order_items	Parts	Customers
Customer inquiry				R
Order inquiry	R	R		
Order entry	I	I	R	R

Transactions / Tables	Orders	Order_items	Parts	Customers
Customer inquiry				cust_number
Order inquiry	order_number	order_number		
Order entry	order_number	order_number	parts_number	cust_number

Data integrity enforcement using declarative referential integrity should also be included. Foreign key constraints will access other tables in the database and there is nothing magic about them. If an appropriate index is not present they will scan the whole table like any other query.

Once the transaction analysis has been performed the database designer should have a good understanding of the tables that are accessed frequently, in which mode and with which key. From this information one can begin to derive

▶ Which tables are accessed the most and therefore experience the most disk I/O.

▶ Which tables are written to frequently by many transactions and therefore might experience the most lock contention.

▶ For a given table, which columns are used to access the required rows, that is, which common column combinations form the search arguments in the queries.

In other words *where are the hot spots in the database?*

The database designer, armed with this information, should now be able to make informed decisions about the estimated disk I/O rates to tables, the type of indexes required on those tables and the columns used in the indexes.

Relational databases, and SQL Server is no exception, are reasonably easy to prototype so there is no excuse for not testing out the physical design that you are considering. Load data into your tables, add your indexes and stress your database with some representative Transact-SQL. See how many transactions a second you can perform on a given server or, to look at it another way, how much disk I/O does a named transaction generate? What resource -CPU or disk do you run out of first?

Start stress testing off with simple experiments. Jumping in at the deep end with many users testing complex functionality is likely to just confuse the issue. Begin with simple transactions issued by one user and then try more complex transactions.

Do not forget multi-user testing! Lock contention cannot be tested unless some kind of multi-user testing is performed. In its simplest form this might involve persuading a number of potential users to use the test system concurrently by following set scripts while performance statistics are monitored. In its more sophisticated form this might involve the use of a multi-user testing product that can simulate many users while running automated scripts.

Transaction analysis and performance testing can be approached in a much more sophisticated way than has been described above. The important point, however, is that it should be done, the level of sophistication being determined by the available resource be it time or money.

Again, note that physical design and performance testing are on-going activities. Systems are usually in a constant state of flux because business requirements are usually in a constant state of flux. Therefore performance should be regularly monitored and, if necessary, the database tuned.

1.2.3 Hardware Environment Considerations

The previous section described pre-production performance testing. This should have given the database designer a feel for the hardware requirements of the production system. Obviously there is a hardware budget for any project but it is clearly critical to have sufficient hardware to support the workload of the system. It is also critical to have the correct balance and correct type of hardware.

For example, there is no point in spending a small fortune on CPU power if only a small amount of money is spent on the disk subsystem. Similarly, there is no point in spending a small fortune on the disk subsystem if only a small amount of money is spent on memory. Would the application benefit from a multiprocessor configuration or a single powerful processor?

If the application's main component is a single report that runs through the night but must be finished before 9:00 a.m., a single powerful processor might be a better choice. On the other hand, if the application consists of a large number of users in an OLTP system, a more cost-effective solution would probably be a multiprocessor configuration.

Take a step back and look at the application and its hardware as a whole. Make sure the system resource is not unbalanced and do not forget the network!

1.2.4 Where To Next?

Once we have performed our data volume and transaction analysis we can start to consider our physical design. We will need to decide what transactions need to be supported by indexes and what type of index we should use. Chapter 3 discusses indexes in detail, but before we look at indexes we need a more general view of the storage structures used in SQL Server and these are now covered in the next chapter.

2

SQL Server Storage Structures

2.1 Introduction

A developer of application code is probably quite content to consider an SQL Server as a collection of databases which, in turn, contain tables, indexes, triggers, stored procedures and views. As a database designer and a person who will be responsible for the performance of those databases it is useful to be able to look a little deeper at the storage structures in SQL Server. A lot of the internals of SQL Server are hidden and undocumented but there is a fair amount that we can still learn about the way the product works. This chapter investigates the storage structures that SQL Server uses and the methods available to view them.

2.2 Devices and Databases

A database resides in one or more Windows NT operating system files that may reside on FAT or NTFS partitions. These operating system files are known in SQL Server terminology as *database devices*. There can be as many as 256 database devices per SQL Server and the maximum size for each device is 32 Gigabytes.

To create a device the SQL Enterprise Manager can be used or the Transact-SQL *DISK INIT* statement. The *New Database Device* dialog box in the SQL Enterprise Manager is shown in Figure 2.1. An example of the DISK INIT Transact-SQL statement is shown below:

```
DISK INIT
    NAME = 'InsuranceDataDev1',
    PHYSNAME = 'd:\sqldevices\InsuranceDataDev1.dat',
    VDEVNO = 23,
    SIZE = 51200
```

This creates a 100 Mb database device allocating virtual device number 23.

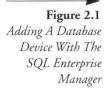

Figure 2.1
Adding A Database
Device With The
SQL Enterprise
Manager

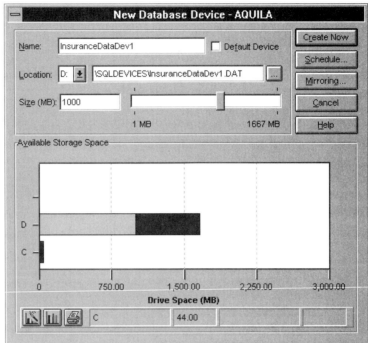

When creating a database, the database devices on which it is to reside are specified as well as the size of the database. It is recommended that the transaction log belonging to a database (the *syslogs* system table) is placed on a database device that is separate from the one on which the data is stored. This is so the transaction log and the database data can be stored on different disk drives or disk arrays providing the capability to implement transaction log based recovery. In a development environment where the ability to recover up to date data is not as critical, the transaction log can be placed on the same database device as the database data.

To create a database the SQL Enterprise Manager can be used or the Transact-SQL *CREATE DATABASE* statement. The *New Database* dialog box in the SQL Enterprise Manager is shown in Figure 2.2.

An example of the *CREATE DATABASE* Transact-SQL statement is shown below:

```
CREATE DATABASE InsuranceDB
   ON InsuranceDataDev1 = 100
   LOG ON InsuranceLogDev1 = 100
```

This creates a 200 Mb database with the data and the transaction log on separate database devices.

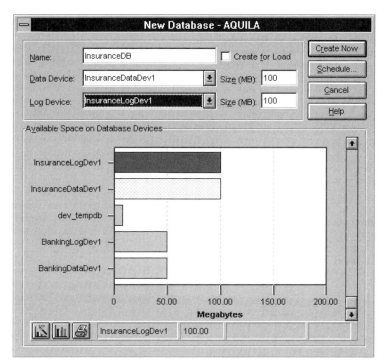

Figure 2.2

Adding A Database With The SQL Enterprise Manager

More than one database can reside in a database device although to simplify administration or if SQL Server 6.5 Fallback Support is required, this is not recommended. It is usually simpler to place the database data on one device and the transaction log on another, a total of two devices in all.

Strictly speaking, then, the relationship between databases and database devices is a many to many relationship. A database device can hold many databases and a database can reside on many database devices. This is modeled in the MASTER database as three tables:

▶ sysdevices

▶ sysdatabases

▶ sysusages

The *sysdevices* table holds one row for every database (and dump) device present on the SQL Server. The *sysdatabases* table holds one row for every database present on the SQL Server and the *sysusages* table resolves the many to many relationship between the *sysdevices* table and the *sysdatabases* table. Each row in *sysusages* is known as a *device fragment*.

The columns in the *sysdevices* table are shown in Table 2.1.

Table 2.1 *The Sysdevices Table*

Column	Datatype	Description
low	int	First virtual page number on a database device.
high	int	Last virtual page number on a database device.
status	smallint	A bitmap indicating the type of device: 1 Default disk 2 Physical disk 4 Logical disk 8 Skip header 16 Dump device 32 Serial writes 64 Device mirrored 128 Reads mirrored 256 Half-mirror only 512 Mirror enabled 4096 Read Only 8192 Deferred
cntrltype	smallint	Controller type: 0 Non CD-ROM database device 2 Disk dump device 3 - 4 Diskette dump device 5 Tape dump device 6 Named pipe device
name	varchar(30)	Logical name of the database device (or dump device).
phyname	varchar(127)	Name of the physical device.
mirrorname	varchar(127)	Name of the mirror device.
stripeset	varchar(30)	Reserved for future use.

A device is a range of 2 Kb pages with the value in the *low* and *high* columns representing the first and last page number respectively. The system stored procedure *sp_helpdevice* can be used to interrogate the *sysdevices* system table:

```
sp_helpdevice

device_name   physical_name                     description
-----------   -------------                     ----------
BigDataDev1   D:\SQLDEVICES\BigDataDev1.DAT special, physical
                                            disk,1100 MB
```

```
BigLogDev1       D:\SQLDEVICES\BigLogDev1.DAT  special, physical disk,
                                                 550 MB
diskdump         nul                           disk, dump device
diskettedumpa  a:sqltable.dat                  diskette, 1.2 MB,
                                                 dump device
diskettedumpb  b:sqltable.dat                  diskette, 1.2 MB, dump
                                                 device
master           C:\MSSQL\DATA\MASTER.DAT      special, physical
                                                 disk, 40 MB
MSDBData         C:\MSSQL\DATA\MSDB.DAT        special, physical
                                                 disk, 6 MB
MSDBLog          C:\MSSQL\DATA\MSDBLOG.DAT     special, physical
                                                 disk, 2 MB

Status       cntrltype    device_number    low            high
------       ---------    -------------    ----           -----
2            0            1                16777216       17340415
2            0            2                33554432       33836031
16           2            0                0              20000
16           3            0                0              19
16           4            0                0              19
3            0            0                0              20479
2            0            127              2130706432     2130709503
2            0            126              2113929216     2113930239
```

Note that the output is displayed in one wide screen full. I have broken it into two parts to make it easier to see. Where does *sp_helpdevice* get the virtual device number (*vdevno*) from? It is in fact stored in the high order byte of both the *low* and *high* columns.

The *sysdatabases* system table is shown in Table 2.2.

A number of the database status bits can be set via the SQL Enterprise Manager or the *sp_dboption* system stored procedure.

The *sysusages* system table is shown in Table 2.3.

2.3 Units of Storage

A database is a collection of logical pages each 2 Kb in size. Database pages are always this size and cannot be adjusted by the database designer. The 2 Kb page is the fundamental unit of storage and it is also a unit of I/O and a unit of locking. However, there are other storage units in a database.

Space is allocated to tables and indexes in *extents* as shown in Figure 2.3. An extent is a structure that contains eight database pages (16 Kb). Whenever a table or index is created an extent is allocated to it. As the table or index grows the database pages in the extent fill until the last page becomes full and there is no more space in which to store table rows or index entries. At this point a new extent is allocated to the table or index. When data is removed

Table 2.2   *The Sysdatabases Table*

Column	Datatype	Description
name	varchar(30)	Database name.
dbid	smallint	Unique database identifier.
suid	smallint	Server user ID of the creator of the database.
mode	smallint	While a database is being created or loaded this is used internally as a lock.
status	smallint	Status bits. 2 database is in transition 4 select into/bulkcopy set 8 trunc. log on chkpt set 16 no chkpt on recovery set 32 crashed during database load 64 database not yet recovered 128 database is in recovery 256 database is suspect 1024 read only set 2048 dbo use only set 4096 single user set 8192 database being checkpointed 16384 ANSI null default set 32768 emergency mode
version	smallint	Number representing the internal version of the SQL Server code with which the database was created.
logptr	int	Pointer to the transaction log.
crdate	datetime	Database creation date.
dumptrdate	datetime	Date the last DUMP TRANSACTION was performed.
category	int	Used for replication.

from a table or index a point will be reached when an extent becomes completely empty. At this point the extent is deallocated from the table or index and can then be allocated to a different object if required. There is always one extent allocated to a table or index. As we shall see in later chapters, as well as a 2 Kb page, an extent is also a unit of I/O.

Another unit of storage in a database is an *allocation unit.* An allocation unit is a structure that contains 256 database pages, that is, 32 extents, and is

Table 2.3   *The Sysusages System Table*

Column	Datatype	Description
dbid	smallint	Unique database identifier.
segmap	int	Bitmap of possible segment assignments.
lstart	int	First database page number, this is a logical page number.
size	int	Number of contiguous database pages.
vstart	int	Start virtual page number.

Figure 2.3
Storage Units In A Database

32 Extent or 256 Page
Allocation Unit (0.5 Mb)

8 Page Extent
(16 Kb)

2 Kb
Page

0.5 Mb in size. A device fragment is always a multiple of a whole number of allocation units. The first page of an allocation unit is known as an *allocation page*. The allocation page maps extents to objects. SQL Server is still able to allocate the first extent in an allocation unit to a table or index. However, it will only contain seven usable pages (14 Kb).

To see the space allocated to a table use the system stored procedure *sp_spaceused*:

```
sp_spaceused branches

name        rows    reserved    data    index_size    unused
----        ----    --------    ----    ----------    ------
branches    100     48 KB       20 KB   4 KB          24 KB
```

In the previous example, *sp_spaceused* reports that there are 100 rows in the *Branches* table and that 48 Kb or three extents of space have been reserved for it. Out of the three extents, 10 pages (20 Kb/2) have been used by the table to store rows and another two pages (4 Kb/2) have been used by indexes. Note that the system stored procedure *sp_spaceused* gets its information from the *sysindexes* system table which only holds estimates. It does this to avoid becoming a bottleneck at run time but can become inaccurate. To synchronize the *sysindexes* system table with the real space used, execute a *DBCC CHECKTABLE* or a *DBCC UPDATEUSAGE* statement which will scan the table and indexes. These statements will be described in Chapter 4.

2.4 Database Pages

Database pages are used for a variety of tasks. Database pages that are used to hold table rows and index entries are known as *data pages* and *index pages* respectively. If the table contains columns of the datatype *TEXT* or *IMAGE* then these columns are implemented as chains of *Text/Image* pages. There are other types of pages also. We have already mentioned *allocation pages* and we will meet another type of page called a *distribution page* in Chapter 3 which is used to hold index statistics.

Let us take out a magnifying glass and look closer at a typical page structure. The most common database page we are likely to meet is a data page so we will use a data page as an example.

The basic structure of all types of database page is shown in Figure 2.4. There is a fixed 32 byte page header which contains information such as the page number, pointers to the previous and next page and the object ID of the

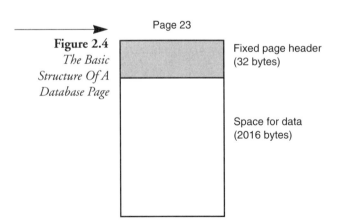

Figure 2.4
The Basic Structure Of A Database Page

Page 23

Fixed page header
(32 bytes)

Space for data
(2016 bytes)

object to which the page belongs. The pointers are needed because pages are linked together as shown in Figure 2.5.

What does a data page look like inside? The internal structure of a data page is shown in Figure 2.6. We can see the data rows but there is also another structure called a *row offset table*. The row offset table contains two byte entries consisting of the row number and the offset byte address of the row in the page. The first row in our page is at byte offset 32 because of the 32 byte page header. Our row (plus overhead) is 20 bytes in length so the next row is at byte offset 52 and so on. The row offset table basically gives us a level of indirection when addressing a row. This is important because, as we shall see in Chapter 3, nonclustered indexes contain pointers to data rows in their leaf level index pages. Such a pointer is known as a *row id* and is made up of a database page number and a row number. The database page number takes SQL Server to an individual page and the row number then takes SQL Server to an entry in the row offset table. In our example, the row id of the row nearest the fixed page header would consist of the page number, 23, and the row number 0.

Entry 0 in the row offset table contains byte offset address 32. SQL Server can then use this offset to retrieve the row. Because the row id is implemented this way we can see that a row can change position in the table without the row id having to change. All that has to change is the offset address in the row offset table entry. Why would a row change position in a page? In Figure 2.6, if *row 1* was deleted *row 2* would move up to *row 0* in order to keep the free space in the page contiguous. The row id for *row 2* would not change.

What does a data row look like inside?

Data rows contain columns of data, as you would expect, but they also contain overhead. The amount of overhead depends on whether the row con-

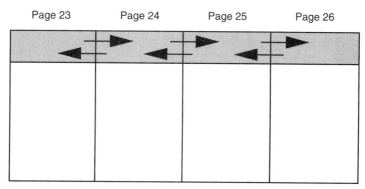

Figure 2.5
Pages Linked In A Chain

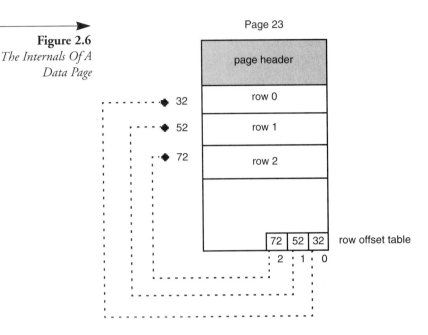

Figure 2.6
*The Internals Of A
Data Page*

tains all fixed length columns or there are also variable length columns. In
Figure 2.7 we have the structure of the *Accounts* table row in our *Banking*
database. The *Accounts* table has 4 fixed length columns. The first 3 columns
are of type *integer* and the last column is of type *money.*

The overhead consists of two bytes. One byte for a field containing the
number of variable length columns which will contain 0 in this example and
another field that contains the row number which can contain a value in the
range 0 to 255 inclusive. The shaded area represents the overhead. Our
Account row that we expected to be 20 bytes in length has turned out to be
22 bytes in length!

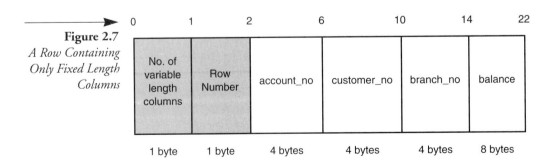

Figure 2.7
*A Row Containing
Only Fixed Length
Columns*

Suppose the last column in our *Accounts* table was not a *money* data type but a *varchar(8)*. The structure of our row containing variable length data is shown in Figure 2.8.

The structure shown in Figure 2.8 assumes that the *balance* column does indeed contain 8 characters. We can immediately see two differences between the structure of a row containing only fixed length columns and a row that also contains variable length columns. First, the fixed length columns are grouped together separately from the variable length columns which are also grouped together and second, there are more overhead bytes.

Looking at the structure, the first overhead field that contains the number of variable length columns now contains the value 1 to represent the balance column. The row number field does not change its function. After this field we find all the fixed length columns followed by a single byte overhead field that contains the total row length, in our example 27. All the variable length columns now follow. At the end of the row are more overhead bytes. An offset table adjust byte (there can be more than 1 depending on the row length), a byte holding the offset from the start of the row to the start of these overhead bytes and a byte containing the offset of the variable length *balance* column (one of these for every variable length column).

Note that the order of the columns in a row that contains variable length columns is not the same order as the table definition. Also note that a fixed length column that allows *null* values is treated as a variable length column.

2.5 Looking into Database Pages

I often find it useful and educational to be able to burrow into the contents of a database page. A useful DBCC statement that will allow you to do this is DBCC PAGE. This DBCC statement is not documented as an option of the DBCC statement in the *Microsoft SQL Server Transact-SQL Reference* manual but it is mentioned in the *Microsoft SQL Server Administrator's* manual in *Part 8 - Troubleshooting*.

Figure 2.8
A Row Containing Fixed And Variable Length Columns

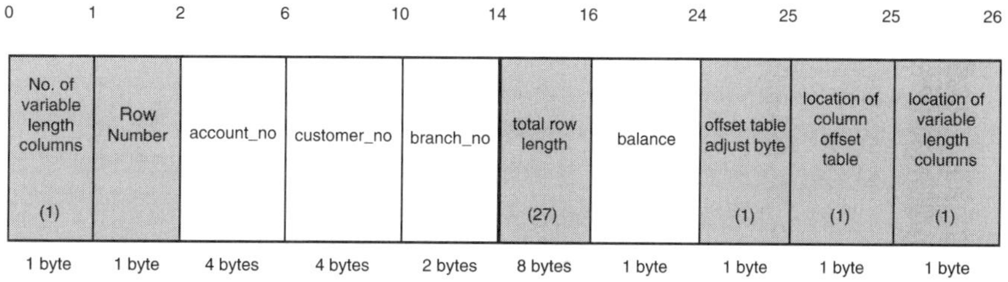

The most useful form of the syntax of this statement is:

```
DBCC PAGE (dbid | dbname, page number)
```

or:

```
DBCC PAGE (dbid | dbname, page number, 1)
```

The first form of the syntax displays the page header, the second format also displays the contents of the page, that is, data in the form of rows and the row offset table.

How do you know the page number to display? One of the columns in the *sysindexes* system table, described in Chapter 3, contains a column *first*. This contains the page number of the first data page in the table if the *sysindexes* entry is a table or clustered index (*indid* = 0 or 1). Also, if the *sysindexes* entry is a table, the *root* column holds the page number of the last data page in the table.

To find the relevant entry in the *sysindexes* table you need to convert the table name to an *object id*. For example, suppose we want to look at pages in the *Accounts* table. First of all we need to find the *object id* of this table.

```
SELECT OBJECT_ID ('accounts')

----------------
1120007021
```

To get the start page number from the *sysindexes* table:

```
SELECT first FROM sysindexes WHERE
    id = 1120007021 AND
    indid IN (0,1)

first
-------
1400
```

To get information out of DBCC PAGE we must initiate tracing to the client:

```
DBCC TRACEON (3604)
```

We are now ready to display the contents of a page, but first of all let us just display the page header so we can see what is in it:

```
DBCC PAGE ('banking',1400)

PAGE:
Page found in cache.

BUFFER:
Buffer header for buffer 0x10d88a0
  page=0x13db800 bdnew=0x10d88a0 bdold=0x10d88a0 bhash=0x0
bnew=0x10d8960
```

```
    bold=0x10d8900 bvirtpg=100664696 bdbid=6 bpinproc=0 bkeep=0
  bspid=0
    bstat=0x1004 bpageno=1400

PAGE HEADER:
Page header for page 0x13db800
pageno=1400 nextpg=1401 prevpg=0 objid=1120007021 timestamp=0001
000c29bf
nextrno=83 level=0 indid=0 freeoff=1858 minlen=22
page status bits: 0x80,0x8,0x1
```

The DBCC PAGE statement immediately tells us whether the page was found in the data cache or not. The data cache is discussed in Chapter 5. The next piece of useful information is the line telling us that this is page 1400 and the next page is page 1401. This is the first page so there is no previous page. This line also tells us what *object id* the page belongs to. Okay, we know this but there are occasions when error messages contain page numbers and in that situation the *object id* is very useful.

The *nextrno* field is the row number that will be used by the next row to be placed on this page. The *level* and *indid* fields are meaningful if this page is an index page. The *level* is the index level where this page resides and *indid* tells us the *id* of the index this page belongs to. The field *freeoff* is the offset of the start of the free space on the page (remember it is a single contiguous chunk) and the *minlen* field tells us the smallest value a row can be.

Let us now look at the contents of the page. I will omit the page header from the example for clarity:

```
DBCC PAGE ('banking',1400,1)

DATA:
Offset 32 -
013db820: 00000019 00002093 0100e803 00000000      ...... .........
013db830: 00001437 4501                             ...7E.

Offset 54 -
013db836: 00010032 0000a09f 0100e803 00000000      ...2............
013db846: 0000000e e700                             ......

:


:

OFFSET TABLE:
Row - Offset
82 (0x52) - 1836 (0x72c), 81 (0x51) - 1814 (0x716),
80 (0x50) - 1792 (0x700), 79 (0x4f) - 1770 (0x6ea),

:


:

2 (0x2) - 76 (0x4c), 1 (0x1) - 54 (0x36),
0 (0x0) - 32 (0x20),
```

We can see, in the *DATA* section, each row and the offset of the row. If we look at the second row at offset 54 we can see that the first 2 bytes are *0001*. These two bytes are the two fields shown in Figure 2.7: one byte for a field containing the number of variable length columns which contains 0 in this example and another field that contains the row number which happens to be 1.

We can see, in the *OFFSET TABLE* section, each entry in the row offset table. Each entry contains a row number and an offset, for example, row number 1 is at offset 54 and the last row offset table entry is for row number 82 at offset 1836. Note that this ties in with the *nextrno=83* field in the page header and the *freeoff=1858* field in the page header (1836 + 22 = 1858 where 22 is the row length).

This chapter has provided an overview of the SQL Server storage structures. In the next chapter we will look at tables and indexes in much more detail. But, now that we have discussed databases, it is time to introduce the *Banking* database used in this book.

2.6 The Banking Database

The *Banking* database is very simple. It consists of just three tables that are created with the following Transact-SQL syntax:

```
CREATE TABLE customers
        (
        customer_no     INT         NOT NULL,
        lname           CHAR(20)    NOT NULL,
        fname           CHAR(20)    NOT NULL
        )

CREATE TABLE accounts
        (
        account_no      INT         NOT NULL,
        customer_no     INT         NOT NULL,
        branch_no       INT         NOT NULL,
        balance         MONEY       NOT NULL
        )

CREATE TABLE branches
        (
        branch_no       INT         NOT NULL,
        branch_name     CHAR(20)    NOT NULL,
        branch_address  CHAR(120)   NOT NULL,
        managers_name   CHAR(20)    NOT NULL
        )
```

The *Banking* database has customers who have one or many bank accounts. A bank account is managed by a branch of the bank at some geographic location. It is as simple as that.

There are 25,000 bank accounts for 12,500 customers. These are managed by 100 branches. There are no primary key constraints or foreign key constraints as we will be adjusting the indexes on a number of occasions. The indexes that are normally present are as follows:

```
CREATE CLUSTERED INDEX accounts_branch_no_idx ON accounts
(branch_no)

CREATE UNIQUE NONCLUSTERED INDEX accounts_account_no_idx ON
    accounts
(account_no)

CREATE NONCLUSTERED INDEX accounts_balance_idx ON accounts
(balance)

CREATE NONCLUSTERED INDEX accounts_customer_no_idx ON accounts
(customer_no)

CREATE UNIQUE CLUSTERED INDEX branches_branch_code_idx ON branches
(branch_no)

CREATE UNIQUE NONCLUSTERED INDEX customers_customer_no_idx ON
    customers
(customer_no)
```

3

Indexing

3.1 Introduction

There are many bells and whistles that can be tweaked to improve SQL Server performance. Some will provide a more positive benefit than others. However, to really improve performance, often with dramatic results, the database designer is well advised to concentrate his or her efforts in the area of indexing. The correct choice of index on a table with respect to the WHERE clause in a Transact-SQL statement such that the query optimizer chooses the most efficient strategy can have sensational results.

I was once asked to look at a query that performed a complex join and had not completed in over 12 hours. Who knows when the query would have completed had it not been cancelled by the user—it may have still been running at the end of the year! Examination of the query showed that a join condition was missing in the WHERE clause as was an index on one of the large tables involved in the join. Making the appropriate changes meant that the query ran in less than 8 minutes!

This magnitude of performance improvement is not likely to be achieved every day but it makes an important point, namely that focusing effort in the area of indexing and query optimization is likely to produce good results for the effort involved and should be high on the database tuner's hit list.

So what are these indexes and why are they so important?

3.2 Data Retrieval with No Indexes

Imagine that this book had no index and you were asked to find references to the topic *page faults*. You would have no choice but to open the book at Page 1, scan the page looking for the topic, turn to Page 2 and continue until you had scanned the last page of the book. You would have to continue your search to the last page in the book as you would not know when you had found the last reference to the topic. You would have read and scanned every page in the book which would probably have taken you a considerable length of time.

SQL Server has to behave in a similar fashion when asked to retrieve rows from a table that has no appropriate index. Suppose we were to execute the following Transact-SQL statement against the *Accounts* table, assuming that there was no suitable index present:

```
SELECT * FROM accounts WHERE branch_no = 1100
```

How would SQL Server find the appropriate rows? It would have to search the *Accounts* table from the start of the table to the end of the table looking for rows which had a *branch_no* that contained the value 1100. This might be fine for small tables containing just a few rows but if the table contained millions of rows the above query would take a very long time to complete.

What is needed is a fast and efficient way of finding the data that conforms to the query requirements. In the case of a book there is usually an index section from which the required topic can be found in an alphabetically ordered list and the page numbers of the pages that feature that topic can then be obtained. The required pages can then be directly accessed in the book.

The method used to directly retrieve the required data from a table in SQL Server is not unlike that used with books. Structures called indexes may be created on a table which enable SQL Server to quickly look up the database pages that hold the supplied key value, in our example the value 1100 for the *branch_no* column.

Unlike a book which normally has one index, a table may have many indexes. These indexes are based on one or more columns in the table. In SQL Server there are two types of index—*clustered* and *nonclustered*—which we shall now compare and contrast. The ultimate decision as to whether an index is used or whether a complete scan of the table is performed is made by a component of SQL Server known as the *query optimizer* which we shall discuss in detail in Chapter 4.

3.3 Clustered Indexes

As a database designer you are only allowed to create one clustered index on a table—you have one chance to play this ace and so you must play it carefully. Why only one clustered index per table? Unlike its nonclustered cousin, described shortly, a clustered index imposes a physical ordering of the table data.

Creating a clustered index forces the data rows in the table to be re-ordered on disk such that they are in the same key sequence order as the clustered index key. For example, if we were to create a clustered index on the *lname* column of the *Customers* table the data rows would be sorted such that their physical order on the disk was in ascending order of the customers' last names, that is, "Adamski" would precede "Tolstoy."

This order would be maintained as long as the clustered index was present. SQL Server would ensure that the insertion of a new data row would cause the row to be placed in the correct physical location in key sequence order.

The structure of a clustered index with its key defined on the *lname* column of the *Customers* table is shown in Figure 3.1. The lowest level of the clustered index is composed of the data pages themselves and in a clustered index the data pages are known as the *leaf level* of the index. The rest of the clustered index is composed of index pages. The index page at the top of the index is known as the index root. Levels in the index between the root page and the leaf level pages are known as intermediate level pages. Another name for an index page is an index *node*. For simplicity we have shown the structure with the ability to hold two data rows per page and three index entries per page. In reality many more rows and index entries are likely to be found.

At any given level in the index the pages are linked together. This is not shown in Figure 3.1 for clarity but can be seen in Figure 3.2.

The entries in the index pages contain a key value and a pointer to the next index page at the next lowest level that starts with that key value, plus some control information. The pointer in a clustered index is a page number. In Figure 3.1 for example, the root page contains an entry that contains a key

Figure 3.1
The Structure Of A Clustered Index

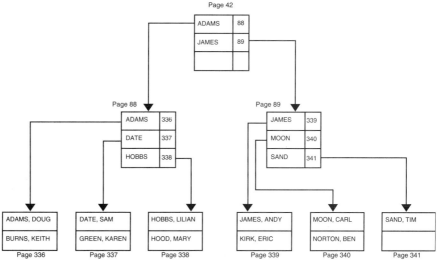

Figure 3.2
*At A Given Level
In The Index The
Pages Are Linked
Together*

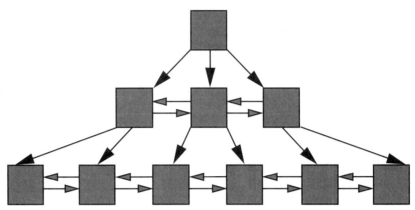

value "Adams" and a page number 88 that points to the intermediate index page 88 whose lowest key value is "Adams."

The reason that there can be only one clustered index on a table is that the clustered index governs the physical placement of the data and the data cannot be in two places at once. There can only be one sequence in which the data can be physically placed.

So how can a clustered index support our requirement to perform fast and efficient data retrieval? The clustered index will help us to avoid table scans as the query optimizer will probably use the clustered index to retrieve data directly. Suppose we issued the following SELECT statement:

```
SELECT * FROM customers WHERE lname = 'Green'
```

Let us assume that the query optimizer decides that the clustered index is the most efficient access path to the data. This is a realistic assumption as the WHERE clause only specifies the *lname* column on which the clustered index is based.

SQL Server will first obtain the page number of the root page from the *sysindexes* table, in our example, page 42. In this root page there will be a number of key values and in our clustered index these are "Adams" and "James." SQL Server will look for the highest key value that is not greater that "Green" which will be "Adams."

In a clustered index an index entry consists of the index key plus a pointer which is a page number. The pointer held in the "Adams" key entry points to page 88 and so index page number 88 will be retrieved.

Again, SQL Server will look for the highest key value that is not greater than "Green." In index page number 88 this is "Date." The pointer held in the "Date" key entry is to page 337, which is a data page, and so this page will be retrieved. The data page is now scanned for a row containing "Green" in the *lname* column. The row is found and returned. Note that SQL Server did not know that the row existed until the data page was obtained.

Clearly, the clustered index in our example has supported fast access to the data row. If we consider the number of I/Os required to traverse the index in this way we can see that one I/O is required to retrieve the root page, one I/O is required to retrieve the intermediate index page and one I/O is required to retrieve the data page—a total of three I/Os. A table scan would probably result in many more I/Os.

Would the three I/Os required to traverse our index be physical I/Os? Probably not. The root page of an index is accessed by every query that needs to traverse the index and so is normally always found in cache if the index is accessed frequently. The intermediate nodes and data pages are less likely to be, but if the data cache is large enough it is possible that they will stay in the cache.

We have looked at a SELECT statement that retrieved a single row. What about a SELECT statement that retrieves a range of rows?

```
SELECT * FROM customers WHERE lname BETWEEN 'Date' AND 'Kirk'
```

In the above example a range of values is specified based on the *lname* column. It can be seen from Figure 3.1 that, because our clustered index is based on the *lname* column and the data is thus in key sequence order, the rows that meet the criteria are all stored together, that is, clustered. In our example, the six rows that meet the criteria of the SELECT statement are found in three data pages and so only three I/Os would be required to retrieve these data pages.

If the clustered index had not been based on the *lname* column the rows would not have been clustered together (unless fate had intervened or the rows were loaded in that fashion with no other clustered indexes on the table). In the worst case, the six rows would have been stored across six data pages resulting in six I/Os to retrieve them.

Note: In the *Banking* database there are about 40 customer rows per data page. So 3 I/Os would return 120 rows and in the worst case, therefore, 120 I/Os would be required to return 120 customer rows if there was no clustered index on *lname*. A not inconsiderable difference!

In a similar fashion, clustered indexes support searches using the LIKE operator. Suppose we execute the following query:

```
SELECT * FROM customers WHERE lname LIKE 'N%'
```

All the customers with last names beginning with 'N' will be returned. Again, our clustered index on *lname* will ensure that these rows are stored together resulting in the least number of I/Os to retrieve them.

Finally, what about returning the data in order? Suppose we execute the following query:

```
SELECT * FROM customers ORDER BY lname
```

The query optimizer will know that the clustered index guarantees that the data is in key sequence order and so there is no need to perform a sort of the rows to satisfy the ORDER BY clause, again saving disk I/O.

3.4 Nonclustered Indexes

Like their clustered counterparts nonclustered indexes are balanced trees with a hierarchy of index pages starting with the index root page at the top, leaf level pages at the bottom and intermediate level pages between the root page and the leaf level pages. Again, at any given level in the index the pages are linked together as was shown in Figure 3.2.

Unlike their clustered counterparts nonclustered indexes have no influence on the physical order of the data and the leaf level of a sorted index is not considered to be the data but is the lowest level of index pages. The structure of a nonclustered index with its key defined on the *fname* column of the *Customers* table is shown in Figure 3.3.

The first observation that we can make is that every data row in the table has a pointer to it from the index leaf level (the dashed lines). This was not the case with the clustered index in Figure 3.1 where the leaf level only contained pointers to the lowest keyed data row in each page. This means that nonclustered indexes are typically larger than their clustered counterparts because their leaf level has to hold many more pointers. There are about 40 customer rows per data page so the leaf level of the nonclustered index will need to hold 40 times more pointers. The typical effect of this is that a nonclustered index on a key will usually have one more level of index pages than a clustered index on the same key.

What do the index entries in a nonclustered index look like? Like a clustered index they contain a key value and a pointer to the relevant index page at the next lowest level. There is also some control information. Eventually, the leaf level points to the data row. However, the pointer in the leaf level of a nonclustered index is a *row id*. A row id is a page number plus a row number. In Figure 3.3 the leaf level index page 96 has an entry for the key "Andy" that points to page 339, row number 1. The intermediate level index pages are

Figure 3.3
The Structure Of A Nonclustered Index

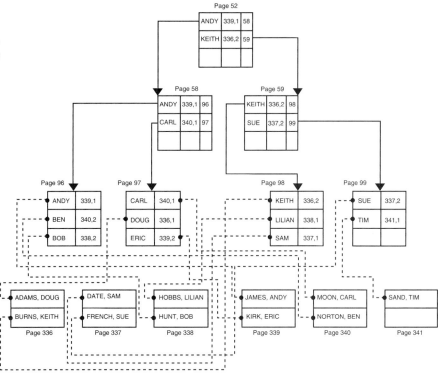

similar to those found in a clustered index in that they contain a page pointer to the relevant index page at the next lowest level but in a nonclustered index they also contain the row id of the data row that the index entry points to. This is an optimization used by SQL Server when rows are deleted.

An important observation to make about Figure 3.3 is that, although the index levels are in key sequence order, the data is not. This means that any kind of range retrieval performed using the sorted index will have to use a logical I/O to follow each relevant leaf level pointer to the data rows themselves. This is an important point which we will revisit later. Note also that once the leaf level has been accessed SQL Server knows whether a row exists or not.

So far we have discussed the behavior of clustered indexes and nonclustered indexes with respect to data retrieval. Let us now look at the behavior of these indexes with respect to data insertion, update and deletion.

3.5 The Role of Indexes in Insertion and Deletion

The existence of indexes on tables is usually considered with respect to query execution time. However, SQL Server indexes, in particular clustered indexes, also affect the behavior of SQL Server when rows are inserted. Consider the *Customers* table as shown in Figure 3.4. The table has been allocated a single eight-page extent of which three pages are full and the fourth page is partly filled.

We will assume, for clarity, that a database page only holds three rows and that only the *lname* and *fname* columns are shown.

Suppose we wish to add a new row. Where is it stored? As the table has no indexes present the new row is inserted at the end of the table on the last page as shown in Figure 3.5. We shall see shortly that this behavior is true even if there are nonclustered indexes present on the table. Only the creation of a clustered index may modify this behavior.

One can imagine that in a multiuser system many users will be attempting to insert customer rows. This will result in a hot spot at the end of the table and this is particularly relevant from the standpoint of locking which will be discussed in Chapter 6. The bottom line is that the presence of such a hot spot can severely degrade performance. So, insertion into a table with no index can be a problem—what about deletion?

Suppose some rows are now deleted as shown in Figure 3.6. Free space, shown in Figure 3.7, is left on the pages from which the rows are deleted.

If a new row is now inserted where will it go? It will be inserted at the end of the table as shown in Figure 3.8. It will not reuse the space freed by the deletion of the rows.

Figure 3.4
The Customers Table With No Indexes Present

Page 336	Page 337	Page 338	Page 339
HOBBS, LILIAN	ADAMS, DOUG	STONE, JOHN	HOOD, MARY
GREEN, KAREN	KIRK, ERIC	KENT, RON	
BURNS, KEITH	JAMES, ANDY	MOON, CARL	

Figure 3.5
Insertion At The End Of A Table

Page 336	Page 337	Page 338	Page 339
HOBBS, LILIAN	ADAMS, DOUG	STONE, JOHN	HOOD, MARY
GREEN, KAREN	KIRK, ERIC	KENT, RON	
BURNS, KEITH	JAMES, ANDY	MOON, CARL	

MOSS, SUE

Figure 3.6
Deleting Rows
From The Table

Page 336	Page 337	Page 338	Page 339
HOBBS, LILIAN	ADAMS, DOUG	~~STONE, JOHN~~	HOOD, MARY
GREEN, KAREN	KIRK, ERIC	~~KENT, RON~~	MOSS, SUE
BURNS, KEITH	JAMES, ANDY	MOON, CARL	

Figure 3.7
Space Freed From
Row Deletion

Page 336	Page 337	Page 338	Page 339
HOBBS, LILIAN	ADAMS, DOUG		HOOD, MARY
GREEN, KAREN	KIRK, ERIC		MOSS, SUE
BURNS, KEITH	JAMES, ANDY	MOON, CARL	

Figure 3.8
Free Space Not
Being Reused

Page 336	Page 337	Page 338	Page 339
HOBBS, LILIAN	ADAMS, DOUG		HOOD, MARY
GREEN, KAREN	KIRK, ERIC		MOSS, SUE
BURNS, KEITH	JAMES, ANDY	MOON, CARL	

DATE, SAM

This means that the space freed by deleting old rows will not be reused by new rows. The end result of this is that the amount of space used by the table may well exceed the space required to store the actual rows. Once all the rows are removed from a page it becomes available for use by the table again. If all the rows are removed from an extent it is deallocated and no longer belongs to the table.

In the worst case, however, many pages could contain mainly free space but still contain one or two rows. In this case the pages cannot become available for use by the table again and the table will appear to be taking up large amounts of space as shown in Figure 3.9.

This situation can be exacerbated by update activity that causes rows to be deleted and reinserted, as described in Chapter 4. In the absence of a clustered index, the deleted row will be reinserted at the end of the table and the space freed by the deleted row will remain unused until the page is completely empty.

Figure 3.9
*A Table Using
Much More Space
Than The Data
Requires*

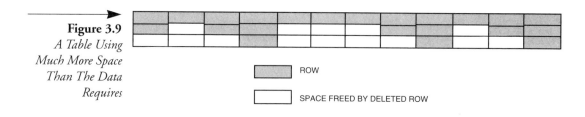

Hint: If a row size is used such that only one row can fit on a page, the deletion of a row will mean that there is no remaining row on the page so the page will immediately become available for reuse and free space will not be wasted.

The previous discussion has highlighted two problems areas:

▶ The non-reuse of free space from deleted rows

▶ The hot-spot caused by the insertion at the end of a table

So how can we avoid these problems? The answer is to create a clustered index on the table.

When rows were inserted at the end of the *Customers* table we saw that space freed by deleted rows could not be reused until all the rows had been deleted from the page. How does our clustered index modify this behavior? Our clustered index is going to ensure that new rows are always inserted in key sequence order, that is, in ascending order of the customer's last name. So let's delete some rows and see what happens.

We'll delete the customers who have last names of "Green" and "Hood." Pages 337 and 338 now have free space in them as shown in Figure 3.10. Let's now insert two new customers "French" and "Hunt." The clustered index will attempt to insert these rows in key sequence order so "French" will need to be inserted after "Date" but before "Hobbs" and "Hood" will need to be inserted after "Hobbs" but before "James."

Well, we are lucky. It just so happens that there is free space on the pages where we want to insert the rows and this space is therefore reused as shown in Figure 3.11.

We can see an immediate advantage to creating our clustered index—space freed by deleting rows can be reused. Of course, if our clustered index key had been an increasing key value such as that generated in a column with the identity property, new rows would always be inserted at the end of the table and space would still not be reused.

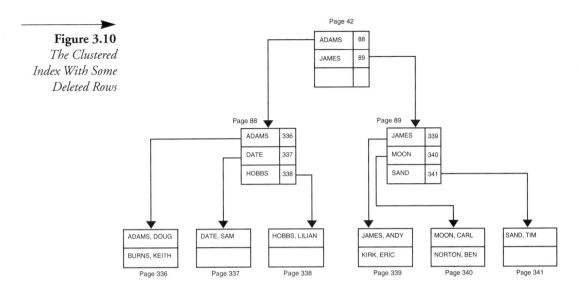

Figure 3.10
The Clustered Index With Some Deleted Rows

Figure 3.11
The Clustered Index With Some Newly Inserted Rows

Our example is, of course, a little contrived as there will be many occasions where there is not going to be free space in the page in which we want to insert the new row and we will deal with this scenario now.

Suppose that our clustered index contains the entries as shown in Figure 3.12. We want to insert a row with a key value of "Jones" which SQL Server must store between the key values "James" and "Kent" but there is obviously insufficient space in page 337 to hold the new row. In this case SQL Server

Figure 3.12
Full Clustered
Index Leaf Pages

Page 336	Page 337	Page 338	Page 339
ADAMS, DOUG	HOBBS, LILIAN	KENT, RON	MOSS, SUE
BURNS, KEITH	HOOD, MARY	KIRK, ERIC	STONE, JOHN
GREEN, KAREN	JAMES, ANDY	MOON, CARL	

Figure 3.13
A 50:50 Page Split

Page 336	Page 337	Page 338	Page 339
ADAMS, DOUG	HOBBS, LILIAN	KENT, RON	MOSS, SUE
BURNS, KEITH	HOOD, MARY	KIRK, ERIC	STONE, JOHN
GREEN, KAREN		MOON, CARL	

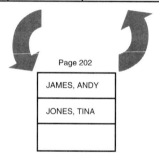

Page 202
JAMES, ANDY
JONES, TINA

must perform a page split. This involves acquiring a new empty page and chaining it into the existing chain of pages.

This type of page splitting is known as a 50:50 split as SQL Server ensures that approximately 50% of the rows on the existing page are moved onto the new page as shown in Figure 3.13. This is only part of the work that SQL Server must do. The intermediate index pages in the clustered index must be updated so that the new page is referenced. This will involve adding a new entry into an index page at the next level up. Of course, if there is insufficient room for the new entry the index page might split also! In our example, a new entry must be made for the key "James" pointing to page 202.

What about any nonclustered indexes that point to the table? Entries must be made for the new row but the existing row with the key "James" has moved to a new page so its leaf level pointer in any nonclustered indexes must also be updated. As one can imagine, this page splitting has caused SQL Server to perform a large amount of work.

Are the split pages going to split again soon? We can see that if inserts continue with key values greater than and less than "James" there will be a delay before page splitting occurs again. This delay is caused by the fact that the page splitting left us with pages that had free space in them. We can store about 40 Customer rows into a data page so in reality the page split will leave us with approximately 20 rows per page and therefore room for another 20 rows more per page which will delay the page splitting. On average we can expect to find pages that range from 50% full having just split to 100% full just before they split giving us an average page fullness of about 75%.

This is fine but suppose the clustered index is based on an ever increasing key value such as that provided by a column with the identity property or a column containing the date and time an order is taken. Insertion of new rows will always happen at the end of the clustered index. In this case there is no point in SQL Server performing a 50:50 split when a new page is chained in as space that is reserved physically before the last row inserted will never be used.

Figure 3.14 shows the insertion of a key value of "Moss." There is no space in which to store this row on page 338 so a new page must be chained in. In this case SQL Server does not shuffle rows from page 338 onto the new page but instead inserts only the new row on the new page as shown in Figure 3.15.

Note that an entry is added into the index page to point to the new key value on the new page. What happens in the case of duplicate key values being added to our clustered index? SQL Server has to be careful how these

Figure 3.14
Insertion At The End Of The Key Range

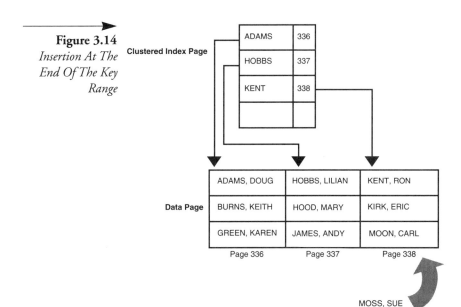

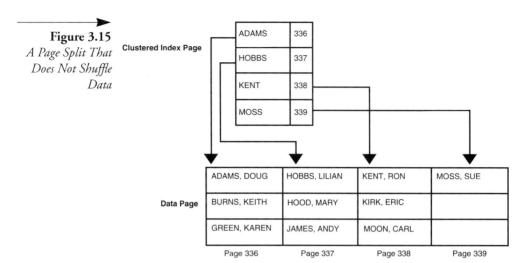

Figure 3.15
*A Page Split That
Does Not Shuffle
Data*

are handled—take the following scenario as shown in Figure 3.16. We are
adding a new row but there is no room on the data page to accommodate it.

Suppose SQL Server handled this the way it handled normal page splits.
We would be left in a situation as shown in Figure 3.17.

In this case the index entry is added to point to the lowest key value in the
new page. The problem is that the entry for "Jessie James" is ignored. Any traversal through the clustered index structure would miss it as SQL Server

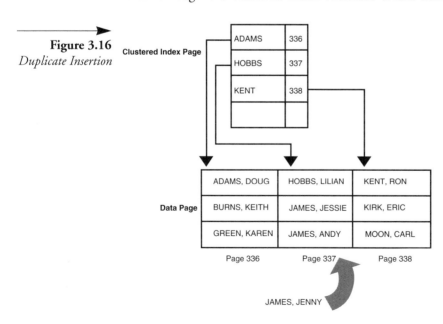

Figure 3.16
Duplicate Insertion

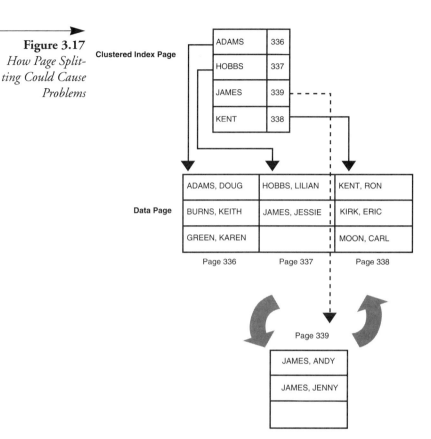

Figure 3.17
How Page Splitting Could Cause Problems

would be directed to page 401 believing that the first entry for "James" started on page 401 which clearly is not the case.

So how does SQL Server handle duplicate key values in a clustered index? In fact, the new page is chained in as described earlier but an entry is not added to the clustered index structure. The chained in page is known as an *overflow page* and is reserved for data rows with the duplicate key values only, as shown in Figure 3.18. When retrieving the rows that have the duplicate key value the clustered index will be traversed until the data page containing the key value is found and then all rows with that key value will be retrieved from that page and any overflow pages.

The action of page splitting is clearly going to give SQL Server some work to do. The new page must be obtained and chained in, rows must be shuffled, entries in most cases will be inserted into clustered index pages and any nonclustered indexes on the table will need to update their index entries to point to the existing rows that have moved to the new page. Also, of course, new entries will have to be added to the nonclustered indexes to point to the new row.

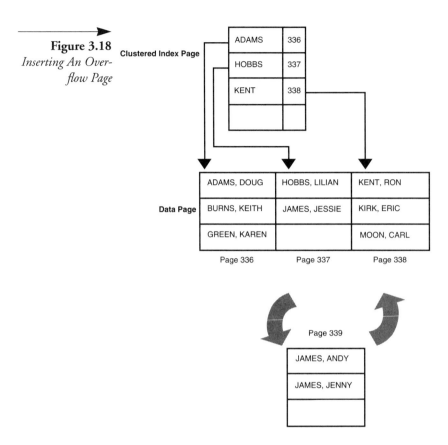

Figure 3.18
Inserting An Over-
flow Page

It would clearly be beneficial to minimize page splitting but how can we achieve this? One obvious way would be to not use clustered indexes, but the benefits they bring usually outweigh the overhead of page splitting. Without clustered indexes, for example, we would always insert at the end of the table causing a potential bottleneck.

Is there another way to minimize page splitting? Fortunately, there is. We can reserve space in a clustered index or a nonclustered index when we create the index using a *fillfactor*. During the creation of the index the index pages have free space reserved in them and, most importantly, in a clustered index free space is reserved in the data pages.

This free space is only reserved during the index creation process. Once the index has been created the free space in the index and data pages can be used for newly inserted rows. The size of the index will be larger if space is reserved in it and in the case of a clustered index the size of the table will also be larger but this does mean that the point when SQL Server needs to page split will be delayed.

When SQL Server starts to split pages *fragmentation* is said to occur. As many rows get inserted into a clustered index many data pages will be chained into the table and the table will become fragmented. This affects both insertion and scan efficiency and so we want to avoid it. We can tell if a table is becoming fragmented by using the *DBCC SHOWCONTIG* statement which will be described shortly.

3.6 So How Do You Create Indexes?

We have discussed the mechanics of indexes and later we will discuss indexes with reference to performance but it is time that we looked at how you create them. Indexes may be created via the Transact-SQL CREATE INDEX statement or the SQL Enterprise Manager. First, let us look at the Transact-SQL options and then we will look at the graphical approach provided by the SQL Enterprise Manager. The Transact-SQL syntax is shown below:

```
CREATE [UNIQUE] [CLUSTERED | NONCLUSTERED] INDEX index_name
    ON [[database.]owner.]table_name (column_name [,
        column_name]...)
[WITH
    [PAD_INDEX, ]
    [[,] FILLFACTOR = fillfactor]
    [[,] IGNORE_DUP_KEY]
    [[,] SORTED_DATA | SORTED_DATA_REORG]
    [[,] IGNORE_DUP_ROW | ALLOW_DUP_ROW]]
[ON segment_name]
```

The different options are described next.

To create a clustered index in Transact-SQL the CREATE INDEX statement is used:

```
CREATE UNIQUE CLUSTERED INDEX accounts_account_no_idx
    ON accounts (account_no)
```

The above example creates a clustered index on the *account_no* column of the *Accounts* table. The *unique* clause ensures that more than one row cannot have the same key value, in this case *account_no*. Note that the table may or may not already contain data. If it does and there are duplicate values the above CREATE INDEX statement will fail:

```
CREATE UNIQUE CLUSTERED INDEX accounts_account_no_idx
    ON accounts (account_no)

Msg 1505, Level 16, State 1
Create unique index aborted on duplicate key. Primary key is
    '1916'
```

Similarly, once the index has been successfully created an attempt to insert or update a row that would result in a duplicate key value will fail:

```
INSERT INTO accounts VALUES (1916, 103424, 1012, 10765)
```

```
Msg 2601, Level 14, State 3
Attempt to insert duplicate key row in object 'accounts' with
    unique index
'accounts_account_no_idx'
Command has been aborted.
```

This is fine as we want the *account_no* column to contain no duplicate values as this is the way we uniquely identify an account. We may wish to index on the *branch_code* column of the *Accounts* table instead. In this case it is highly likely that more than one account may have the same branch code so we will want to create an index that does not enforce unique values:

```
CREATE CLUSTERED INDEX accounts_branch_no_idx ON accounts
(branch_no)
```

As the above example shows, we accomplish this by merely omitting the UNIQUE clause. Note that an index may be created consisting of more than one table column. This is sometimes known as a *composite* index. An index can be created consisting of no greater that sixteen columns which in practical terms is a limit few people are likely to hit. Also, the sum of the column sizes in the index cannot be greater than 900 bytes. It is not a good idea to choose a composite key of 900 bytes in length because very few index entries will be able to fit into an index page and so many index pages will be used in the index. This will ultimately result in *deep* indexes consisting of many index levels. Traversing the index may then require many disk I/Os.

As mentioned previously, only one clustered index can be created on a table, which makes sense as data can only be physically sorted in one order. Any attempt to create a second clustered index will fail:

```
CREATE CLUSTERED INDEX accounts_balance_idx ON accounts
(balance)
```

```
Msg 1902, Level 16, State 1
Cannot create more than one clustered index on table 'accounts'.
   Drop the existing clustered index 'accounts_branch_no_idx'
   before creating another
```

To create a nonclustered index the CREATE INDEX statement is used as it was for creating the clustered index only in this case NONCLUSTERED is specified:

```
CREATE UNIQUE NONCLUSTERED INDEX accounts_account_no_idx
   ON accounts (account_no)
```

If neither CLUSTERED nor NONCLUSTERED is specified a nonclustered index is created.

How do we specify the *FILLFACTOR* option? The FILLFACTOR is a value from 0 to 100. An index created with a FILLFACTOR of 100 will have its index pages completely filled. This is useful if no data is to be entered into the table in the future.

An index created with a FILLFACTOR of 0 will have its leaf pages completely filled but other levels in the index will have enough space for a minimum of another index entry. An index created with a FILLFACTOR of between 0 and 100 will have its leaf pages filled to the FILLFACTOR percentage specified and, again, other levels in the index will have enough space for a minimum of another index entry. Remember that in a clustered index the leaf level is the data.

The default FILLFACTOR value is 0 and this default value can be changed with the *sp_configure* system stored procedure or via the *Configuration* tab in the *Server Configuration/Options* dialog box in the SQL Enterprise Manager. Table 3.1 shows the consequence of different FILLFACTOR values. A FILLFACTOR value of 0 specifies that the leaf level page of the index should be completely filled leaving no free space, however, the non-leaf pages should reserve space for one extra index entry. A FILLFACTOR value of 100% specifies that the leaf level page of the index should be completely filled leaving no free space. There should also be no free space reserved in the index pages. A FILLFACTOR value of 1–99% specifies that the leaf level page of the index should be filled no more than the FILLFACTOR value. The non-leaf pages should reserve space for one extra index entry. Note that for non-unique clustered indexes space is reserved for two index entries.

Care should be taken when choosing a FILLFACTOR as its relevance will depend on the way the application uses the table data. There is little point in

Table 3.1 *The Consequences Of Different Fillfactor Values*

Fillfactor Value %	Non-Leaf Page	Leaf Page
0	one index entry	completely full
1–99	one index entry	<= fillfactor % full
100	completely full	completely full

reserving space throughout an index if the row inserted always has a key greater than the current maximum key value. The following example creates an index with a FILLFACTOR of 50% meaning that each data page (leaf page) will only be filled to 50%. Index pages at the other levels will have room for one or two more index entries.

```
CREATE CLUSTERED INDEX accounts_balance_idx ON accounts
(balance)
WITH FILLFACTOR =50
```

Note that over time, as rows are inserted into the table, the effectiveness of the FILLFACTOR value will vanish and so a planned rebuilding of critical indexes at periodic intervals should be considered if heavy inserts are made to the table. Because SQL Server merges index pages with only one index entry to keep the index compact, the number of items on an index page is never less than two, even if a low value of FILLFACTOR is specified.

SQL Server 6.5 also introduced a new clause *PAD_INDEX* to the CRE-ATE INDEX statement. The PAD_INDEX clause means that the FILLFAC-TOR setting should be applied to the index pages as well as to the data pages in the index.

The ALLOW_DUP_ROW and IGNORE_DUP_ROW options are use-ful when a non-unique clustered index is to be created on a table that con-tains rows with identical values in their columns. Consider the following table and its data:

```
CREATE TABLE tab1 (f1 INT, f2 INT, f3 INT)

SELECT * FROM tab1

f1      f2      f3
---     ---     ---
1       1       1
2       2       2
3       3       3
4       4       4
4       4       4
```

We can create a non-unique clustered index specifying that no options are to be used when dealing with duplicate rows or the ALLOW_DUP_ROW or IGNORE_DUP_ROW options are to be used. If we specify no options when creating a non-unique clustered index on the above table the index creation will fail:

```
    CREATE CLUSTERED INDEX tab1_index ON tab1 (f1, f2, f3)

Msg 1508, Level 16, State 1
Create index aborted on duplicate rows. Primary key is '4'
```

If we specify the ALLOW_DUP_ROW option when creating a non-unique clustered index on the above table the index creation will succeed:

```
CREATE CLUSTERED INDEX tab1_index ON tab1 (f1, f2, f3)
WITH ALLOW_DUP_ROW
```

If we specify the IGNORE_DUP_ROW option when creating a non-unique clustered index on the above table the index creation will succeed; however, any duplicate rows in the table will be eliminated and a warning message will be output:

```
CREATE CLUSTERED INDEX tab1_index ON tab1 (f1, f2, f3)
WITH IGNORE_DUP_ROW

Warning: deleted duplicate row. Primary key is '4'

SELECT * FROM tab1

f1    f2    f3
---   ---   ---
1     1     1
2     2     2
3     3     3
4     4     4
```

The IGNORE_DUP_KEY option is useful when a unique clustered or nonclustered index is to be created on a table that might have rows with duplicate key values inserted into it. If the IGNORE_DUP_KEY option is set, rows containing duplicate key values are discarded but the statement will succeed whereas, if the IGNORE_DUP_KEY option is not set, the statement as a whole will be aborted.

The SORTED_DATA and SORTED_DATA_REORG options specify the amount of work done by SQL Server when a clustered index is created. Using either option skips the step that involves sorting the data as it is assumed that the data is already in the correct sorted order, that is, sorted in key sequence order. If SQL Server finds that this is not the case an error will occur and the index creation will fail.

```
SELECT * FROM tab1

f1     f2     f3
----   ----   ----
4      4      4
1      1      1
2      2      2
3      3      3

CREATE UNIQUE CLUSTERED INDEX tab1_index ON tab1
(f1,f2,f3) WITH SORTED_DATA

Msg 1530, Level 16, State 1
```

```
Create index with sorted_data was aborted because of row out of
     order. Primary key of first out of order row is '1'48
```

The difference between SORTED_DATA_REORG and SORTED_DATA is that SORTED_DATA_REORG physically reorganizes the data which is the case if neither of these options is specified. The SORTED_DATA option does not physically reorganize the data and so the SORTED_DATA option will be quicker than the SORTED_DATA_REORG option because the data is not moved and nonclustered indexes are not rebuilt.

The SEGMENT option allows the database administrator to create the index on a segment different from the table itself. Historically, this was used for nonclustered indexes to spread disk I/O to the index and table across separate disk drives for better performance. Most database administrators typically use a form of disk striping to spread disk I/O nowadays. Disk striping is discussed in Chapter 5.

Indexes can also be created and managed using the SQL Enterprise Manager. To do so, click the required table name with the right mouse button. In the resulting menu select *Indexes*. The *Manage Indexes* window displays and can be edited. This is shown in Figure 3.19.

This window also provides the database administrator with useful index space usage information as well as the facility to update and view the *distribution statistics*. Distribution statistics may assist the query optimizer in choosing a good query strategy as discussed in Chapter 4.

Figure 3.19
Using The SQL Enterprise Manager To Manage Indexes

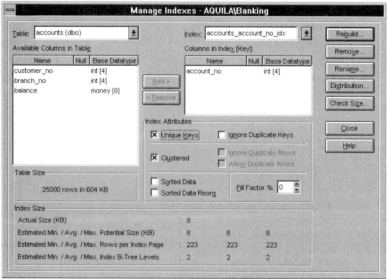

3.6.1 Dropping Indexes

Both clustered and nonclustered indexes can be dropped with the *DROP INDEX* Transact-SQL statement:

```
DROP INDEX accounts.accounts_balance_idx
```

Indexes may also be dropped by using the SQL Enterprise Manager. To do so merely click the *Remove* button shown in Figure 3.19.

3.6.2 Rebuilding Indexes

Prior to SQL Server 6.5, rebuilding an index really meant dropping it and then recreating it. This is fine unless the index is created because a primary key constraint is defined on a table. In this case it is not possible to drop the index directly as it can only be dropped as part of the removal of the primary key constraint. Unfortunately, as many a frustrated database administrator has found, dropping a primary key constraint is not possible if it is referenced by foreign key constraints. To drop the index means dropping the primary key constraint which means dropping foreign key constraints. This can get complicated and time consuming. SQL Server 6.5 introduced a new DBCC statement to avoid this problem:

```
DBCC DBREINDEX ('branches', accounts_branch_no_idx, 70)

Clustered index 'accounts_branch_no_idx' is being rebuilt.
Non-clustered index 'accounts_account_no_idx' is being rebuilt.
Non-clustered index 'accounts_balance_idx' is being rebuilt.
```

The DBCC DBREINDEX statement rebuilds a specific index or all the indexes on the table. Note that if a clustered index is rebuilt all the nonclustered indexes are automatically rebuilt. This must happen as the clustered index rebuild will move the data onto new pages so the pointers in the leaf level of the nonclustered indexes are now invalid.

The options SORTED_DATA and SORTED_DATA_REORG can also be used with the DBCC DBREINDEX statement. For an explanation of what they mean see the discussion of the CREATE INDEX statement earlier in this chapter.

3.6.3 Renaming Indexes

Indexes may be renamed by using the *sp_rename* system stored procedure:

```
sp_rename 'accounts.accounts_balance_index', accounts_balance_idx
```

(Note the use of the single quotes.)

Indexes may also be dropped by using the SQL Enterprise Manager. To so, click the *Rename* button shown in Figure 3.19.

3.6.4 Finding Out Index Information

Information can be graphically displayed by using the SQL Enterprise Manager. However, the SQL Enterprise Manager only displays so much. It is useful to be able to gather more information from Transact-SQL statements.

The System Stored Procedure *sp_helpindex*

The indexes that are present on a table can be listed by using the *sp_helpindex* system stored procedure:

```
sp_helpindex authors

index_name            index_description          index_keys
----------            -----------------          ----------
accounts_branch_no_i  clustered located on       branch_no
                         default
accounts_account_no_  nonclustered, unique       account_no
                         located on default
accounts_balance_idx  nonclustered located       balance
                         on default
```

3.6.5 The System Table Sysindexes

The stored procedure *sp_helpindex* looks in the system table *sysindexes* which contains much useful information about indexes. *Sysindexes* is present in every database. The definition of the table is shown in Table 3.2 below:

Table 3.2 *System Table Sysindexes*

Column	Datatype	Description
name	varchar(30)	Name of table (for indid = 0 or 255). Else index name.
id	int	ID of table (for indid = 0 or 255). Else, the ID of table on which the index is created.
indid	smallint	Index ID: 0 = Table, 1 = Clustered index, >1 Nonclustered Index, 255 = text or image data.
dpages	int	If indid = 0 or indid = 1, dpages is the count of used data pages. If indid > 1 or < = 250 dpages is the count of index leaf pages.
reserved	int	If indid = 0 or indid = 1, the total of pages allocated for all indexes and data pages. If indid > 1 or < = 250, the total pages allocated to this index. If indid = 255, the total pages allocated for text or image data.

Table 3.2 *System Table Sysindexes (continued)*

Column	Datatype	Description
used	*int*	If indid = 0 or indid = 1, the total of pages used for all indexes and data pages. If indid > 1 or < = 250, the total pages used by this index. If indid = 255, the total pages used for text or image data.
rows	*int*	If indid >= 0 and indid <= 250 the number of rows in the table else this is set to 0.
first	*int*	If indid = 0 or indid = 1, pointer to first data page. If indid >1 or < = 250, pointer to first leaf page. If indid = 255, pointer to first text or image page.
root	*int*	If indid > 0 or < = 250, pointer to root page. If indid = 0 or indid = 255, pointer to last page.
distribution	*int*	If indid = 1 or < = 250, pointer to distribution page.
OrigFillFactor	*tinyint*	The original fillfactor value used when the index was created.
segment	*smallint*	Segment number in which this object is placed.
status	*smallint*	Internal system-status information: 1 = Terminate command if attempt to insert duplicate key. 2 = Unique index. 4 = Terminate command if attempt to insert duplicate row. 16 = Clustered index. 64 = Index allows duplicate rows. 2048 = Index created to support PRIMARY KEY constraint. 4096 = Index created to support UNIQUE constraint.
rowpage	*smallint*	Maximum number of rows that can be stored per page.
minlen	*smallint*	Minimum length of a row.
maxlen	*smallint*	Maximum length of a row.
maxirow	*smallint*	Maximum length of a non-leaf index row.
keycnt	*smallint*	Number of key columns in the index.
keys1	*varbinary(255)*	Description of index key columns.
keys2	*varbinary(255)*	Description of index key columns.

Table 3.2 *System Table Sysindexes (continued)*

Column	Datatype	Description
soid	*tinyint*	If character data in key, sort order ID that the index was created with, else 0.
csid	*tinyint*	If character data in key, character set ID that the index was created with, else 0.
UpdateStamp	*varbinary*	Used for internal synchronization of row/page count changes.

The example below shows a *sysindexes* entry for the clustered index on the *Accounts* table. The column headings have been edited and moved for clarity.

```
SELECT * FROM sysindexes WHERE name = 'accounts_branch_no_idx'

name                id        indid   dpages    reserved    used   rows
----------------    --------  -----   -------   --------    ----   -----
accounts_branch     16003088  1       400       888         869    25000
   _no_idx

first root distribution OrigFillFactor segment status rowpage minlen maxlen
----- ---- ------------ -------------- ------- ------ ------- ------ ------
3728  3736 3737              70             1      144     93      22     22

maxirow       keycnt       keys1                                    keys2
-------       ------       ----------------------------------       -----
9             1            0x0000030038040101000a00000000000000     (null)

soid          csid         UpdateStamp
----          -----        ------------------
0             0            0x0000000100000001
```

The *indid* is 1 which shows that this is a clustered index. The number of data pages *dpages* is 400. There are 888 pages *reserved* for all the indexes and data of which 869 are *used*. There are 25000 rows and as they contain fixed length datatypes the minimum size of the row (minlen) and the maximum size of the row (maxlen) is the same value 22. Note that 22 is 20 bytes of user data plus 2 bytes overhead. The maximum rows per page is 93.

The maximum size of a non-leaf index row is 9 bytes which is made up of 4 bytes for the *account_no* column, 4 bytes for the page pointer and 1 byte that holds the number of variable length fields.

The first page of the table is 3728, the root page of the index is 3736 and the page number of the distribution page is 3737. The original fillfactor was 70%.

3.6.6 The DBCC Statement DBCC SHOWCONTIG

This DBCC statement is used primarily to observe the level of fragmentation that has occurred in a table, in other words the level of page splitting. The following DBCC SHOWCONTIG output was from the *Accounts* table after it had been loaded with 12500 rows with even values in the *account_no* column. A clustered index was created on the *account_no* column and then 12500 rows with odd values in the *account_no* column were loaded. This results in page splitting as the even numbered rows now have odd numbered rows inserted between them. Note that DBCC SHOWCONTIG expects the *object_id* of the table as a parameter not the name. This can be obtained from the following SELECT statement:

```
SELECT OBJECT_ID ('accounts')
```

If no index id is specified the page chain at the data level is scanned else the page chain at the leaf level of the specified index.

Output after loading 12500 rows with even values in the account_no column:

```
DBCC SHOWCONTIG (16003088)
DBCC SHOWCONTIG scanning 'accounts' table...
[SHOW_CONTIG - SCAN ANALYSIS]
--------------------------------------------------------
Table: 'accounts' (16003088) Indid: 1 dbid:6
TABLE level scan performed.
- Pages Scanned...............................: 151
- Extent Switches............................: 18
- Avg. Pages per Extent......................: 7.9
- Scan Density [Best Count:Actual Count]......: 100.00% [19:19]
- Avg. Bytes free per page...................: 27.2
- Avg. Page density (full)...................: 98.65%
- Overflow Pages.............................: 0
- Disconnected Overflow Pages................: 0
```

The first line of output *Pages Scanned* is the number of pages in the page chain, in our example the number of pages in the table (*dpages* in *sysindexes*). Another way of looking at this item is that it has taken 151 pages to hold the 12500 rows. As a page will hold about 91 rows (2016 free bytes per page/22 bytes row length) this is in the right ball park.

Extent switches is the number of times the DBCC statement moved off an extent while it was scanning the pages in the extent. We would expect an extent switch to happen after the whole extent had been scanned and a new extent needed to be scanned next. As we have 151 pages the best we can hope for is *(number of pages/8 pages per extent)* extents to hold the data. In our case 151/8 is 18.9 and therefore the best we can hope for is to hold the data in 19 extents. Our extent switches is 18 which is perfect as the jump onto the first extent is not counted.

The *Avg. Pages per Extent* is merely the average number of pages per extent which is the *(number of pages/number of extents)*. In our example (151/19) which gives us 7.9.

Perhaps the most useful line of output is the *Scan Density [Best Count:Actual Count]*. This is our measure of fragmentation. The *Best Count* is the ideal number of extent changes if everything is contiguously linked whereas the *Actual Count* is the actual number of extent changes. DBCC seems to count every extent in this line of output, hence, 19! The *Scan Density* is the ratio of these two values expressed as a percentage. In other words *((Best Count/Actual Count)*100)*. In our example *Scan Density* is ((19/19)*100) giving 100% which is perfect.

The *Avg. Bytes free per page* and *Avg. Page density (full)* are a measure of the average free bytes on the pages in the chain and the percentage fullness respectively. These are values that are affected by the fillfactor used.

Output after loading 12500 rows with odd values in the account_no column:

```
DBCC SHOWCONTIG scanning 'accounts' table...
[SHOW_CONTIG - SCAN ANALYSIS]

------------------------------------------------

TABLE level scan performed.
- Pages Scanned..............................: 452
- Extent Switches............................: 302
- Avg. Pages per Extent......................: 8.0
- Scan Density [Best Count:Actual Count]......: 18.81% [57:303]
- Avg. Bytes free per page...................: 629.2
- Avg. Page density (full)...................: 68.76%
- Overflow Pages.............................: 0
- Disconnected Overflow Pages................: 0
```

After loading our second batch of 12500 rows we can see that the situation has deteriorated. We have doubled the number of rows in the table but the *Pages Scanned* value has increased by a factor of three!

It should take (452/8 = 57) extents to hold the rows. But the actual number of extent changes measured was 303 giving the *Scan Density* value of ((57/303)*100) or 18.81%. Note also that our page fullness has dropped. The bottom line here is that there is much page fragmentation. Many pages are chained in and SQL Server would have to jump around to scan this table. Note also that the page fullness is about 3/4 full. This is common when page splitting is occurring and is due to the fact that 50:50 splitting is taking place as mentioned earlier in this chapter. An index rebuild, preferably with an appropriate fillfactor value would be advisable here.

3.7 Using Indexes to Retrieve Data

Now that we have seen how indexes are put together and how they behave when data is retrieved and added we can investigate how indexes can be used to support good performance.

The choice of whether to use an index or not and if so which index is a decision that the query optimizer makes. We will investigate the query optimizer in detail in Chapter 4 but we need to look at the different mechanisms of using an index to understand what the query optimizer is thinking when it is in the process of making its decision.

If there are no indexes on a table there is only one way in which the data can be accessed and that is by means of a table scan. When a table scan is performed each page in the table is read starting at the first page and ending at the last page. To read each page SQL Server performs a logical I/O. If the page is not found in the data cache this results in a physical I/O to disk. Each time a query is run the physical I/O generated by the query is likely to change because data will be cached from the previous execution of the query. For this reason, when comparing the work performed by different query optimizer strategies, it is better to compare the logical I/O values.

The table scan is a useful *baseline* as we know that we can always access our data in the number of logical I/Os the table scan requires. Anything more is a poor strategy. With this in mind let us consider different types of index access.

We will use a simplified diagram of our two index types.

Figure 3.20 shows a simplified clustered index and Figure 3.21 shows a simplified nonclustered index. Note that, as is commonly found, the clustered index contains one less level than the nonclustered index.

We will assume that in one scenario we have a clustered index on the *account_no* column of the *Accounts* table and in the other scenario there is a nonclustered index on it instead.

3.7.1 Retrieving a Single Row

This is sometimes called a *direct key lookup*. We are attempting to retrieve a single row as opposed to a range of rows. Often this is a result of using the equality operator (=) on a primary key, for example:

```
SELECT balance WHERE account_no = 736979
```

In the case of the clustered index SQL Server will first obtain the page number of the root page from the *sysindexes* table. In this root page there will

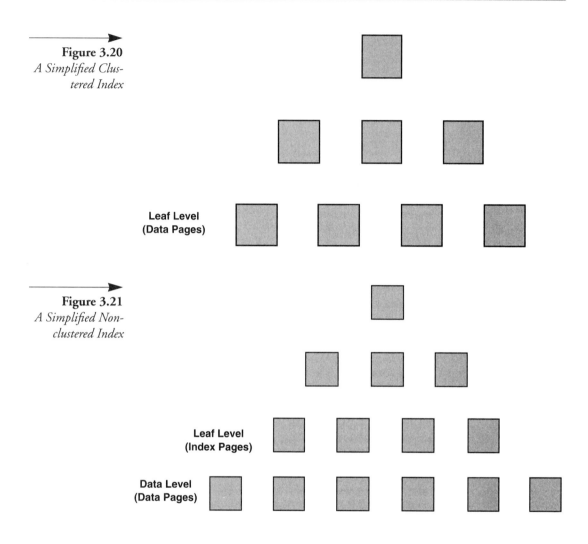

Figure 3.20
*A Simplified Clus-
tered Index*

**Leaf Level
(Data Pages)**

Figure 3.21
*A Simplified Non-
clustered Index*

**Leaf Level
(Index Pages)**

**Data Level
(Data Pages)**

be a number of key values and SQL Server will look for the highest key value that is not greater than the key we wish to retrieve.

As we have already seen, in a clustered index an index entry consists of the index key plus a pointer which is a page number, so the index key retrieved in the root page will point to an intermediate index page.

Again, SQL Server will look for the highest key value that is not greater than the key we wish to retrieve. In our diagram, the key found will now contain a page pointer to a data page, and so this page will be retrieved. The data page is now scanned for a row containing the key we wish to retrieve. The row is either found and returned or SQL Server will return a message stating "*(0 row(s) affected)*." This is shown graphically in Figure 3.22.

Figure 3.22
*A Direct Key
Lookup In A Clus-
tered Index*

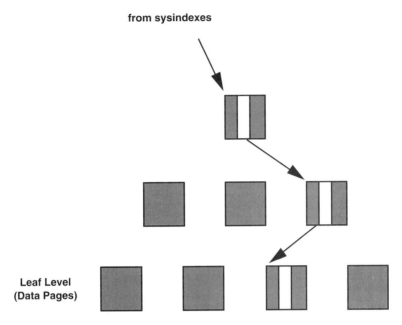

In the case of a nonclustered index the traversal of the index is performed in a similar fashion. However, once the leaf level is reached the key value of the key we wish to retrieve is found and this leaf level index entry will contain the *row id* of the data row so SQL Server will go directly to it in the appropriate data page.

The nonclustered index has taken one more logical I/O. Is this important? Taken on its own, probably not. However, if this is a query we are trying to highly optimize for an Online Transaction Processing System (OLTP) with a large user population it might just influence our design. On the whole though, the difference between using a clustered index or a nonclustered index for a single row retrieval is slim.

3.7.2 Retrieving a Range of Rows

We shall now attempt to retrieve a range of rows as opposed to a single row. Often this is a result of using operators such as BETWEEN, <, > and LIKE, for example:

```
SELECT balance WHERE account_no BETWEEN 78901 AND 78903
```

In the case of the clustered index SQL Server will first obtain the page number of the root page from the *sysindexes* table. In this root page there will be a number of key values and SQL Server will look for the highest key value that is not greater than the lowest key we wish to retrieve.

Figure 3.23
*A Direct Key
Lookup In A Non-
clustered Index*

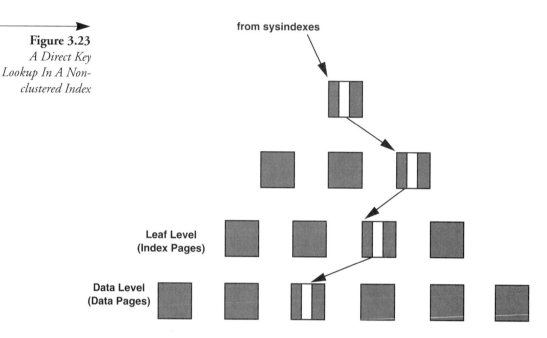

from sysindexes

Leaf Level
(Index Pages)

Data Level
(Data Pages)

The page pointer will be followed to the intermediate index page. Again, SQL Server will look for the highest key value that is not greater than the lowest key we wish to retrieve. In our diagram, the key found will now contain a page pointer to a data page, and so this page will be retrieved. The data page is now scanned for a row containing the lowest key we wish to retrieve. The row is retrieved and so is the next row and so on until the key value of a retrieved row is found to be higher than the range we require.

This is shown graphically in Figure 3.24 with the query returning 3 rows. Note that SQL Server is directed to the data page that contains the lowest key value in the range. Once there, SQL Server needs only to retrieve the rows sequentially until the range is exhausted. SQL Server can do this because the clustered index has ensured that the rows are in key sequence order.

In the case of a nonclustered index the traversal of the index is performed in a similar fashion. However, once the leaf level is reached the key value of the key we wish to retrieve is found and this leaf level index entry will contain the *row id* of the data row so SQL Server will go directly to it in the appropriate data page. Now the leaf level of the nonclustered index is in key sequence order but the data is not. What this means is that the key values in the range are found next to one another in the index leaf pages but it is highly unlikely that the data rows will be. In Figure 3.25 the query has returned three rows. The leaf level of the nonclustered index contains the three index entries next to one another but the data rows are on different data pages.

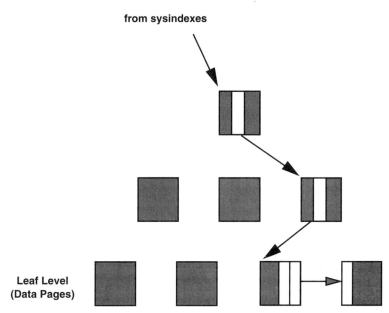

Figure 3.24
A Range Retrieval
In A Clustered
Index

from sysindexes

Leaf Level
(Data Pages)

This is a very important point and is a fundamental difference between the behavior of a clustered index and a nonclustered index with range retrievals. In our example the clustered index has required less logical I/Os to retrieve the data than the nonclustered index because in the clustered index the data rows are adjacent.

We have only retrieved three data rows in our example but suppose we had retrieved 90. We can hold 90 rows from the *Accounts* table in one page so the clustered index could theoretically retrieve the 90 data rows in one logical I/O. The nonclustered index may take as many as 90 logical I/Os which could equate to 90 physical I/Os if the data rows were all on their own separate data pages.

Suppose one data page happened to hold ten of the rows that satisfied the range? The nonclustered index would have ten pointers addressing that page and would still generate 10 logical I/Os to it. If the query optimizer decided that the number of logical I/Os needed to traverse the nonclustered index, scan the relevant leaf level pages and retrieve the data was greater than the number of pages in the table, a table scan would be performed.

3.7.3 Covered Queries

The leaf level of a clustered index contains the data rows whereas the leaf level of a nonclustered index contains only the key and a pointer and as long as the

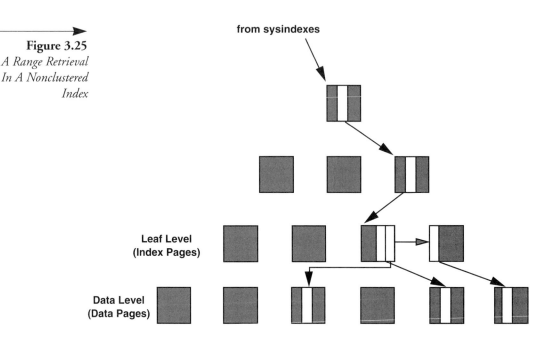

Figure 3.25
*A Range Retrieval
In A Nonclustered
Index*

key is only a small portion of the total row we can see that a database page
will hold more key values than complete data rows.

We can use this fact to provide fast access for certain queries using a nonclustered index. Suppose we have created a *composite* index, that is, an index
that consists of more than one column. An example of this might be the following:

```
CREATE INDEX accounts_account_no_bal_idx
   ON accounts (account_no, balance)
```

Now suppose we execute the following query:

```
SELECT balance FROM accounts
   WHERE account_no BETWEEN 24000 AND 24500
```

The query optimizer will realize that this is a covered query and that the
index named *accounts_account_no_bal_idx* is a *covering index*. This means
that SQL Server does not have to go to the data level to satisfy the query. It
only needs to go down as far as the leaf level of the clustered index as shown
in Figure 3.26.

This is very efficient. In the example above there were 500 rows satisfying
the query but SQL Server only used eight logical I/Os to satisfy the query.
Although clustered indexes are often more efficient than their nonclustered
cousins, when a nonclustered index is used as a covering index it is normally

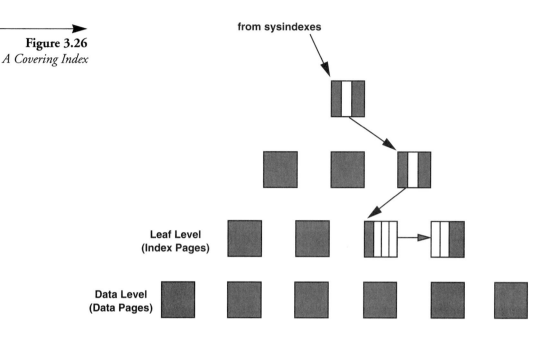

Figure 3.26
A Covering Index

from sysindexes

Leaf Level
(Index Pages)

Data Level
(Data Pages)

more efficient than an equivalent clustered index and, like a table scan, scanning the leaf level of an index activates the *read ahead manager* and so a parallel data scan is initiated.

3.8 Choosing Indexes

The choice of indexes can dramatically affect performance and can mean the difference between data being retrieved in seconds with few disk I/Os or minutes, even hours, with many disk I/Os. Choosing the optimum number of indexes that support the critical queries is therefore an extremely important task.

3.8.1 Why Not Create Many Indexes?

If queries can be assisted by indexes why not create lots of indexes on every table? Unfortunately, like so many areas in database technology, there are swings and roundabouts concerning the use of indexes. On one hand indexes can speed up access to data, but on the other hand, they can slow down table insertions, updates and deletions. This is because SQL Server has more work to do maintaining all the indexes to ensure that they always truly reflect the current data in the table. Indexes also take up disk space.

Clearly, if disk space is plentiful and the database is read only there are good reasons to create many indexes. In reality most databases experience a mixture of read and write activity so the correct choice of indexes is critical to good performance. The choice of appropriate indexes should be a product of good up front design and transaction analysis.

We have already seen the affect that inserts can have on a clustered index. If the index key is not an increasing key value, that is, the newly inserted key is not always higher than existing key values, data rows will be inserted throughout the page chain. This avoids the hot spot at the end of the table but will cause page splitting to occur.

Either way, row insertion means that SQL Server must perform work to maintain the clustered index. If there are also nonclustered indexes on the table, which is usually the case, each nonclustered index must also be maintained when rows insertions occur. Every nonclustered index must accommodate a new index entry which may cause page splitting to occur in the index pages.

What about row deletion? In a clustered index a row may be deleted from a data page and if there is no index entry pointing to it because it is not the lowest key value in the page, little maintenance activity need be performed. In the case of nonclustered indexes there will always be maintenance activity if a row is deleted. Every nonclustered index must remove the index entry. If this leaves a single row in an index page SQL Server will merge the index page with another in order to keep the index compact. Again, this means work for SQL Server.

The behavior of updates will be covered in Chapter 4. But it is possible that an update to a row may result in the row being deleted and then re-inserted which has the overhead of deletion and insertion.

The bottom line is that too many indexes on a table can be disastrous for the performance of transactions that write to the table. How many indexes should there be on a table? There is no correct answer but for a volatile table I start to worry if someone wants to put more than three on it.

3.8.2 Online Transaction Processing Versus Decision Support

Online Transaction Processing Systems (OLTP) have characteristics that are different from Decision Support Systems (DSS) and you should have a good appreciation of where your application fits into this spectrum.

OLTP systems tend to involve a high frequency of short, pre-defined transactions that affect small amounts of data. More often than not, OLTP systems change data by insertion, update and deletion. OLTP systems frequently support large user populations and provide guaranteed response times in the sub-second range.

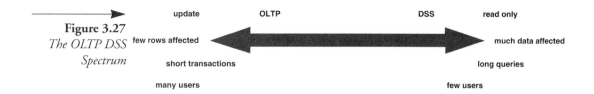

Figure 3.27
*The OLTP DSS
Spectrum*

update   OLTP   DSS   read only

few rows affected   much data affected

short transactions   long queries

many users   few users

DSS systems tend to be read only. They tend to involve a low frequency of long, complex, ad hoc queries that affect large amounts of data. Usually DSS systems do not support large user populations and the response time of queries may be measured in minutes or even hours. Unlike OLTP systems, DSS systems are often not mission critical.

Examples of OLTP systems are sales order entry systems and travel booking systems whereas examples of DSS systems might be anything from MIS reporting systems to large data warehousing systems.

Given the differences in the two application types it is clear that the indexing strategies are going to be different. In the case of OLTP there are likely to be high transactions rates involving transactions that change data. Having too many indexes will adversely affect the performance of OLTP systems and so the designer should limit the number of indexes to those that are really necessary. In the case of DSS the system is likely to be predominantly read only and therefore the designer can use as many indexes as are needed to support the query mix. Unlike OLTP transactions, DSS queries are ad hoc by nature and so the designer will often be unable to perform much up front transaction analysis in order to arrive at a fixed indexing strategy, therefore, using a good mix of indexes is frequently desired.

3.8.3 Choosing Sensible Index Columns

When the query optimizer is investigating different access strategies it will cost each strategy to determine the number of logical I/Os the strategy will use. This will be an estimate but, depending on the choice of columns in an index, the query optimizer might decide very quickly that an index is not worth bothering with.

When we are choosing index columns we should be looking for a combination of columns that support our queries but we should also be considering the number of duplicate values in the index column or columns. Suppose we were to index a column that could contain only the code "M" (male) and "F" (female). Would this be a good column to index? It would not be a good column to index because probably half the rows would contain

"M" and half would contain "F." We can say that the following query is not very *selective*:

```
SELECT * FROM table9 WHERE col5 = 'F'
```

If there were a nonclustered index on *col5* the query optimizer would not use it.

Another example would be the *state* column in a table holding client information. If we executed the following query on a 100,000 row table how many rows would be returned?:

```
SELECT * FROM clients WHERE state = 'CA'
```

If our company were based in San Francisco we might expect that most of our clients were located in California and therefore 90% of the rows in the table might be returned. However, if our company were based in Boston we might expect that few of our clients were located in California and therefore 5% of the rows in the table might be returned.

We can define *selectivity* as the percentage of the rows returned. For example:

```
selectivity = (the number of rows returned / the count of rows in
    the table) * 100
```

If 5,000 of the rows in our 100,000 row table were returned the selectivity of our query would be:

```
selectivity = (5000 / 100000) * 100 = 5%
```

If 90,000 of the rows in our 100,000 row table were returned the selectivity of our query would be:

```
selectivity = (90000 / 100000) * 100 = 90%
```

The more selective a query the fewer rows returned and the more likely that an index will be chosen by the query optimizer. In the example where 90% of the rows in the table are returned the query optimizer would probably choose a table scan in preference to a nonclustered index on the *state* column. In the example where 5% of the rows in the table are returned the query optimizer would probably choose to use a nonclustered index on the *state* column.

How does the query optimizer know that 5% or 90% of the rows in a table will be returned by a query? We shall see later that each index usually has a *distribution page* that helps the query optimizer estimate the number of rows returned.

Another value associated with selectivity is *density*. The density is the average fraction of duplicate index key values in the index. We can easily work out the density by finding the reciprocal of the count of unique values in the index key. Suppose in our example we had clients in 40 states; the index density would be 1/40 = 0.025.

Once the index density is known, by multiplying the total count of rows in the table by it, we can obtain the likely number of rows hit by specifying a given value, in our example:

```
row hits = 100000 * 0.025 = 2500
```

This is obviously an approximation as it does not take into account the fact that we might have many or few column values of "CA" so index density is only used when a distribution page cannot be.

Note: These terms can be confusing. A high *selectivity* refers to few duplicates but a high *density* refers to many duplicates.

SQL Server 6.0 and 6.5 hold multiple index densities for a composite index and we can picture the fact that adding more columns to an index is likely to increase the number of unique values in the index key.

Suppose, in our example, the index is not based on the *state* column alone but is based on the *state* and *city* columns. Whereas previously 10,000 clients may have been located in California, only 10 may be located in Oakland. The selectivity of a query specifying both the *state* and *city* columns will be higher than the selectivity of a query specifying only the *state* column.

SQL Server will hold the index densities for the *state* column and the *state* and *city* columns combined, that is, two density values. The query optimizer can access these values when working out its strategy.

How can we easily find information on the density of an index key? DBCC comes to the rescue with the *DBCC SHOW_STATISTICS* statement:

```
DBCC SHOW_STATISTICS (accounts, accounts_ branch_ cust_idx)

Updated                    Rows          Steps          Density
-------                    --------      --------       ----------
Dec 14 1996 3:43PM         25000         329            0.0

All density      Columns
-----------      --------------------
0.01             branch_no
4e-005           branch_no, customer_no

Steps
-------
1000
1000
1000
```

```
1000
1001
1001
:
```

This DBCC statement displays information about the distribution page. Most of this information will be discussed with respect to the query optimizer later. However, there is some information referred to as *All density* and this is the index density that we have been discussing. Our index is a composite index of two columns which are *branch_no* and *customer_no*. The *branch_no* column has a density value of 0.01 which is representative of the fact that we have 100 unique *branch_no* values (density = 1/100).

The density of both columns combined is very low (4e-005 or 0.00004). There are 25,000 rows in the *Accounts* table so a query containing:

```
WHERE branch_no = 1000
```

would return (25000 * .01 = 250) rows whereas a query containing:

```
WHERE branch_no = 1000 AND customer_no = 34667
```

would return (25000 * 0.00004 = 1) row.

3.8.4 Choosing A Clustered Index or A Nonclustered Index

As we have seen, a table can only have one clustered index and so it is important that we use it carefully—it's our ace and we want to play it at the right time! So when is a clustered index useful?

Consider using a clustered index when:

▶ It is desired to avoid hot spots caused by insertions into the last page of the table.

▶ The physical ordering supports the range retrievals of important queries or equality returns many duplicates.

▶ The clustered index key is used in the ORDER BY clause or GROUP BY clause of critical queries.

▶ The clustered index key is used in important joins to relate the tables, that is, it supports the foreign key.

▶ The clustered index columns are not changed regularly.

If there is no obvious candidate for the clustered index, because the clustered index structure is small and compact, it is a shame not to use it. Maybe the clustered index could be used to support the primary key constraint.

Consider using a nonclustered index when:

▶ A single or few rows will be retrieved, that is, the query is highly selective.

▶ The nonclustered index key is used in the ORDER BY clause or GROUP BY clause of critical queries.

▶ The nonclustered index key is used in important joins to relate the tables.

▶ A covered query is required.

Also consider that many applications will require the selection of a row by its primary key. This is a single row selection and therefore would normally benefit from the creation of an index containing the same columns as the primary key. As it is less common to request ranges of primary keys a nonclustered index is probably the best option. Also, rows are often inserted in ascending primary key order, especially if the primary key value is system generated, such as an invoice number or sales number. In this case, a clustered index would not eliminate the hot spot on the last page as rows would be added to the *end* of the index.

There are occasions when neither a clustered index or nonclustered index should be used. If the table is tiny the query optimizer will probably choose a table scan anyway and if the index has a low selectivity the query optimizer might always ignore it. Creating an index in these instances just increases disk space usage and maintenance overhead.

The choice of index and index columns is often a compromise. In my experience, regardless of the database product, this choice is perhaps the most critical one the database designer must face as incorrect indexes will result in potentially much greater disk I/O, CPU, locking contention and a lower caching efficiency.

4

The Query Optimizer

4.1 Introduction

When we execute a query, whether by typing a Transact-SQL statement or by using a tool such as Microsoft Access, it is highly likely we will require that rows are read from one or more database tables. Suppose we require that SQL Server performs a join of two tables, table *A* containing a dozen rows and table *B* containing a million rows. How should SQL Server access the required data in the most efficient fashion? Should it access table *A* looking for rows that meet the selection criteria and then read matching rows from table *B* or should it access table *B* first? Should it use indexes if any are present or do a table scan? If indexes are present and there is a choice of index, which one should SQL Server choose?

The good news is that SQL Server contains a component known as the *query optimizer* which will automatically take a query passed to it and attempt to execute the query in the most efficient way. The bad news is that it is not magic and it does not always come up with the best solution. A database administrator should be aware of the factors that govern query optimization, what pitfalls there are and how the query optimizer can be assisted in its job. Database administrators who know their data well can often influence the optimizer with the judicious use of indexes to choose the most efficient solution.

What do we mean by efficient in the context of the query optimizer? Basically, the query optimizer is looking to minimize the number of logical I/Os required to fetch the required data. The query optimizer is the SQL Server AutoRoute Express™ choosing the best route to the data.

The query optimizer's main task, therefore, is to minimize the work required to execute a query whether it is a query that retrieves data from a single table or a query that retrieves data from multiple tables participating in a join. The query optimizer also has another job which is to determine the type of update that is performed, for example, direct versus deferred. We will look at different update strategies later in this chapter.

Note that, although we have referred only to queries, the query optimization process is necessary for SELECT, INSERT, UPDATE and DELETE Transact-SQL statements as the UPDATE and DELETE Transact-SQL statements will often contain a WHERE clause and the INSERT statement may contain a SELECT clause.

4.1.1 When Is the Query Optimized?

When a query is submitted to SQL Server various phases of processing occur. First of all the query is parsed where it is syntax checked and converted into a *parsed query tree* that the standardization phase can understand. The standardization phase takes the parsed query tree and processes it to remove redundant syntax and to flatten subqueries. This phase essentially prepares the parsed query tree for query optimization. The output of this phase is a *standardized query tree*. This phase is sometimes known as *normalization*.

The query optimizer takes the standardized query tree and investigates a number of possible access strategies, finally eliminating all but the most efficient query plan. In order to formulate the most efficient query plan the query optimizer must carry out a number of steps. These are query analysis, index selection and join order selection.

Once the most efficient query plan is produced, the query optimizer must translate this into runnable code that can execute under Windows NT. This code can then access the appropriate indexes and tables to produce the result set.

How does the query optimizer work out the most efficient query plan? We will look at the way it does it next. We shall see that it takes in the information available to it in the form of the query itself, indexes and distribution pages, size of the table and rows per page and then calculates the logical I/O cost given a possible access path.

4.2 Query Optimization

The query optimization phase is the phase that we will concern ourselves with in this chapter. This phase can be broken down into a number of steps:

► Query Analysis
► Index Selection
► Join Order Selection

Figure 4.1
The Phases In Query Processing

SELECT customer_no, balance FROM accounts
WHERE balance > 100

Phase 1: Parsing
Phase 2: Standardization
Phase 3: Query Optimization
Phase 4: Query Compilation
Phase 5: Query Execution

```
customer_no         balance
-------------------  -----------
456789              567.87
898776              644.65
   :                   :
```

Let us investigate each step in sequence.

4.2.1 The First Step: Query Analysis

The first step that the query optimizer performs during the query optimization phase is query analysis. In this step the query optimizer examines the query for *search arguments (SARGs),* the use of the OR operator and join conditions.

4.2.1.1 Search Arguments

A search argument is that part of a query that restricts the result set. If indexes have been chosen carefully, an index can be used to support the search argument. Examples of search arguments are:

```
account_no = 7665332
balance > 30
lname = 'Burrows'
```

The AND operator can be used to connect conditions so another example of a valid search argument would be:

```
balance > 30 AND lname = 'Burrows'
```

Examples of common operators that are valid in a search argument are =, >, <, <= and >=. Other operators such as BETWEEN and LIKE are also valid because the query optimizer can represent them with the common operators listed above. For example, a BETWEEN can always be represented as >= AND <=. For example:

```
balance BETWEEN 1000 AND 10000
```

becomes:

```
balance >= 1000 AND balance <= 10000
```

A LIKE can always be represented as >= AND < For example:

```
lname LIKE 'Burr%'
```

becomes:

```
lname >= 'Burr' AND lname < 'Burs'
```

Hint: The expression balance BETWEEN 1000 AND 10000 is not equivalent to balance BETWEEN 10000 AND 1000. The query optimizer will not detect the mistake and switch the values.

There are a number of expressions that are not considered to be search arguments. The NOT operator is an example:

```
NOT IN ('CA', 'NH', 'TX')
customer_no != 9099755
balance <> 78000
```

Another example of this is the use of NOT EXISTS.

The NOT is not considered to be a search argument because it does not limit the search. Whereas *account_no = 100000* specifies a single value in a table that may potentially be efficiently retrieved using an index, *account_no != 100000* will cause SQL Server to look at every row in the table to ensure that the *account_no* column does not contain this value.

There are other expressions that are also not considered to be search arguments. If a column is used instead of an operator the expression is not considered to be a search argument. For example:

```
loan < loan_agreed
```

How can SQL Server use such an expression to restrict the result set? It cannot as the *loan_agreed* value is not known until the row is read and until it is known it cannot be used to compare against the *loan* column. This will normally result in a table scan even if the query is covered.

Another example of an expression that is not considered to be a search argument is one that involves mathematics or functions, for example:

```
balance * 1.175 > 10000

upper(lname) = 'SHARMAN'
```

As long as we have just a column on the left hand side of an appropriate operator we have a search argument. We can often compare the column with an *expression* such that the query optimizer will be able to use the distribution steps in the distribution page for the index rather than just the density values. Distribution pages will be covered shortly. This is true as long as the expression can be evaluated before the query execution phase, in other words, before the query actually runs. An example of such a search argument would be:

```
monthly_yield = 36234/12

yearly_amount = 50 * 365

sell_by_date > DATEADD (DAY, -10, GETDATE())
```

If the query optimizer cannot evaluate the expression until the query runs, that is until after the query optimization phase has completed, then SQL Server has no chance of making use of distribution steps. A classic example of this is where variables are used:

```
DECLARE @date_calculated DATETIME

SELECT @date_calculated = DATEADD (DAY, -10, GETDATE())

SELECT qty, brand
    FROM stock WHERE sell_by_date > @date_calculated
```

In one of my databases, the above example used a table scan instead of the nonclustered index on *sell_by_date* that the previous date arithmetic without variables example used. Note that this is different from stored procedure parameters which will be discussed later in this chapter.

4.2.1.2 OR Clauses

The query optimizer also checks the query for ORs. The OR clause links multiple search arguments together. For example, we might have a query that looked like the following:

```
SELECT * FROM customers WHERE
    age > 40        OR
```

```
      height < 2        OR
      weight < 200      OR
      state = 'NH'      OR
      city = 'Manchester'
```

Any row matching any of the above conditions will appear in the result set. A customer will be displayed who lives in the city of "Manchester" in the United Kingdom or who lives in "Nashua" in New Hampshire. In other words, it is likely that many rows in the table will meet one or more of these criteria.

Compare the following query:

```
SELECT * FROM customers WHERE
      age > 40          AND
      height < 2        AND
      weight < 200      AND
      state = 'NH'      AND
      city = 'Manchester'
```

The number of rows in the table that meet all the criteria is likely to be far less. The ANDs restrict the result set whereas the ORs widen it. For this reason a query containing ORs is handled in a particular way which will be discussed later. Because of this the query optimizer looks for OR clauses in the query analysis step.

There may be OR clauses in the query that are hiding. Take the following query:

```
SELECT lname, fname FROM employees
      WHERE state IN ('CA', 'IL', 'KS', 'MD', 'NY', 'TN', 'TX')
```

At first glance there are no ORs in this query. The query optimizer sees this, however, as a number of OR clauses:

```
SELECT lname, fname FROM employees
      WHERE
            state = 'CA'      OR
            state = 'IL'      OR
            state = 'KS'      OR
            state = 'MD'      OR
            state = 'NY'      OR
            state = 'TN'      OR
            state = 'TX'
```

4.2.1.3 Join Clauses

After looking for search arguments and OR clauses the query optimizer looks for any join conditions. When more than one table is processed in a query a join clause is usually found. The join clause may be in the WHERE clause or, if SQL Server 6.5 is being used, ANSI-standard join clauses are supported.

SQL Server Join Example:

```
SELECT fname, lname FROM customers, accounts
    WHERE customers.customer_no = accounts.customer_no AND
    balance > 10000
```

ANSI Join Example:

```
SELECT fname, lname FROM customers INNER JOIN accounts
    ON customers.customer_no = accounts.customer_no
    WHERE balance > 10000
```

Note that in SQL Server 6.5 the following ANSI-standard join clauses are supported:

▶ JOIN

▶ CROSS JOIN

▶ INNER JOIN

▶ LEFT OUTER JOIN

▶ RIGHT OUTER JOIN

▶ FULL OUTER JOIN

Sometimes a table may be joined with itself. This is sometimes known as a *self-join* or *reflexive* join. Although only one table is being accessed, the table is mentioned in the query more than once and so a join clause is used. The classic self-join is the *Employees* table containing a column *supervisor_id* which holds a value found in the *employee_id* elsewhere in the table. In other words, a supervisor is an employee. The *Employees* table might be defined as follows:

```
CREATE TABLE employees (
                employee_id    char(8),
                lname          char(10),
                fname          char(10),
                supervisor_id  char(8)
                )
```

A query to retrieve the last name of the employee and the last name of their supervisor would be:

```
SELECT e1.lname AS employee, e2.lname AS supervisor
    FROM employees e1, employees e2
    WHERE e1.supervisor_id = e2.employee_id
```

4.2.2 The Second Step: Index Selection

Having identified the search arguments in the query the next step that the query optimizer performs during the query optimization phase is index selection. In this step the query optimizer takes each search argument and checks to see if it is supported by one or more indexes on the table. The selectivity of the indexes is taken into consideration and based on this the query optimizer can calculate the cost of a strategy that uses that index in terms of logical and physical I/Os. This cost is used to compare strategies that use different indexes and a strategy that uses a table scan.

4.2.2.1 Does A Useful Index Exist?

To obtain information on the indexes present on a table and their characteristics, SQL Server can check the *sysindexes* system table. From the *sysindexes* table the query optimizer can quickly establish the indexes present on the table by checking the rows that have a value in the *id* column equal to the object id of the table (as defined in the *sysobjects* system table) and an *indid* column value > 0 and < 255. The *keycnt, keys1* and *keys2* columns help the query optimizer determine on which columns the index is based.

The query optimizer will look for an index based on the same column as the search argument. If the index is a composite index the query optimizer determines if the first column in the index is specified in the search argument.

If a search argument has no matching index then no index can be used to support the search argument and so the query optimizer will look for indexes supporting other search arguments. If it is the only search argument then a table scan will be performed.

4.2.2.2 How Selective Is the Search Argument?

Suppose the following query is presented to the query optimizer:

```
SELECT account_no FROM accounts WHERE
          branch_no = 1005 AND
          balance > 5000 AND
          customer_no BETWEEN 10000 AND 110000
```

If there are indexes present on the *branch_no, balance* and *customer_no* columns how can the query optimizer decided which is the most efficient index to use, that is, which is the index that will use the least number of I/Os to return the data?

The query optimizer has a number of mechanisms by which it can determine this information. The most accurate method is to use statistical information available in the *distribution page* (sometimes called the *statistics page*) associated with the index. We will look at distribution pages soon. If the distribution page does not exist the query optimizer applies a weighting to each operator. For example, the = operator has a weighting of 10% which means that the query optimizer will assume that 10% of the rows in the table will be returned.

The weightings of some common operators are shown in Table 4.1.

As you might imagine, these weightings are very general estimates and can be wildly inaccurate so it is always best if the query optimizer is able to use the distribution statistics associated with an index.

If we have a unique index matching the search argument then the query optimizer knows immediately the number of rows returned by the = operator. Because of the unique index the query optimizer knows that at most one row can be returned (of course, zero rows could be returned) so this figure is used rather than the 10% weighting.

4.2.2.3 The Distribution Page

A distribution page is usually created when an index is created, the one exception to this being when an index is created on an empty table, otherwise an index has exactly one distribution page. Note that the indexes on a table that has been truncated will also have no distribution page. The page number of the distribution page can be found by looking at the *distribution* column in the *sysindexes* system table for the row representing the index whose distribution page we wish to find. If this column is empty then there is no distribution page associated with the index.

The distribution page holds distribution statistics information for the index to allow the query optimizer to quickly estimate the proportion of rows that will be returned by a search argument. Suppose we execute the following query on the *Accounts* table that holds information for 25,000 accounts:

```
SELECT account_no FROM accounts WHERE balance > 9999
```

Will 25,000 rows be returned, or 1000 rows, or 25 rows or 0 rows? The query optimizer needs to know this information so it can decide whether a nonclustered index on the *balance* column is interesting.

Table 4.1 *The Weightings Of Common Operators*

Operator	Weighting
=	10%
<	33%
>	33%
BETWEEN	25%

In the *Banking* database there are, on average, less than 10 accounts that have a balance greater than 9,999 and so an indexed access should be more efficient than a table scan. But how can the query optimizer know this? It could count the number of rows that satisfied the search argument before it actually executed the query but that would rather defeat the object!

This is where the distribution page comes into its own. It holds a series of samples across the index key range which the query optimizer can check. Based on these samples the query optimizer can quickly estimate the percentage of the rows in the table that will be returned by the search argument using that index.

The distribution page actually holds a number of key values as shown in Figure 4.2. The number of key values held in the distribution page are a function of the key size as the free space on the distribution page is effectively a constant. The distribution page is 2 Kb in size like any other database page. We can subtract 32 bytes from this 2 Kb to allow for the fixed page header leaving 2016 bytes free to store the key values.

Suppose we have an index key that is an integer such as the *account_no* column in our *Accounts* table. An integer datatype is 4 bytes and therefore we could expect to be able to store 2016/4 = 504 samples, that is, key values. The initial key value found in the index is the first one to be sampled and stored in the distribution page so we will have a distribution page as shown in Figure 4.3.

We can see that the number of distribution steps will be one less than the number of key values stored in the distribution page. Unless there are very few rows in the table, a distribution step will represent a sample over a number of key values.

The equation to calculate the size of a step is:

```
(rows per table - 1) / (key samples per distribution page - 1)
```

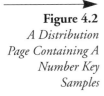

Figure 4.2
A Distribution Page Containing A Number Key Samples

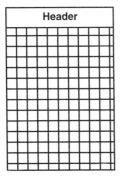

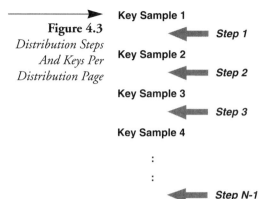

Figure 4.3
*Distribution Steps
And Keys Per
Distribution Page*

Key Sample 1

◀ *Step 1*

Key Sample 2

◀ *Step 2*

Key Sample 3

◀ *Step 3*

Key Sample 4

⋮

⋮

◀ *Step N-1*

Key Sample N

In our *Accounts* table there are 25,000 rows so we can estimate that there are:

```
(25000-1)/(504 - 1) = 49
```

rows per step. This means that every step in the distribution page represents 49 rows. We can see that if we had a key value that was 30 bytes in size we would only be able to store 2016/30 = 67 key values on the distribution page, giving:

```
(25000-1)/(67 - 1) = 378
```

rows per step. The sample interval is hence greater and consequently less accurate. The distribution page, therefore, is most useful if the key size of the associated index is small.

What about composite indexes? SQL Server only stores distribution steps for the first column. This means that it is better to choose as the first column of an index the most selective column, that is, the column with the least number of duplicate values. Of course, the first column of the index needs to be specified in the query and so choosing the most selective column will need to be done with this in mind.

How can we study a distribution page? One method is to use the SQL Enterprise Manager. If we display the *Manage Indexes* dialog box for a table we can then mouse click the *Distribution* button to display the *Index Distribution Statistics* as shown in Figure 4.4.

Another method is to use DBCC SHOW_STATISTICS. The format of this DBCC statement is:

```
DBCC SHOW_STATISTICS (table_name, index_name)
```

Figure 4.4
Index Distribution
Statistics Via The
SQL Enterprise
Manager

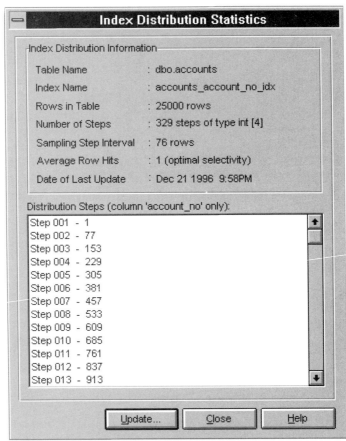

To use this DBCC statement to display the information as shown by the SQL Enterprise Manager in Figure 4.4:

```
DBCC SHOW_STATISTICS (accounts, accounts_account_no_idx)

Updated                  Rows          Steps          Density
------------------       -----         ------         -------
Dec 21 1996 9:58PM       25000         329            4e-005

All density              Columns
-----------              -----------
4e-005                   account_no

Steps
-------
    1
   77
  153
```

```
229
305
381
457
533
```

The distribution page shown above is associated with the nonclustered index based on the *account_no* integer column in the *Accounts* table. The distribution statistics, irrespective of which utility displayed them, indicate that there are 329 steps. This conflicts with the 503 we calculated earlier. Why is this?

The reason is that we have assumed that the entries in the distribution page are equal in size to the key. This is not so. Suppose we obtain the page number of the distribution page from the *sysindexes* system table and dump it using DBCC PAGE (the database ID of the *Banking* database on this SQL Server is 6):

```
DBCC TRACEON (3604)
DBCC PAGE (6, 2388, 1)
```

```
PAGE:
Page found in cache.

BUFFER:
Buffer header for buffer 0x10e4360
  page=0x14d4800 bdnew=0x1182e68 bdold=0x1182e68 bhash=0x11040a0
bnew=0x10e6220
  bold=0x10e42a0 bvirtpg=100665684 bdbid=6 bpinproc=0 bkeep=0
bspid=0
  bstat=0x1004 bpageno=2388

PAGE HEADER:
Page header for page 0x14d4800
pageno=2388 nextpg=0 prevpg=0 objid=384004399 timestamp=0001
0002ff62
nextrno=329 level=0 indid=2 freeoff=2012 minlen=6
page status bits: 0x8000,0x80,0x40

DATA:
Offset 32 -
014d4820: 00000100 0000 ......

Offset 38 -
014d4826: 00014d00 0000 ..M...

Offset 44 -
014d482c: 00029900 0000
    :
    :
```

Note the data entries at the various offsets. These samples are not 4 bytes long but 6 bytes long! The two bytes are overhead used by SQL Server.

Using this new entry size we can say that the number of steps is in fact more like (2016/6 − 1) = 335 samples. This is much closer to the number reported by the utilities. The small discrepancy is caused by other overhead such as the space required to hold index density information.

4.2.2.4 Updating Distribution Pages

When does the distribution page get updated? Statistics are not automatically updated when transactions that change the index commit. This would cause the distribution page to become a bottleneck. The distribution page is accurate when it is first constructed as part of the index creation (assuming there is data in the table). After that, on a volatile index, the distribution statistics will diverge from reality. It is the responsibility of the database administrator to ensure that the distribution page is updated to reflect reality and there are various ways to achieve this. The most common method is to use the Transact-SQL statement UPDATE STATISTICS. The format of this statement is:

```
UPDATE STATISTICS table_name [index_name]
```

If both the table name and index name are specified, the distribution page for that index is updated. If only the table name is specified, the distribution pages for all indexes present on the table are updated.

One might imagine that omitting the table name would cause the distribution pages on all of the indexes on all of the tables in the database to be updated. Not so, this will result in a syntax error. A convenient way of doing this might be to use a Transact-SQL cursor:

```
DECLARE tables_cursor CURSOR FOR
    SELECT name FROM sysobjects WHERE type = 'U'

OPEN tables_cursor

DECLARE @tablename varchar(30)

FETCH NEXT FROM tables_cursor INTO @tablename

WHILE (@@fetch_status <> -1)

    BEGIN

        EXEC ('UPDATE STATISTICS ' + @tablename)
        FETCH NEXT FROM tables_cursor INTO @tablename

    END

PRINT 'The distribution pages of all indexes in the database have
    been updated.'

CLOSE tables_cursor

DEALLOCATE tables_cursor
```

The above cursor creates a result set of all the user tables and then proceeds to update the distribution pages of all the indexes on each one.

Another method of updating distribution pages is to use the *Database Maintenance Plan Wizard*. This is a wizard that first appeared in SQL Server 6.5 to allow a database administrator to easily and quickly set up a routine to backup and integrity check a database as well as to reorganize indexes and update distribution pages. The section of the wizard that is concerned with data optimization is shown in Figure 4.5.

Updating distribution pages can also be achieved using the *Distributed Management Objects (DMO)* interface. The *Table* object has a method named *UpdateStatistics* that can be used to update the distribution page of all the indexes on a table and the *Index* object has a method named *UpdateStatistics* that can be used to update the distribution page of an index.

How can we easily tell when a distribution page was last updated? As Figure 4.4 shows, the *Index Distribution Statistics* information displayed in the SQL Enterprise Manager contains the *Date of Last Update*. This information is also displayed by DBCC SHOW_STATISTICS. However, there is also a function *STATS_DATE* that can be used. The format of this function is:

```
STATS_DATE(table_id, index_id)
```

Figure 4.5
The Database Maintenance Plan Wizard

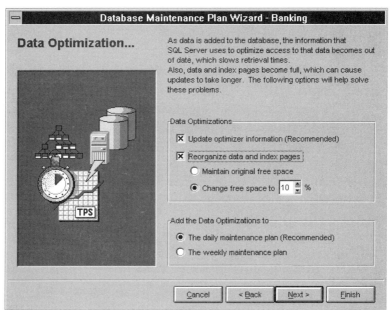

To check the date the distribution pages were last updated on all the indexes on a given table the following Transact-SQL can be used:

```
SELECT
    ind.name AS 'Table Index',
    STATS_DATE(ind.id, ind.indid) AS 'Date Last Updated'
    FROM sysobjects tab, sysindexes ind
    WHERE tab.id = ind.id
    AND tab.name = 'accounts'
```

This might give the following output:

```
Table Index              Date Last Updated
----------------------   ------------------
accounts_branch_no_idx   20 Dec 1996 23:32
accounts_account_no_idx  21 Dec 1996 22:41
accounts_balance_idx     21 Dec 1996 18:05
```

Note that if there is no distribution page created for an index, because the index was created on an empty table, the *Date Last Updated* column will contain *null*. This should be a red warning light to a database administrator who should run UPDATE STATISTICS without delay!

Whichever method is chosen, the distribution page for an index on a table that is written to should be updated regularly or the query optimizer will start to use inaccurate information. An extreme example of this would be an index that was created on a table containing a single row that then had a million rows added. Most cases are not so extreme but it is easy to forget to update distribution pages if no automated mechanism such as a scheduled task is set up. When the query optimizer chooses a strategy that you would not expect, the date the distribution page was last updated is often the first information to check.

4.2.2.5 When Can the Distribution Page Not Be Used?

The distribution page cannot be used by the query optimizer if it is not there! As we have said, this occurs if the index was created on an empty table. Even if it is present it may not be used. When we discussed search arguments earlier in this chapter we introduced cases where the query optimizer cannot evaluate the expression in the WHERE clause until the query runs, that is, until after the query optimization phase has completed. An example of this as we have seen is using a variable:

```
DECLARE @bal MONEY

SELECT @bal = 4954.99

SELECT * FROM accounts WHERE balance = @bal
```

In this case distribution steps cannot be used and the query optimizer will use the *index density* information present in the distribution page. Index density was discussed in Chapter 3 and is the average fraction of duplicate index key values in the index. It is the reciprocal of the count of unique values in the index key.

Suppose we have a *Supplier* table with a *country_code* column and we deal with suppliers from 20 countries. The index density would be 1/20 = 0.05.

Once the index density is known, by multiplying the total count of rows in the table by it, we can obtain the likely number of rows hit by specifying a given value. Suppose our table contains 5000 suppliers:

```
row hits = 5000 * 0.05 = 250
```

However, this does not take into account the fact that we might have many or few column values of "UK" and so index density is a poor substitute for being able to use distribution steps.

An even poorer substitute are the weightings we saw earlier in this chapter and shown in Table 4.1. These are used if there is no statistics page.

However, note that the query optimizer will use the weightings even if there is a distribution page if the operator used is not the = operator. In the above example if we were to substitute > for = the query optimizer would use the 33% weighting.

4.2.2.6 Translating Rows To Logical I/Os

When the query optimizer has found a particular index interesting and it has used the selectivity of the search argument to assess the number of rows returned, it translates this value into logical I/Os. The way it does this translation depends on the index type, clustered or nonclustered, and whether there is actually an index present.

4.2.2.7 No Index Present

If we have no suitable index on the table a table scan must be performed as shown in Figure 4.6.

The number of logical I/Os a table scan will use is easy to calculate. All we have to do is find the number of database pages used by the table. We can find this information from the *sysindexes* system table by looking at the *dpages* column. In the *Banking* database the *Accounts* table uses 400 pages.

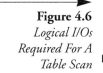

Figure 4.6
Logical I/Os
Required For A
Table Scan

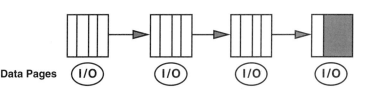

Data Pages

This is an *extremely important number.* We immediately know that we can retrieve all the rows from the *Accounts* table in 400 logical I/Os. This establishes a baseline value against which the query optimizer measures the cost of index access.

4.2.2.8 A Clustered Index Present

What if we can use a clustered index? SQL Server will have to traverse the index until the appropriate data page is reached. Because the data is in key sequence this data page and any other relevant pages will then be retrieved. The cost of using a clustered index is then the cost of the index traversal plus the data pages scanned as shown in Figure 4.7.

We can estimate the number of data pages scanned from the *sysindexes* system table by looking at the *rowpage* column. In the *Banking* database the *Accounts* table has a value in this column of 93.

To find the number of logical I/Os used to traverse the clustered index we need to know the number of levels in the index. This is known as the *depth* of the index. The quickest way of finding the depth of the index is to check the *Manage Indexes* dialog box which will give an estimate as to the number of index levels.

4.2.2.9 A Nonclustered Index Present

If there is a nonclustered index present, SQL Server will have to traverse the index until the appropriate leaf pages are reached. The pointers from the leaf pages will then have to be followed to each row pointed at by an index entry

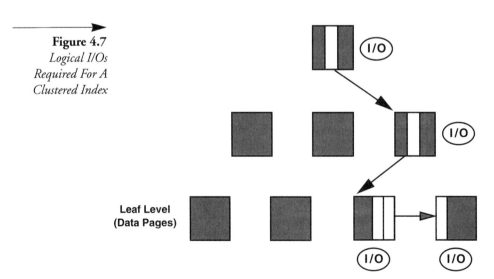

Figure 4.7
*Logical I/Os
Required For A
Clustered Index*

Leaf Level
(Data Pages)

in the leaf page. In the worst case each data row will be on its own data page. The cost of using a nonclustered index is then the cost of the index traversal plus the leaf pages scanned plus the cost of retrieving each row as shown in Figure 4.8.

This could result in many logical I/Os. If the query returns a range of rows, say 500, the query optimizer will assume that this will cost the number of logical I/Os to traverse the nonclustered index plus the number of logical I/Os to scan the relevant leaf pages plus 500 logical I/Os to retrieve the data rows. We can immediately see that, in the case of our *Accounts* table, this is greater than our baseline value for a table scan.

Clearly, if the query is only going to return one row, for example when we use the = operator with a unique index, the cost is the index traversal plus the cost of retrieving the single data page as shown in Figure 4.9. Compared to performing the same operation using a clustered index, the nonclustered index will usually take only one extra logical I/O.

We have previously mentioned the covered query where all the information necessary is satisfied from the index leaf level without visiting the data. SQL Server will have to traverse the index until the leaf level is reached and then the relevant leaf level pages are scanned as shown in Figure 4.10.

4.2.3 The Third Step: Join Order Selection

If the query contains more than one table or the query performs a self join the query optimizer will derive the most efficient strategy for joining the tables.

Figure 4.8
Logical I/Os Required For A Nonclustered Index

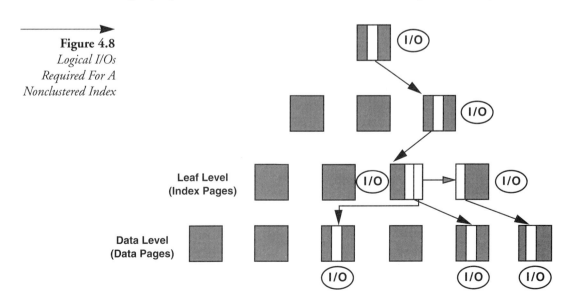

Figure 4.9
*Logical I/Os
Required For A
Nonclustered
Index And A Single
Row Retrieval*

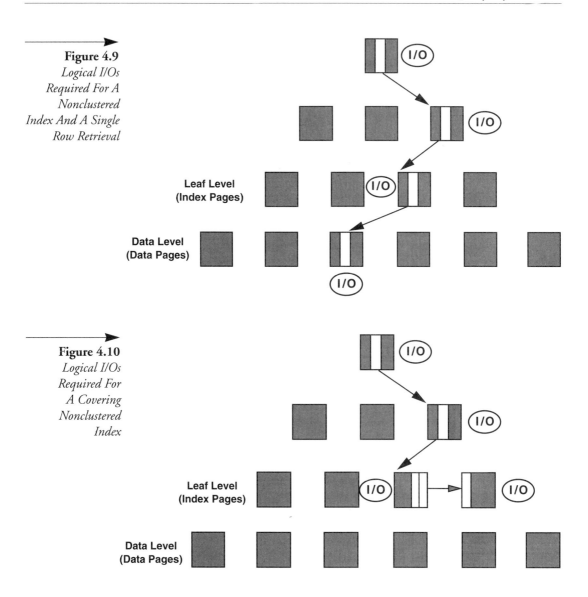

Figure 4.10
*Logical I/Os
Required For
A Covering
Nonclustered
Index*

The order in which tables are joined can have a large impact on performance. For example, suppose we wish to run the following query that joins the *Accounts* table with the *Customers* table:

```
SELECT * FROM accounts, customers
WHERE accounts.customer_no = customers.customer_no
AND balance > 9990
```

Both tables have a nonclustered index on *customer_no*. Suppose the *Customers* table was accessed first. There is no restriction on the *customer_no* column and so all 12,500 customer rows would be retrieved and for each of these rows the *Accounts* table would be accessed. It would, therefore, be accessed 12,500 times and each customer has two accounts so 25,000 account rows would be retrieved. Each one would then be tested for the restriction > 9990.

Suppose, instead, the *Accounts* table was accessed first. The restriction would be applied which in fact removes the majority of rows in the *Accounts* table leaving only 25 rows with the *balance* column containing a value > 9990. This means that the *Customers* table will only be accessed 25 times, considerably reducing the logical I/Os needed to execute the query. In fact in our *Banking* database this join order needed 103 logical I/Os against the 25,333 logical I/Os needed by the first join order.

The query optimizer can use information in the distribution page to help it choose an efficient strategy. We have already seen that the distribution page contains index density information and it is this information that the query optimizer uses to estimate how many rows from one table will join with rows from another table, that is the *join selectivity*. The distribution page not only holds index density for a single column in a composite index but also the index densities of some of the column combinations. If the composite index contained three columns COL1, COL2 and COL3 then the index densities held would be for the combinations:

```
COL1                    index density value (a)
COL1, COL2              index density value (b)
COL1, COL2, COL3        index density value (c)
```

Suppose the distribution page is not present. In this case the query optimizer uses a formula to work out the join selectivity. It is the reciprocal of the number of rows in the smaller table. If we had a query that joined the *Accounts* table (25,000 rows) with the *Customers* table (12,500 rows) the join selectivity would be (1/12500) = 0.00008. For each row in the *Customers* table we would expect a match to (0.00008 * 250000) = 2 rows in the *Accounts* table.

Joins are processed as a series of nested loops which are known as *nested iterations*. In a two table join every row selected from the outer table (the table in the outer loop) causes the inner table (the table in the inner loop) to be accessed. This is known as a *scan* (not to be confused with table scan). The number of times the inner table is accessed is known as its *scan count*. The outer table will have a scan count of 1, the inner table will have a scan count equal to the number of rows selected in the outer table. This is depicted graphically in Figure 4.11 for a three table join.

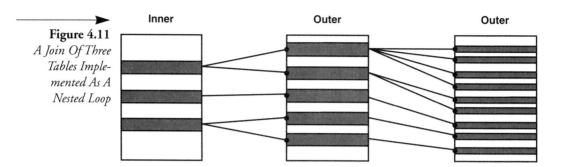

Figure 4.11
*A Join Of Three
Tables Imple-
mented As A
Nested Loop*

The outer table will use an index to restrict the rows if it can whereas the inner table will use an index on the join column if it can.

How many ways are there of joining two tables A and B? There are in fact two ways, AB and BA. What about three tables? There are six ways, ABC, ACB, BAC, BCA, CAB and CBA. What about four tables? The answer is 4! or $1 * 2 * 3 * 4 = 24$.

The number of ways, then, to join X tables is X! or factorial X. A query can join a maximum of 16 tables so we are talking 20,922,789,888,000 possible ways of performing this join. A join of 10 tables would have 3,628,800 possible combinations.

The query optimizer uses techniques internally to minimize the number of possible combinations but the fact still remains, the more tables in a join the longer the query optimizer will take to work out the most efficient access strategy. Also, any inefficiency will be magnified enormously as we are basically placing loops within loops within loops.

If you are going to execute a query that joins many tables, test it! Check what the final query plan is. Check the number of logical I/Os. Check the elapsed time. If you are not happy then break the join down into parts, perhaps joining a subset of the tables into a temporary table and then joining that with the remaining tables.

One useful rule of thumb is to make sure that if the number of tables in the query is N, then the number of join conditions is at least N − 1. For example, suppose we join three tables TAB1, TAB2 and TAB3 and the join is over a column we will call C1. Suppose the query is:

```
SELECT * FROM TAB1, TAB2, TAB3 WHERE
    TAB1.C1 = TAB2.C1
```

Applying our rule of thumb we can see that there are three tables in the join so there should be at least two join conditions. There is only one join condition in the query which is below the minimum number. This will result in SQL Server performing a lot of extra work joining all the rows in TAB3 with all the rows in the result set from the join of TAB1 and TAB2 or some combination of this. Depending on the form of the SELECT statement the answer returned may be correct, for example if a DISTINCT was used. The time taken to process the query, though, would be much greater than necessary.

Applying our rule of thumb we can see that the query should be written:

```
SELECT * FROM TAB1, TAB2, TAB3 WHERE
    TAB1.C1 = TAB2.C1 AND
    TAB2.C1 = TAB3.C1
```

However, if it makes sense to add a third join condition then do not be afraid to do so as it will give the query optimizer more options to work with:

```
SELECT * FROM TAB1, TAB2, TAB3 WHERE
    TAB1.C1 = TAB2.C1 AND
    TAB2.C1 = TAB3.C1 AND
    TAB1.C1 = TAB3.C1
```

4.2.4 Tools for Investigating Query Strategy

We have now discussed the steps that the query optimizer performs during query optimization, namely:

▶ Query Analysis

▶ Index Selection

▶ Join Order Selection

To facilitate performance, tuning and optimization it is essential that we are able to see the decisions that the query optimizer has made so that we can compare the decisions with *what we expect*. We also need to be able to measure the work done in executing the query so we can compare the effectiveness of different indexes.

Hint: You should always calculate a rough estimate of the logical I/Os a query should use. If the logical I/Os used differs by a large amount it could be that your estimate is very inaccurate or more likely the query plan is not what you expected!

There are a number of tools at our disposal for checking what the query optimizer is doing. There are various options we can set in ISQL/w and there are also a number of trace flags that can be used.

4.2.4.1 SET SHOWPLAN

In ISQL/w we can request the display of the query optimizer strategy for a query with the SET SHOWPLAN ON statement:

```
SET SHOWPLAN ON

SELECT * FROM branches
STEP 1
The type of query is SETON
STEP 1
The type of query is SELECT
FROM TABLE
branches
Nested iteration
Table Scan

branch_no   branch_name   branch_address              managers_name
---------   -----------   ------------------------    --------------
1000        Ropley        The High St, Ropley,        Ken England
                          Hampshire
1001        Epsom         The Main St, Epsom, Surrey  Nigel Stanley
1002        Chandlers     Elm St, Chandlers Ford,     Lilian Hobbs
            Ford          Hampshire
1003        Reading       Station St, Reading,        Keith Burns
                          Berkshire
1004        Bracknell     Oak Rd., Bracknell,         Andrew
                          Berkshire                       Phillips
:
:
```

The above example of a *showplan* shows that a SELECT statement has been executed against the *Branches* table and that the strategy chosen by the query optimizer is a table scan. We will look at a number of possible strategies in more detail shortly. Note that a query optimizer strategy will also be generated when statements other than SELECT are executed such as DELETE or UPDATE.

Sometimes the database administrator will wish to examine query optimizer strategies but not actually access the table data, that is, to terminate the query after the query optimizer has selected a strategy but before the execution of the query using that strategy takes place. To do this the SET NOEXEC ON statement can be used:

```
SET SHOWPLAN ON
SET NOEXEC ON
SELECT * FROM branches

STEP 1
The type of query is SELECT
FROM TABLE
branches
Nested iteration
Table Scan
```

Hint: Take care with the use of the SET NOEXEC ON statement as it can drive you crazy! Once you specify it, NO statement is executed until you specify SET NOEXEC OFF. This includes other SET statements. It is very easy to forget you have specified a SET NOEXEC ON statement and wonder why a query is taking an eternity or a SET statement seems to have stopped working.

4.2.4.2 SET STATISTICS IO

Another SET statement that is useful when investigating different query optimizer strategies is SET STATISTICS IO ON. This displays the count of table scans, logical and physical reads and read ahead reads for each Transact-SQL statement:

```
SET STATISTICS IO ON
SELECT * FROM branches

branch_no   branch_name     branch_address           managers_name
----------  -------------   ----------------         --------------
1000        Ropley          The High St, Ropley,     Ken England
                            Hampshire
1001        Epsom           The Main St, Epsom,      Nigel Stanley
                            Surrey
1002        Chandlers Ford Elm St, Chandlers Ford, Lilian Hobbs
                            Hampshire
1003        Reading         Station St, Reading,     Keith Burns
                            Berkshire
1004        Bracknell       Oak Rd., Bracknell,      Andrew Phillips
                            Berkshire
:
:

Table: branches scan count 1, logical reads: 10, physical reads:
   0, read ahead reads: 0
```

Similarly, the SET STATISTICS TIME ON statement displays the time that SQL Server took to parse the command, compile the query optimizer strategy and execute the command:

```
SET STATISTICS TIME ON
SELECT * FROM branches

SQL Server Parse and Compile Time:
cpu time = 10 ms.

SQL Server Execution Times:
cpu time = 0 ms. elapsed time = 0 ms.

branch_no   branch_name     branch_address           managers_name
----------  -------------   ----------------------   --------------
1000        Ropley          The High St, Ropley,     Ken England
                            Hampshire
```

```
1001      Epsom           The Main St, Epsom,    Nigel Stanley
                          Surrey
1002      Chandlers Ford  Elm St, Chandlers Ford, Lilian Hobbs
                          Hampshire
1003      Reading         Station St, Reading,   Keith Burns
                          Berkshire
1004      Bracknell       Oak Rd., Bracknell,    Andrew Phillips
                          Berkshire
:
:

SQL Server Execution Times:
  cpu time = 0 ms. elapsed time = 491 ms.
```

I personally do not tend to use this statement. Whereas logical I/Os is a constant and will be the same for a given access strategy at any time irrespective of other work on the server, this is not true for the statistics time. For that reason I do not find it useful. If I really want to compare the elapsed times of queries I tend to use my own statements:

```
DECLARE
  @time_msg CHAR(255),
  @start_time DATETIME

SELECT @start_time = GETDATE()

-- Execute the query we wish to test

SELECT * FROM accounts

SELECT @time_msg ='Query time (minutes:seconds) ' +
                  CONVERT(CHAR(2), DATEDIFF(ss,@start_time,
                    GETDATE())/60) +
                  ':' +
                  CONVERT(CHAR(2), DATEDIFF(ss,@start_time,
                    GETDATE())%60)
print @time_msg

account_no    customer_no    branch_no    balance
----------    -----------    ---------    --------
1             100001         1001         9,396.95
6401          103201         1001         6,375.32
12801         106401         1001         3,389.39
:
:

Query time (minutes:seconds) 1 :16
```

The ISQL/w window also contains the facility to view the resource usage for a query in a graphical fashion.

The Transact-SQL that generated this output is shown below:

```
SELECT * FROM accounts, customers, branches WHERE
        accounts.customer_no = customers.customer_no AND
        accounts.branch_no = branches.branch_no AND
```

```
balance > 8000 AND
customers.lname LIKE '%na%'
```

Figure 4.12 shows the statistics I/O output from the above query. The histogram shows the *scan count* which is the number of times a table was accessed, the *logical reads* which are the number of database pages needed from the table and its indexes to satisfy the query and the *physical reads* which are the number of database pages actually read from disk. This is usually less than the logical reads value as database pages will often be held in cache.

The graphical outputs can be useful when analysing queries to quickly see if a different query design or index design can result in less I/O but usually I prefer the less visually stimulating text output from SHOW STATISTICS IO.

4.2.4.3 Example Showplan Outputs

The following section will show some example showplans. We will use two tables from the *Banking* database, the *Accounts* table and the *Branches* table. To remind ourselves, the *Accounts* table has a row count of 25,000 whereas the *Branches* table has a row count of 100. The definitions of the tables are as follows:

```
CREATE TABLE accounts (
                        account_no      int      not null,
                        customer_no     int      not null,
                        branch_no       int      not null,
                        balance         money    not null
                       )
```

Figure 4.12
A Graphical Statistics I/O Output

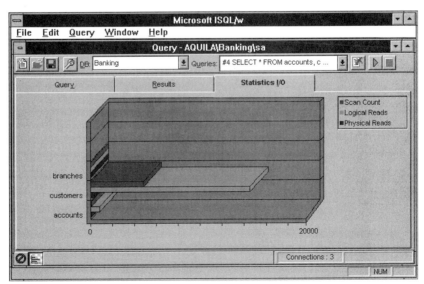

```
CREATE TABLE branches  (
                        branch_no       int        not null,
                        branch_name     char(20)   not null,
                        branch_address  char(120)  not null,
                        managers_name   char(20)   not null
                        )
```

We will define these indexes on the tables for the purpose of the following examples:

```
CREATE CLUSTERED INDEX accounts_branch_no_idx ON accounts
(branch_no)
```

```
CREATE UNIQUE NONCLUSTERED INDEX accounts_account_no_idx ON
   accounts
(account_no)
```

```
CREATE NONCLUSTERED INDEX accounts_balance_idx ON accounts
(balance)
```

```
CREATE UNIQUE CLUSTERED INDEX branches_branch_code_idx ON branches
(branch_no)
```

Why did we choose these particular indexes? Perhaps we know that the application has some frequently used transactions that query the *Accounts* table by *account_no* or groups by *branch_code*.

```
Query 1 - Find the balance of the customer with a customer_no of
   111651

SELECT balance FROM accounts WHERE customer_no = 111651

STEP 1
The type of query is SELECT
FROM TABLE
accounts
Nested iteration
Table Scan
balance
-------------------------
6,942.35
5,863.83

(2 row(s) affected)

Table: accounts scan count 1, logical reads: 400, physical reads:
   0, read ahead reads: 0
```

Let us investigate what has happened here. The first line of the showplan display is *STEP 1*. Every query is resolved in a number of steps, often just one as above. Some queries cannot be resolved in a single step and so *STEP* will appear a number of times. We shall see this later.

The type of query is SELECT shows that for this *STEP* a SELECT statement was issued. The type of query is often SELECT, INSERT, UPDATE or

DELETE but other query types may also be seen. For example, a DROP TABLE statement would display *The type of query is TABDESTROY.*

FROM TABLE accounts shows that the query is retrieving rows from the table *Accounts.* Sometimes the table name displayed is *worktable* indicating that SQL Server is retrieving data from a temporary worktable that it has created. The order that the *FROM TABLE* lines appear in the showplan output is important. It reflects the order in which the query optimizer has chosen to join the tables.

Nested iteration refers to the mechanism that SQL Server uses to return rows from a table or to join tables. It is usually not a useful line of display output. The line displaying *Table Scan* is perhaps the most important line. It shows the table access strategy the query optimizer has chosen and it may not be what you expect.

In our example a table scan has been chosen. This means that the query optimizer has chosen to read every page in the table in order to search for the rows that were requested. This might be fine for a small table but may be unacceptable for a large one. Note that SQL Server must read *every* row in the table from the first to the last as it cannot know when it has retrieved the last row that satisfies the criteria.

Why was a table scan chosen? The query optimizer had no other choice as there were no indexes it could use. This underlines a fundamental point. If there are no appropriate indexes, the query optimizer is forced to choose a table scan.

The statistics I/O display shows that 400 logical I/Os were needed to satisfy the query. This is what we expect as the *Accounts* table is 400 pages in size.

Suppose that this query is frequently used. It might be worth creating a new index. Suppose that we replace the index *accounts_account_no_idx* with an index that contains customer_no as the second column:

```
CREATE UNIQUE NONCLUSTERED INDEX accounts_account_no_idx ON
   accounts
(account_no,
customer_no)
```

We now rerun the query:

```
SELECT balance FROM accounts WHERE customer_no = 111651

STEP 1
The type of query is SELECT
FROM TABLE
accounts
```

```
Nested iteration
Table Scan
balance
--------------------------
6,942.35
5,863.83

(2 row(s) affected)

Table: accounts scan count 1, logical reads: 400, physical reads:
    0, read ahead reads: 0
```

A table scan is still chosen by the query optimizer. This is because the *customer_no* column is the second column, in the index definition. As we have not specified the first column *account_no* in the query, to use this index SQL Server would have to scan every leaf index node finding the row ids of the rows that satisfied the query and, for each row id, it would have to read in the data pages. If the query optimizer decides that it is less costly to choose a table scan it will do so.

Let us add an index *accounts_customer_no_idx* that contains *customer_no* as the only column:

```
CREATE NONCLUSTERED INDEX accounts_customer_no_idx ON accounts
(customer_no)

SELECT balance FROM accounts WHERE customer_no = 111651

STEP 1
The type of query is SELECT
FROM TABLE
accounts
Nested iteration
Index : accounts_customer_no_idx
balance
--------------------------
6,942.35
5,863.83

(2 row(s) affected)

Table: accounts scan count 1, logical reads: 5, physical reads: 2,
    read ahead reads: 0
```

Instead of seeing a table scan we now see the line *Index : accounts_customer_no_idx* displayed in the showplan output. This line shows that a nonclustered index, in this case *accounts_customer_no_idx*, has been used to satisfy the query. Note the reduction in logical I/Os. For retrieving *Accounts* table rows when only the *customer_no* is known this is clearly a very efficient access method using the nonclustered index *accounts_customer_no_idx*. However, remember that although indexes help operations that retrieve data from the database, they may hinder operations that write to the database. Adding this new index will slow down the insertion of new accounts and may exacerbate lock conflict. The addition of an index is often a balancing act!

Is the logical I/O count of 5 expected? The number of levels in this index as obtained from the SQL Enterprise Manager is 3. There are 2 data rows. SQL Server will need 3 logical I/Os to traverse the index structure and then 2 logical I/Os to read the 2 data rows.

```
Query 2 - Find the customers with accounts managed by branch 1009

SELECT customer_no FROM accounts WHERE branch_no = 1009

STEP 1
The type of query is SELECT
FROM TABLE
accounts
Nested iteration
Using Clustered Index
customer_no
-----------
102305
105505
108705
:
:
106655
109855

(500 row(s) affected)

Table: accounts scan count 1, logical reads: 9, physical reads: 0,
    read ahead reads: 0
```

As there is a clustered index on *branch_no* the query optimizer has chosen to use it. The clustered index has sequenced the data on *branch_no* and so only 9 logical reads were needed to fetch all the 500 rows from the *Accounts* table that satisfied the query. The showplan output shows the fact that a clustered index is chosen by displaying the *Using Clustered Index* line.

```
Query 3 - Find the customers with accounts managed by branch 1009
    that have a balance > 1000

SELECT customer_no FROM accounts where branch_no = 1009 AND bal-
    ance > 1000

STEP 1
The type of query is SELECT
FROM TABLE
accounts
Nested iteration
Using Clustered Index
customer_no
-----------
102305
```

```
105505
:
:
106655
109855

(454 row(s) affected)

Table: accounts scan count 1, logical reads: 9, physical reads: 0,
    read ahead reads: 0
```

In the above example the clustered index is again chosen. The query optimizer now had to make a choice between a table scan, the clustered index on *branch_no* and the nonclustered index on *balance*. We already know that a table scan requires 400 logical I/Os so can any other access method improve on this? As there are likely to be 100 different values in the *branch_no* column (there are 100 branches) and there is a clustered index on *branch_no* that will store the account rows with a branch number of 1009 physically next to one another it would seem reasonable to assume that using the clustered index would use fewer logical I/Os than the table scan as only part of the table would have to be retrieved. But what about the nonclustered index?

The nonclustered index is present on the balance. The query optimizer should be able to look at the distribution page for this index to work out how many rows have a value in the *balance* column > 1000. The query optimizer will then assume every row will result in a logical I/O. It will then compare this costing with that for the clustered index. Generally, the clustered index will win.

In the *Accounts* table there are in fact 22,517 rows that have a value in the *balance* column > 1000. The query optimizer would estimate the logical I/O cost to be the number of logical I/Os required to traverse the index, scan the leaf level and retrieve each of the rows. The value would be far greater than a table scan (in fact if we measure it using the nonclustered index on the *balance* column would need 22,688 logical I/Os).

```
Query 4 - Find the details of the branch that holds account number
    1604

SELECT branch_name, managers_name FROM branches, accounts
WHERE accounts.account_no = 1604 AND
branches.branch_no = accounts.branch_no

STEP 1
The type of query is SELECT
FROM TABLE
accounts
Nested iteration
Index : accounts_account_no_idx
FROM TABLE
```

```
branches
Nested iteration
Using Clustered Index
branch_name    managers_name
-----------    -------------
Reading        Keith Burns

(1 row(s) affected)

Table: branches scan count 1, logical reads: 2, physical reads: 0,
   read ahead reads: 0
Table: accounts scan count 1, logical reads: 4, physical reads: 0,
   read ahead reads: 0
```

In the above example we have a join of two tables. We can see that the query optimizer has chosen to process the *Accounts* table first and the line *Index : accounts_account_no_idx* shows that a nonclustered index has been used to access the table to retrieve the rows that satisfy the selection criteria, in this case, *account_no = 1604*. The *Branches* table is then accessed to retrieve the matching row. The query optimizer has taken this approach to reduce the number of *Accounts* table rows as much as possible before accessing the *Branches* table. It knows that there is a unique nonclustered index on the *account_no* column and that, at most, one row will satisfy the criteria. The *Branches* table will, therefore, only be scanned once. Also, there is a clustered index on the *Branches* table that can be used in the join clause and there is no other restriction on the *Branches* table. The *Accounts* table is, therefore, chosen as the outer table.

Note that the SHOWPLAN output is in the order that the join is performed, that is, table *Accounts* then table *Branches*. The STATISTICS I/Os output is in the order that the tables are listed in the query NOT the order they are processed.

```
Query 5 - Find the details of the branches that hold accounts with
   balances < $10
SELECT branches.branch_no, branch_name, managers_name,
   account_no FROM branches, accounts
WHERE accounts.balance < 10 AND
branches.branch_no = accounts.branch_no

STEP 1
The type of query is SELECT
FROM TABLE
accounts
Nested iteration
Index : accounts_balance_idx
FROM TABLE
branches
Nested iteration
Using Clustered Index
```

```
branch_no     branch_name        managers_name      account_no
---------     ---------------    ---------------    ----------
1097          Gillingham         Douglas Adams      198
1041          High Bickington    Cliff England      7542
1001          Epsom              Nigel Stanley      11901
1021          Lynmouth           Tricia Gay         121
1011          Battle             Mike England       22211
1051          Capel Curig        Pat Burridge       5552
1015          Greater Tandoori   Angus Lilburn      17215
1089          Selbourne          Peter May          14989
1023          Oxford             Mike Cash          23924
1093          Medstead           June May           23094
1069          East Worldham      Kevin Roche        2669
1071          Bradford           Mike Sandbach      5171
1049          Watford            Stuart Hudson      10850
1055          Sandwich           Graham Hunt        17656
1021          Lynmouth           Tricia Gay         24221
1061          Calver             Dave Jacob         1261
1003          Reading            Keith Burns        4904
1075          Dover              Mary Green         7175
1039          Beech              Margaret England   19540
1083          Maidenhead         Keith Evans        15783
1025          Paignton           Martin Pope        1525
1097          Gillingham         Douglas Adams      24598
1081          Chesterfield       Andy Rydlewski     4282
1027          Bristol            Graham Hawkins     13828
1027          Bristol            Graham Hawkins     3428

(25 row(s) affected)

Table: branches scan count 25, logical reads: 50, physical reads:
   0, read ahead reads: 0
Table: accounts scan count 1, logical reads: 26, physical reads:
   0, read ahead reads: 0
```

In the above example we have a join of the same two tables as in the previous example. We can see that the query optimizer has chosen to process the *Accounts* table first and the line *Index : accounts_balance_idx* shows that a non-clustered index has been used to access the table to retrieve the rows that satisfy the selection criteria, in this case, *balance < 10.* The *Branches* table is then accessed to retrieve the matching row.

The query optimizer has taken this approach to reduce the number of *Accounts* table rows as much as possible before accessing the *Branches* table. It knows from the distribution page for the *accounts_balance_idx* index that there are few rows that satisfy the criterion. The *Branches* table will, therefore, only be scanned a few times, in this case 25. Again, the clustered index on the *Branches* table is used.

```
Query 6 - Find the details of the branches that hold accounts with
   balances < $99
```

```
SELECT branches.branch_no, branch_name, managers_name,
    account_no FROM branches, accounts
WHERE accounts.balance < 99 AND
branches.branch_no = accounts.branch_no

STEP 1
The type of query is SELECT
FROM TABLE
branches
Nested iteration
Table Scan
FROM TABLE
accounts
Nested iteration
Using Clustered Index
branch_no      branch_name     managers_name     account_no
---------      -----------     -------------     ----------
1001           Epsom           Nigel Stanley     2902
1001           Epsom           Nigel Stanley     11901
1001           Epsom           Nigel Stanley     8101
1003           Reading         Keith Burns       4904
:
:
1099           Beech           Margaret England  2800

(225 row(s) affected)

Table: branches scan count 1, logical reads: 9, physical reads: 0,
    read ahead reads: 0
Table: accounts scan count 100, logical reads: 892, physical
    reads: 0, read ahead reads: 0
```

Again, we have a join of the same two tables as in the previous example. However, in this example, we have changed the restriction to *balance* < 99. The query optimizer has decided, based on information in the distribution page of the index *accounts_balance_idx*, that a number of rows now meet this criterion and so it is actually better to use the *Branches* table as the outer table and the *Accounts* table as the inner table. There is no restriction on the *Branches* table so a table scan is performed. The whole table can be retrieved in 9 logical I/Os. For each row the *Accounts* table is accessed, resulting in a scan count of 100. The clustered index *accounts_balance_idx* is then used to access the account rows for a given branch.

4.2.4.4 Trace Flags

Another method of checking what the query optimizer is doing is to use trace flags. Whereas the showplan output tells us the final decision that the query optimizer has made, the query plan, the trace flags give us more insight into why the query optimizer has arrived at its decision.

Hint: Trace flags are not part of the supported feature set of SQL Server and, as such, Microsoft states that future compatibility or continued use is not assured.

Trace flags can be set by using one of four available mechanisms. The DBCC statement can be used, the -T option with the *sqlservr* command-line executable, in SQL Server setup choosing *Set Server Options* and then *Parameters* or using the SQL Enterprise Manager choosing *Server Configuration/Options* and then *Parameters*.

Once set, trace flags are in effect until they are turned off if using DBCC or until the SQL Server is stopped and restarted without the trace flag if using the *sqlservr* command-line executable.

Setting a trace flag with DBCC is accomplished with the DBCC TRACEON statement:

```
DBCC TRACEON (3604)
```

Turning off a trace flag with DBCC is accomplished with the DBCC TRACEOFF statement:

```
DBCC TRACEOFF (3604)
```

To start SQL Server with a trace flag, use the -T option on the command line:

```
sqlservr -dc:\mssql\data\master.dat -ec:\mssql\log\errorlog -T302
```

To start SQL Server with a number of trace flags, use multiple -T options on the command line:

```
sqlservr -dc:\mssql\data\master.dat -ec:\mssql\log\errorlog -
    T302 -T310
```

The same format is used in the SQL Enterprise Manager or setup program as shown in Figure 4.13.

The trace flags that are most relevant to the operation of the query optimizer are shown in Table 4.2.

So let us investigate some queries using trace flags. Some are more useful than others and some display very cryptic output. I find the most useful trace flag to be 302. We will use the DBCC statement to set the trace flags but first we need to set a trace flag to make sure that the trace output is displayed at the client. This trace flag is 3604. We could also (or instead of) send trace output to the SQL Server errorlog using trace flag 3605.

Before these queries execute we will issue:

```
DBCC TRACEON (3604, 302)

SET SHOWPLAN ON
```

Figure 4.13
*Setting Trace Flags
In The Enterprise
Manager/Setup
Program*

Table 4.2 *Query Optimizer Trace Flags*

Flag	Information Produced
302	Displays information about whether the statistics page is used, the actual selectivity (if available), and what SQL Server estimated the physical and logical I/O would be for the indexes.
310	Displays information about join order.
330	Enables full output when using the SET SHOWPLAN option, which gives detailed information about joins.

First of all let us issue a simple query that looks up account numbers for a given balance:

```
Query 7 - Find the account numbers with balances = 1789.30
    SELECT account_no FROM accounts WHERE balance = 1789.30
```

The somewhat cryptic output from this query is as follows:

```
*******************************
Leaving q_init_sclause() for table 'accounts' (varno 0).
The table has 25000 rows and 400 pages.
```

```
Cheapest index is index 0, costing 400 pages per scan.

*******************************
Entering q_score_index() for table 'accounts' (varno 0).
The table has 25000 rows and 400 pages.
Scoring the search clause:
AND (!:0x1a5acd0) (andstat:0xa)
EQ (L:0x1a5acbc) (rsltype:0x3c rsllen:8 rslprec:19 rslscale:4
opstat:0x0)
VAR (L:0x1a5ac4a) (varname:balance varno:0 colid:4
coltype(0x3c):MONEY colen:8 coloff:14 colprec:19 colscale:4
vartypeid:11 varnext:1a5ab4c varusecnt:1 varlevel:0 varsubq:0)
MONEY (R:0x1a5aca2) (left:0x1a5acaa len:8 maxlen:4 prec:6
scale:2 value:1789.30)
Scoring clause for index 3
Relop bits are: 0x80,0x4
Qualifying stat page; pgno: 1768 steps: 199
Search value: MONEY value:1789.30
No steps for search value--qualpage for LT search value finds
value between steps 35 and 36--use betweenSC
Estimate: indid 3, selectivity 7.058240e-005, rows 1 pages 5
Cheapest index is index 3, costing 5 pages and generating 1 rows per
scan.
Search argument selectivity is 0.000071.
*******************************
STEP 1
The type of query is SELECT
FROM TABLE
accounts
Nested iteration
Index : accounts_balance_idx
account_no
-----------
16455
19202
4616

(3 row(s) affected)
```

We can see from the showplan output that the query optimizer decided to use the nonclustered index *accounts_balance_idx*. Let us see how this relates to the trace flag output remembering, while we do, that this trace flag output was originally intended for the benefit of the SQL Server engineers.

The first lines of interest are:

```
The table has 25000 rows and 400 pages.
Cheapest index is index 0, costing 400 pages per scan.
```

This is telling us that the *Accounts* table contains 25,000 rows and is 400 pages in size and that a table scan (index 0) would take 400 logical I/Os. This is our baseline against which other access strategies will be measured. Note that these figures are taken from the *sysindexes* system table which, as we have mentioned previously, are estimates and can be inaccurate. See later for how to correct this.

```
Entering q_score_index() for table 'accounts' (varno 0).
The table has 25000 rows and 400 pages.
Scoring the search clause:
```

This indicates that we have a search argument and we are now going to look for the most efficient index.

```
EQ (L:0x1a5acbc) (rsltype:0x3c rsllen:8 rslprec:19 rslscale:4
opstat:0x0)
VAR (L:0x1a5ac4a) (varname:balance varno:0 colid:4
coltype(0x3c):MONEY colen:8 coloff:14 colprec:19 colscale:4
vartypeid:11 varnext:1a5ab4c varusecnt:1 varlevel:0 varsubq:0)
MONEY (R:0x1a5aca2) (left:0x1a5acaa len:8 maxlen:4 prec:6
scale:2 value:1789.30)
```

This output refers to the different search arguments in the WHERE clause. In our query there is only one search argument *balance = 1789.30*. We can see the *EQ* representing this search argument. The name of the column is shown *varname:balance*, the datatype of the column *MONEY* and its value *value:1789.30*. This output would be repeated for every search argument in the WHERE clause.

Having found all of the search arguments, each one is linked with indexes present on the table and a cost generated for an access strategy that uses that index.

```
Scoring clause for index 3
Relop bits are: 0x80,0x4
Qualifying stat page; pgno: 1768 steps: 199
Search value: MONEY value:1789.30
No steps for search value--qualpage for LT search value finds
value between steps 35 and 36--use betweenSC
Estimate: indid 3, selectivity 7.058240e-005, rows 1 pages 5
```

Index 3 has been linked to the search argument *Search value: MONEY value:1789.30*. The phrase *Index 3* refers to the index on the table with a value of 3 in the *indid* column in the *sysindexes* system table. This is the index *accounts_balance_idx*.

The phrase *Qualifying stat page; pgno: 1768 steps: 199* is showing us that distribution statistics are available and they can be found in the distribution page on page 1768. There are 199 distribution steps.

```
No steps for search value--qualpage for LT search value finds
value between steps 35 and 36--use betweenSC           .
```

This shows that the value *1789.30* was not found on the distribution page but was found between distribution steps 35 and 36.

The phrase *Estimate: indid 3, selectivity 7.058240e-005, rows 1 pages 5* tells us that the query optimizer estimates the number of rows matching the search argument for this index to be 1 and it estimates that 5 pages will need to be retrieved to fetch the row. This refers to index pages and data pages. The selectivity of the index represents the fraction of rows in the table that match the search argument. This is the index density and was described earlier.

As we can see in this example, the logical I/O cost of 5 pages is less than the table scan which cost 400 logical I/Os and so this index is chosen:

```
Cheapest index is index 3, costing 5 pages and generating 1 rows
    per scan.
```

Let us now modify this query slightly by placing a computation on the column.

```
Query 8 - Find the account numbers where twice the balance =
    3578.60
```

This query is functionally equivalent to the previous query and will return the same answer.

```
SELECT account_no FROM accounts WHERE balance*2 = 3578.60
```

However, a table scan has been performed. Why? If we look at the trace flag output below we see that there is no information on search arguments. This is because the query optimizer has not found any. As we discussed earlier in this chapter, any use of computation or use of functions on the column means that this will not be treated as a search argument and so an index will not be used.

```
*******************************
Leaving q_init_sclause() for table 'accounts' (varno 0).
The table has 25000 rows and 400 pages.
Cheapest index is index 0, costing 400 pages per scan.
STEP 1
The type of query is SELECT
FROM TABLE
accounts
Nested iteration
Table Scan
account_no
-----------
19202
4616
16455

(3 row(s) affected)

Query 9 - Find the account numbers where the balance = a variable
```

If a variable is used the query optimizer does not know the value of the search argument at query optimization time:

```
DECLARE @bal MONEY

SELECT @bal = 1789.30

SELECT account_no FROM accounts WHERE balance = @bal
```

The output is similar to Query 7 with one main exception:

```
*******************************
Leaving q_init_sclause() for table 'accounts' (varno 0).
The table has 25000 rows and 400 pages.
Cheapest index is index 0, costing 400 pages per scan.

*******************************
Entering q_score_index() for table 'accounts' (varno 0).
The table has 25000 rows and 400 pages.
Scoring the search clause:
AND (!:0x1a5af54) (andstat:0xa)
EQ (L:0x1a5af40) (rsltype:0x3c rsllen:8 rslprec:19 rslscale:4
opstat:0x8)
VAR (L:0x1a5af06) (varname:balance varno:0 colid:4
coltype(0x3c):MONEY colen:8 coloff:14 colprec:19 colscale:4
vartypeid:11 varnext:1a5ae08 varusecnt:1 varlevel:0 varsubq:0)
MONEY (R:0x1a5aaca) (left:0x1a5aad2 len:8 maxlen:8 prec:19
scale:4 constat:0x4 value:0.00)

Scoring clause for index 3
Relop bits are: 0x80,0x4
SARG is a subbed VAR or expr result or local variable (constat =
4)--use magicSC or densitySC
Estimate: indid 3, selectivity 7.058240e-005, rows 1 pages 5
Cheapest index is index 3, costing 5 pages and generating 1 rows per
scan.
Search argument selectivity is 0.000071.
*******************************
STEP 1
The type of query is DECLARE
STEP 1
The type of query is SELECT
STEP 1
The type of query is SELECT
FROM TABLE
accounts
Nested iteration
Index : accounts_balance_idx

(1 row(s) affected)

account_no
-----------
16455
19202
```

```
4616
```

```
(3 row(s) affected)
```

The following lines of output show that variable is being used and, as such, the distribution steps cannot be used. However, as the distribution page is available the index density can be used.

```
SARG is a subbed VAR or expr result or local variable (constat =
4)--use magicSC or densitySC
Estimate: indid 3, selectivity 7.058240e-005, rows 1 pages 5
```

Suppose we do not use equality but instead use another operator such as >, < or BETWEEN, for example:

```
Query 10 Find the account numbers where the balance > a variable
```

Here we use a query similar to Query 9 but with the > operator.

```
DECLARE @bal MONEY

SELECT @bal = 9999.00

SELECT account_no FROM accounts WHERE balance > @bal
```

Note the following fragment of output. In this case we have not used the index density but instead we have used a built in weighting (a magic number) of 33% as described earlier in the chapter.

```
SARG is a subbed VAR or expr result or local variable (constat =
4)--use magicSC or densitySC
Estimate: indid 3, selectivity 3.300000e-001, rows 8250 pages 8315
Cheapest index is index 0, costing 400 pages and generating 8250
   rows
per scan.
Search argument selectivity is 0.330000.
```

Note that using this weighting, the query optimizer has decided that the cost of using the index is far greater than the table scan and so the table scan is used. In fact there are only two rows in the *Accounts* table that have a balance > 9999.00!

```
Query 11 Find the balance of an account given the account number
```

In this example there is a unique index *accounts_account_no_idx* that can be used to satisfy the query. The query optimizer can make use of this fact.

```
SELECT balance FROM accounts WHERE account_no = 24000

********************************
Leaving q_init_sclause() for table 'accounts' (varno 0).
The table has 25000 rows and 400 pages.
Cheapest index is index 0, costing 400 pages per scan.
```

```
******************************
Entering q_score_index() for table 'accounts' (varno 0).
The table has 25000 rows and 400 pages.
Scoring the search clause:
AND (!:0x1a5acac) (andstat:0xa)
EQ (L:0x1a5ac98) (rsltype:0x38 rsllen:4 rslprec:10 rslscale:0
opstat:0x0)
VAR (L:0x1a5ac46) (varname:account_no varno:0 colid:1
coltype(0x38):INT4 colen:4 coloff:2 colprec:10 colscale:0
vartypeid:7 varnext:1a5ab4a varusecnt:1 varlevel:0 varsubq:0)
INT4 (R:0x1a5ac7e) (left:0x1a5ac86 len:4 maxlen:4 prec:5 scale:0
value:24000)

Unique nonclustered index found--return rows 1 pages 3
Cheapest index is index 2, costing 3 pages and generating 1 rows
  per
scan.
Search argument selectivity is 0.000040.
******************************
STEP 1
The type of query is SELECT
FROM TABLE
accounts
Nested iteration
Index : accounts_account_no_idx
balance
--------------------------
9,685.96

(1 row(s) affected)
```

Note the fragment of output:

```
Unique nonclustered index found--return rows 1 pages 3
Cheapest index is index 2, costing 3 pages and generating 1 rows per
scan.
Search argument selectivity is 0.000040.
```

The query optimizer has spotted the unique index and so it immediately knows that only one row will be returned.

Hint: Make sure that you specify the keyword UNIQUE when creating an index if you know the column can never contain duplicate values. This gives the query optimizer extra information that it can use.

4.2.5 More Optimizer Strategies

We have previously mentioned the fact that the query optimizer can use special techniques when it comes across OR clauses. In fact there are a number of cases where the query optimizer uses special techniques and we will now have a look at some of these. The cases we will look at are:

▶ The OR Strategy

▶ Join Processing Strategies

▶ Aggregates

▶ Group By

▶ Order By

4.2.5.1 The OR Strategy

Suppose we have the following query:

```
SELECT account_no FROM accounts WHERE
                customer_no IN (100009, 100055, 100077)
```

As we have mentioned previously in this chapter this is equivalent to:

```
SELECT account_no FROM accounts WHERE
                customer_no = 100009 OR
                customer_no = 100055 OR
                customer_no = 100077
```

What access strategy can the query optimizer create to efficiently execute the query? If there is no index on the *customer_no* column then a table scan will be performed and each row will be checked to see if any of the three values in the query are present in the *customer_no* column. However, if there is a useful index the query optimizer can use an OR strategy.

It will create a work table in *tempdb* to hold row ids for every row that satisfies any part of the OR clause. Because a row may satisfy more than one part of the OR clause this worktable may end up holding duplicate row ids so it is then sorted and duplicates are eliminated. This work table is then treated as a *dynamic index* and the row ids are used to retrieve the rows from the table. The work table is then deleted. Let us execute our query to demonstrate this:

```
SELECT account_no FROM accounts WHERE
                customer_no IN (100009, 100055, 100077)

STEP 1
The type of query is SELECT
FROM TABLE
accounts
Nested iteration
Index : accounts_customer_no_idx
FROM TABLE
accounts
Nested iteration
```

```
Index : accounts_customer_no_idx
FROM TABLE
accounts
Nested iteration
Index : accounts_customer_no_idx
FROM TABLE
accounts
Nested iteration
Using Dynamic Index
account_no
-----------
154
153
109
110
17
18
(6 row(s) affected)

Table: accounts scan count 3, logical reads: 21, physical reads:
  0, read ahead reads: 0
Table: Worktable scan count 5, logical reads: 90, physical reads:
  5, read ahead reads: 0
```

We can see that each of the three ORs (elements in the IN clause) resulted in an indexed access, in this case using the index *accounts_customer_no_idx*. We can see that the final work was done through the dynamic index. The *Accounts* table was accessed four times: three times to populate the work table with row ids and then the work table containing the row ids, the dynamic index, accesses the table a final time to retrieve the data rows. The total number of logical I/Os is 111 which is less than the number of logical I/Os required to perform a table scan of the *Accounts* table (we know this is 400 from previous examples).

We can reference other columns from the same table in the OR clause:

```
SELECT account_no FROM accounts WHERE
                customer_no IN (100009, 100055, 100077) OR
                balance BETWEEN 5000 AND 5010

STEP 1
The type of query is SELECT
FROM TABLE
accounts
Nested iteration
Index : accounts_customer_no_idx
FROM TABLE
accounts
Nested iteration
Index : accounts_balance_idx
FROM TABLE
accounts
```

```
Nested iteration
Index : accounts_customer_no_idx
FROM TABLE
accounts
Nested iteration
Index : accounts_customer_no_idx
FROM TABLE
accounts
Nested iteration
Using Dynamic Index
account_no
-----------
154
14161
:
:
5283
(33 row(s) affected)
Table: accounts scan count 4, logical reads: 78, physical reads:
   0, read ahead reads: 0
Table: Worktable scan count 6, logical reads: 125, physical reads:
   6, read ahead reads: 0
```

Again, as there is a useful index on both columns the OR strategy can be used. As long as the OR strategy is cheaper than a table scan it will be used. This is a rare example of the query optimizer using a strategy that makes use of more than one index. Notice that if any of the OR clauses are not supported by an index a table scan will be performed.

4.2.5.2 Join Processing Strategies

We have already seen some of the logic that the query optimizer adopts when considering a join of one or more tables. There are some special cases where the query optimizer makes use of some special strategies and we will now look at these.

4.2.5.3 The Reformatting Strategy

Suppose we were to join two tables and there were no indexes present that the query optimizer could use. With no indexes present, the usual fallback is to execute table scans. In this case we would perform one scan of the outer table and for every row in the outer table that we were interested in the inner table would be accessed, again, via a table scan. So if the outer table had 100 rows in it that satisfied the query, then 100 table scans would be performed against the inner table. Expressed as an equation, if O is the number of pages in the outer table, R is the number of rows in the outer table that satisfy the query and I is the number of pages in the inner table, then:

```
number of logical I/Os to perform query = O + (R * I)
```

The *Accounts* table consists of 400 pages holding 25,000 rows and the *Branches* table consists of 10 pages, holding 100 rows. Therefore to join these two tables, using the smaller *Branch* table as the outer table, without any other selection criteria would need:

```
O + (R * I) = 10 + (100 * 400) = 40010 logical I/Os
```

This is clearly a large number of logical I/Os and so in this situation the query optimizer considers another strategy known as a *reformatting* strategy.

The idea behind the reformatting strategy is that, given a join with no useful indexes, it may be more efficient to actually build a clustered index on the inner table in tempdb as part of the access strategy. Clearly, work will be required to build the index but if this is less than the work saved by executing multiple table scans it may well be worth it. The query optimizer will have to cost this and make a decision.

Suppose we join the *Accounts* table and *Branches* table with no useful indexes present:

```
SELECT * FROM branches, accounts
    WHERE branches.branch_no = accounts.branch_no

STEP 1
The type of query is INSERT
The update mode is direct
Worktable created for REFORMATTING
FROM TABLE
accounts
Nested iteration
Table Scan
TO TABLE
Worktable 1
STEP 2
The type of query is SELECT
FROM TABLE
branches
Nested iteration
Table Scan
FROM TABLE
Worktable 1
Nested iteration
Using Clustered Index
account_no    branch_name
----------    ------------
6400          Ropley
12800         Ropley
:
:
12799         Beech
19199         Beech

(25000 row(s) affected)
```

```
Table: branches scan count 1, logical reads: 10, physical reads:
    0, read ahead reads: 0
Table: accounts scan count 1, logical reads: 400, physical reads:
    0, read ahead reads: 0
Table: Worktable scan count 100, logical reads: 399, physical
    reads: 201, read ahead reads: 0
```

In the above example the query optimizer has decided to use the reformatting strategy. Is this a good idea? The total number of logical reads is (10 + 400 + 399) = 809 which is considerably less than the 40,010 logical reads required if table scans are used. In this case, the reformatting strategy has saved us a great deal.

Looking at the showplan output, the query is executed in two steps represented by *STEP 1* and *STEP 2*. The first step involves executing a table scan against the *Accounts* table and inserting the results into a worktable and *The type of query is INSERT* shows that rows are to be inserted into a table rather than selected. *The update mode is direct* shows that the most efficient insertion method is being used by SQL Server. The phrase *Worktable created for REFORMATTING* means that the reformatting strategy is being used in which case a clustered index will be built on the worktable.

In the second step the join of the *Branches* (outer) table is performed with the (inner) work table using the clustered index to access the work table. The work table is then dropped from tempdb.

Suppose a query is executed frequently that uses a reformatting strategy. It might be better to create a permanent index on a table which the query optimizer can then use rather than have it copy the table and build an index on it every time the query is executed. If you spot that the query optimizer is using a reformatting strategy this should be a warning light hinting that an index is missing.

4.2.5.4 Outer Joins

In the joins presented so far, only matching rows are included in the result set, that is, only rows with values in the specified columns that satisfy the join condition. This type of join is known as an *inner join*. If we want to include nonmatching rows in the result set of a join we can make use of an *outer join*.

The outer joins supported by SQL Server 6.5 are the:

► LEFT OUTER JOIN

► RIGHT OUTER JOIN

► FULL OUTER JOIN

The left outer join includes all the rows from the left table that have matching rows in the right hand table and the rows from the left table that do not have matching rows in the right hand table. Columns from the right hand table are nulled. For example, suppose we want information on all the customers in the database, including their balance. An inner join would return only those customers that had accounts whereas an outer join would also return customers who had no accounts as shown in the example below:

```
SELECT customers.customer_no, lname, balance
    FROM customers LEFT OUTER JOIN accounts
    ON customers.customer_no = accounts.customer_no
    WHERE lname LIKE 'W%'

customer_no    lname        balance
-----------    --------     --------
100077         Williams     1,323.89
100077         Williams     188.60
100155         Walker       3,009.43
100155         Walker       790.12
112501         Wright       (null)

(5 row(s) affected)
```

In the above example Wright has not yet had a bank account set up.

The right outer join includes all the rows from the right table that have matching rows in the left hand table and the rows from the right table that do not have matching rows in the left hand table. Columns from the left hand table are nulled.

The full outer join preserves the unmatched rows from both the left and the right table and can be considered to be a left outer join plus a right outer join.

Let us look at the showplan output for a left outer join.

```
SELECT customers.customer_no, lname, balance
    FROM customers LEFT OUTER JOIN accounts
    ON customers.customer_no = accounts.customer_no
    WHERE lname LIKE 'W%'

STEP 1
The type of query is SELECT
FROM TABLE
customers
Nested iteration
Index : customers_lname_idx
LEFT OUTER JOIN : nested iteration
FROM TABLE
accounts
Nested iteration
Index : accounts_customer_no_idx
```

```
customer_no    lname      balance
-----------    --------   --------
100077         Williams   1,323.89
100077         Williams   188.60
100155         Walker     3,009.43
100155         Walker     790.12
112501         Wright     (null)

(5 row(s) affected)

Table: customers scan count 1, logical reads: 6, physical reads:
   2, read ahead reads: 0
Table: accounts scan count 3, logical reads: 13, physical reads:
   0, read ahead reads: 0
```

For each row in the left table SQL Server will access the right table and will return all rows that meet the specified search condition for the join. If no rows meet the search condition, a single row with all columns set to null is returned for the right table. The showplan output for the right table follows the *LEFT OUTER JOIN* phrase and is indented to segregate the steps for the right table from the steps for the outer query.

What about a right outer join? The query optimizer will always transform a right outer join into a left outer join:

```
SELECT lname, account_no
   FROM customers RIGHT OUTER JOIN accounts
   ON customers.customer_no = accounts.customer_no
   WHERE balance = 0

STEP 1
The type of query is SELECT
FROM TABLE
accounts
Nested iteration
Index : accounts_balance_idx
LEFT OUTER JOIN : nested iteration
FROM TABLE
customers
Nested iteration
Index : customers_customer_no_idx
lname     account_no
-------   ------------
(null)    25001
Jones     200

(2 row(s) affected)
```

For a full outer join a work table is created:

```
SELECT customers.customer_no, lname, balance
   FROM customers FULL OUTER JOIN accounts
   ON customers.customer_no = accounts.customer_no
```

```
STEP 1
The type of query is INSERT
The update mode is direct
Worktable created for REFORMATTING
FROM TABLE
customers
Nested iteration
Table Scan
TO TABLE
Worktable 1
STEP 2
The type of query is SELECT
FROM TABLE
accounts
Nested iteration
Table Scan
FULL OUTER JOIN : nested iteration
FROM TABLE
Worktable 1
Nested iteration
Using Clustered Index
customer_no   lname    balance
-----------   ------   -----------
103200        Pearce   2,132.33
```

The query optimizer will invariably insert the rows from one of the tables in the full outer join into a worktable. The optimizer then transforms the full outer join so that the worktable is the right table of the full outer join.

This is accomplished in two steps. Firstly, for each row in the left table SQL Server will access the right table and will return all rows that meet the specified search condition for the join. If no rows meet the search condition, a single row with all columns set to null is returned for the right table. All these rows are then written into a work table. SQL Server also flags each of these rows by updating a column in the row that has been added to the worktable for this reason.

Secondly, SQL Server processes the right table again, and returns all rows in the right table that were not returned in the first step with a row from the left table with all columns set to NULL.

4.2.5.5 Aggregates

The aggregate operators are AVG, COUNT, COUNT(*), MAX, MIN, SUM. The showplan output is modified accordingly by these operators:

```
SELECT MAX(lname) FROM customers
STEP 1
The type of query is SELECT
Scalar Aggregate
```

```
FROM TABLE
customers
Nested iteration
Table Scan
STEP 2
The type of query is SELECT


--------------------
Wright

(1 row(s) affected)
```

The phrase *Scalar Aggregate* refers to the fact that the query returns a single value. The query optimizer will use an index if it can:

```
SELECT SUM(balance) FROM accounts
STEP 1
The type of query is SELECT
Scalar Aggregate
FROM TABLE
accounts
Nested iteration
Index : accounts_balance_idx
STEP 2
The type of query is SELECT


-------------------------
125,170,935.31

(1 row(s) affected)
```

Invariably, if the query optimizer can use an index it covers the query by definition and is likely to be efficient.

An index cannot be traversed more than once. Suppose we have the following query:

```
SELECT MIN(balance) AS MinBal, MAX(balance) AS MaxBal FROM
    accounts
```

The entire leaf level of the index will be scanned:

```
STEP 1
The type of query is SELECT
Scalar Aggregate
FROM TABLE
accounts
Nested iteration
Index : accounts_balance_idx
STEP 2
The type of query is SELECT
MinBal   MaxBal
------   ---------
0.00     10,000.00
```

```
(1 row(s) affected)

Table: accounts scan count 1, logical reads: 189, physical reads:
    0, read ahead reads: 0
```

Note the logical reads. We can force two index traversals by doing the following:

```
SELECT MIN(balance) AS MinBal,
    (SELECT MAX(balance) AS MaxBal FROM accounts)
    FROM accounts

STEP 1
The type of query is SELECT
Scalar Aggregate
FROM TABLE
accounts
Nested iteration
Index : accounts_balance_idx
STEP 2
The type of query is SELECT
Scalar Aggregate
FROM TABLE
accounts
Nested iteration
Index : accounts_balance_idx
STEP 3
The type of query is SELECT
MinBal
-------   ---------
0.00      10,000.00

(1 row(s) affected)

Table: accounts scan count 1, logical reads: 3, physical reads: 0,
    read ahead reads: 0
Table: accounts scan count 1, logical reads: 1, physical reads: 0,
    read ahead reads: 0
```

Note the difference in logical reads. This can be quite a saving on a large table.

4.2.5.6 Aggregates with Group By

We have seen that aggregate functions return a single value which is called a *Scalar Aggregate* in the showplan output. If we use a *GROUP BY* clause we are now returning a number of aggregate values. This is represented by the phrase *Vector Aggregate* in the showplan output.

```
SELECT branch_no, SUM(balance) FROM accounts GROUP BY branch_no

STEP 1
The type of query is SELECT (into a worktable)
GROUP BY
```

```
Vector Aggregate
FROM TABLE
accounts
Nested iteration
Table Scan
TO TABLE
Worktable 1
STEP 2
The type of query is SELECT
FROM TABLE
Worktable 1
Nested iteration
Table Scan
branch_no
---------    ---------------
1000        1,240,401.57
1001        1,240,775.50
:
:
1098        1,241,086.45
1099        1,335,014.80

(100 row(s) affected)

Table: accounts scan count 1, logical reads: 400, physical reads:
   0, read ahead reads: 0
Table: Worktable scan count 1, logical reads: 202, physical reads:
   0, read ahead reads: 0
```

When a GROUP BY is being processed a work table is built. The query is executed in two steps represented by *STEP 1* and *STEP 2* in the showplan output above. The first step involves executing the query and inserting the results into a worktable. The worktable is then read and the rows grouped as required by the GROUP BY before returning data to the user.

The query optimizer will use indexes if it can to build the work table. If the CUBE or ROLLUP clauses are used this will be represented in the showplan output:

```
SELECT branch_no, SUM(balance) FROM accounts GROUP BY branch_no
   WITH ROLLUP

STEP 1
The type of query is INSERT
The update mode is direct
FROM TABLE
accounts
Nested iteration
Table Scan
TO TABLE
Worktable 1
STEP 2
The type of query is SELECT
```

```
FROM TABLE
Worktable 2
GROUP BY WITH ROLLUP
Vector Aggregate
FROM TABLE
Worktable 1
Using GETSORTED Table Scan
TO TABLE
Worktable 2
branch_no
--------        ---------------
1000            1,240,401.57
:
:
1099            1,335,014.80
(null)          125,170,935.31

(101 row(s) affected)
```

4.2.5.7 Order By

If the result of a query is to be ordered by a column or group of columns the query optimizer can place the results of the query into a work table and then sort it or it can use an index if a useful index is present.

```
SELECT lname, fname FROM customers ORDER BY lname

STEP 1
The type of query is INSERT
The update mode is direct
Worktable created for ORDER BY
FROM TABLE
customers
Nested iteration
Table Scan
TO TABLE
Worktable 1
STEP 2
The type of query is SELECT
This step involves sorting
FROM TABLE
Worktable 1
Using GETSORTED Table Scan
lname       fname
--------    ------
Aardvark    Walter
Abalone     Pat
:
```

The query above is executed in two steps represented by *STEP 1* and *STEP 2* in the showplan output. The first step involves executing the query as a table scan. Instead of returning the rows to the user, however, they are

inserted into a work table. The work table is then read and the results sorted
before returning data to the user.

```
SELECT account_no, branch_no FROM accounts ORDER BY branch_no

STEP 1
The type of query is SELECT
FROM TABLE
accounts
Nested iteration
Table Scan
account_no    branch_no
-----------   ----------
6400          1000
12800         1000
:
```

In the above example there is no mention of a work table or indeed any
mention of a sort. This is because the query optimizer has detected that a
clustered index is present on the *branch_no* column and so a scan of the leaf
level of the clustered index will return the rows in the desired order. Note that
there is no mention of the clustered index in the showplan output.

```
SELECT account_no, balance FROM accounts ORDER BY balance

STEP 1
The type of query is INSERT
The update mode is direct
Worktable created for ORDER BY
FROM TABLE
accounts
Nested iteration
Table Scan
TO TABLE
Worktable 1
STEP 2
The type of query is SELECT
This step involves sorting
FROM TABLE
Worktable 1
Using GETSORTED Table Scan
account_no    balance
-----------   -------
200           0.00
7544          1.83
:
```

Note that in the above example SQL Server has chosen to execute the
query as a table scan followed by a sort even though there is a nonclustered
index on balance. This is often the case as the query optimizer costs the table
scan and sort to use less logical I/Os than scanning the nonclustered index
and retrieving the rows. In the case of a table scan and sort no rows will be

returned until the result set has been sorted. If the nonclustered index was chosen by the query optimizer the first row could be returned immediately. This behavior can be forced with the FASTFIRSTROW query optimizer hint:

```
SELECT account_no, balance FROM accounts (FASTFIRSTROW) ORDER BY
    balance

STEP 1
The type of query is SELECT
FROM TABLE
accounts
Nested iteration
Index : accounts_balance_idx
account_no    balance
----------    ----------
200           0.00
7544          1.83
:
```

The penalty for this rapid returning of the first row is usually a slower query response time overall caused by more disk I/Os.

4.2.6 Influencing the Query Optimizer

The query optimizer works out a strategy for executing a query independent of the syntax of the query. By this we mean that the order of the tables in the query are ignored by the optimizer so the developer can avoid worrying about the order in which the tables are written in the query. Even so, it is worth experimenting with queries and showplan output to see if the addition or omission of columns and operators in the query might influence the query optimizer into choosing a less costly strategy.

It is possible to force the query optimizer to join tables in the order that they are written in the query with the SET FORCEPLAN ON statement. For example, consider the following query.

```
SELECT branch_name, managers_name, account_no FROM accounts,
    branches
WHERE accounts.balance < 10 AND
branches.branch_code = accounts.branch_code

STEP 1
The type of query is SELECT
FROM TABLE
accounts
Nested iteration
Index : accounts_balance_idx
FROM TABLE
branches
Nested iteration
```

```
Using Clustered Index
branch_name    managers_name    account_no
-----------    -------------    ----------------
Ropley         Ken England      25001
Ropley         Ken England      200
Oxford         Mike Cash        123
Bracknell      Andrew Phillips  7544
Reading        Keith Burns      11903

:
```

The *Accounts* table is processed before the *Branches* table. If we place the *Branches* table first in the query and use SET FORCEPLAN ON we can force the query optimizer to process the *Branches* table first:

```
SET FORCEPLAN ON

SELECT branch_name, managers_name, account_no FROM branches,
    accounts
WHERE accounts.balance < 10 AND
branches.branch_no = accounts.branch_no

STEP 1
The type of query is SETON
STEP 1
The type of query is SELECT
FROM TABLE
branches
Nested iteration
Table Scan
FROM TABLE
accounts
Nested iteration
Using Clustered Index
branch_name    managers_name    account_no
-----------    -------------    ----------
Ropley         Ken England      24600
Ropley         Ken England      25001
Ropley         Ken England      200
Reading        Keith Burns      11903
```

The above showplan output shows that the *Branches* table is processed first.

Another way of influencing the optimizer is to ensure that it has access to the latest statistics concerning the distribution of key values in the indexes. Information is accurate just after an index has been created or rebuilt but the statistics can diverge from reality over time and cause the query optimizer to make a less than perfect decision. To ensure that the statistics are recalculated the UPDATE STATISTICS statement can be executed as discussed earlier in this chapter.

Another DBCC statement that can help the query optimizer by ensuring that statistics are accurate is DBCC UPDATEUSAGE. The format of this DBCC statement is:

```
DBCC UPDATEUSAGE ({0 | database_name} [, table_name [, index_id]])
[WITH COUNT_ROWS]
```

The DBCC UPDATEUSAGE statement corrects inaccuracies in the *sysindexes* system table, namely the *used, reserved*, and *dpages* columns for any clustered indexes. Using 0 in place of *database_name* runs DBCC UPDATEUSAGE in the current database.

The *WITH COUNT_ROWS* clause means that the *rows* column of *sysindexes* is updated with the current count of the number of rows in the table. This only applies to *sysindexes* rows that have a value of 0 or 1 in the *indid* column.

It is possible to specify which index should be used by the query optimizer. Suppose we have the following query:

```
select branch_name from branches where managers_name = 'Andy
    James'

STEP 1
The type of query is SELECT
FROM TABLE
branches
Nested iteration
Table Scan
branch_name
--------------------
Poole

(1 row(s) affected)
```

The query optimizer has chosen to use a table scan to access the table. If there is an index on managers_name we can force the query optimizer to use it:

```
SELECT branch_name FROM branches (INDEX=branches_managers_name_idx)
    WHERE managers_name = 'Andy James'
```

The INDEX keyword allows us to specify an index name to be used by the query optimizer. If we specify a value 1 instead of an index name, the clustered index is used if there is one present or if we specify a value 0 a table scan is used.

These query optimizer hints should be used in moderation. If the distribution pages are up to date and any other information used by the query optimizer is up to date, the query optimizer should arrive at a good decision. If a query optimizer hint is used it might be that a point is reached where the latest data distribution means that the hint is not the most efficient access strategy.

4.2.7 Stored Procedures and the Query Optimizer

Stored procedures are found everywhere in SQL Server. There are many system stored procedures and a typical SQL Server development department will also create and use many stored procedures. There are a number of benefits to using stored procedures, such as:

▶ Function Encapsulation

▶ Security

▶ Performance

By function encapsulation I mean that complex logic can be placed into a stored procedure and hidden from the client software which then only has to call the stored procedure, passing appropriate parameters. The stored procedure logic can be changed, perhaps to encompass a database modification, without having to change client application software or at least minimizing any change. We can say that stored procedures insulate the client application software from the database structure.

Many sites take a stance that updates to database data can only be made through stored procedures and cannot be made directly to the tables by the client issuing Transact-SQL statements. This model of processing is shown in Figure 4.14.

This brings us to the second benefit of stored procedures, that of security. Taking the model shown in Figure 4.14, we can see that, in order to implement it, we need a security mechanism that allows us to prohibit client software from directly accessing tables and other objects but allows indirect access in a way that we can define and control. Stored procedures provide this benefit by means of *ownership chains*.

As long as the owner of the stored procedure is the owner of all the objects referenced by the stored procedure then execute access on that stored procedure can be granted to database users and they can perform all of the actions defined in the stored procedure even though they have no direct access to the underlying objects. For example, a database user may be granted execute access to a stored procedure that deletes from one table and inserts into another. As long as the ownership of the stored procedure and tables is the same the database user needs no permissions on the tables.

The most important benefit of stored procedures from the perspective of this book is performance and it is this aspect of stored procedures on which

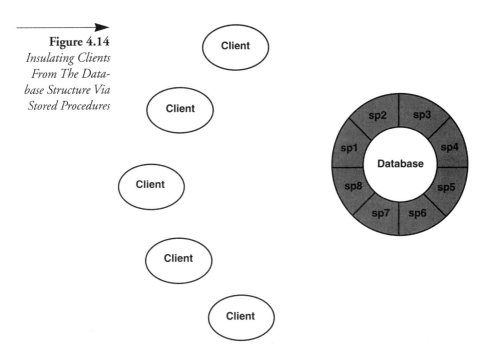

Figure 4.14
Insulating Clients From The Database Structure Via Stored Procedures

we will now concentrate. Generally speaking, stored procedures save us the time and effort spent syntax checking Transact-SQL, optimizing it and they reduce network load because they minimize the amount of traffic sent to and from the server.

The stages in stored procedure processing are shown in Figure 4.15. This figure can be compared with Figure 4.1 which shows the stages in query processing. The principal difference is that when a Transact-SQL query is submitted all the phases are performed. If the query is submitted 100 times these phases are performed for each submission.

With a stored procedure this is not the case. When the stored procedure is initially created the Parsing and Standardization phases are performed in which activities such as syntax checking take place. The output from the Standardization phase is a *query tree* which is stored in the *sysprocedures* system table found in every database. Note that the Transact-SQL source code is stored in the *syscomments* system table found in every database and is not used again in stored procedure processing.

When a stored procedure is executed the query tree is retrieved from *sysprocedures* and so we can see that we immediately have a performance gain as we do not have to perform the Parsing and Standardization phases.

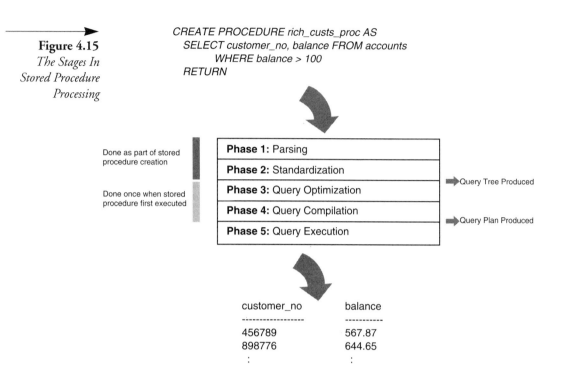

Figure 4.15
The Stages In Stored Procedure Processing

The first time the stored procedure is executed after SQL Server starts, the query tree is retrieved from *sysprocedures* and the query optimizer creates a query plan for the Transact-SQL in the stored procedure and compiles it. Query optimization takes place as we have already seen in this chapter. However, once the query plan has been created and compiled it is stored in a special area of memory known as the *procedure cache*. It is then available for the next user.

If another user wishes to execute the stored procedure SQL Server can now skip the Query Optimization and Query Compilation phases as the query plan is ready and waiting in the procedure cache. This can increase the performance benefit of the stored procedure quite substantially. How useful the performance advantage of skipping the Parsing, Standardization, Query Optimization and Query Compilation phases is depends on how long it takes to perform these phases relative to the execution time of the stored procedure and how often the stored procedure is executed. For a complex stored procedure that is frequently executed the performance advantage is not insignificant.

Because the query plan of a stored procedure can be utilized by many users we say that stored procedures are *reusable*. However, a stored procedure is not *re-entrant*. This means that only a single user can be using a plan at a given time. If two users wish to simultaneously execute a stored procedure, two plans must be made available in the procedure cache which means that the second user will experience the overhead of the Query Optimization and Query Compilation phases.

In reality, a steady state is usually reached so that if 50 users, on average, concurrently execute a stored procedure, there will be 50 query plans for that stored procedure in the procedure cache.

There is one disadvantage to the stored procedure mechanism compared to executing Transact-SQL queries outside of a stored procedure.

Suppose we execute the following query outside of a stored procedure:

```
SELECT account_no, balance FROM accounts
    WHERE balance BETWEEN 8000 AND 8100
```

What strategy will the query optimizer choose? Let us have a look:

```
STEP 1
The type of query is SELECT
FROM TABLE
accounts
Nested iteration
Index : accounts_balance_idx
account_no   balance
----------   ----------
7880         8,000.43
12053        8,000.43
:
:
Table: accounts scan count 1, logical reads: 256, physical reads:
   0, read ahead reads: 0
```

The query optimizer has chosen to use a nonclustered index to access the data and has taken 256 logical reads to do so. Now suppose we execute the query:

```
SELECT account_no, balance FROM accounts
    WHERE balance BETWEEN 8000 AND 9000
```

What strategy will the query optimizer now choose?

```
STEP 1
The type of query is SELECT
FROM TABLE
accounts
Nested iteration
Table Scan
account_no   balance
----------   ----------
22800        8,729.21
19500        8,784.45
:
```

```
:
Table: accounts scan count 1, logical reads: 400, physical reads:
   0, read ahead reads: 0
```

The query optimizer has now chosen to use a table scan, taking 400 logical reads to do so. None of this should surprise us given what we have learned in this chapter. The query optimizer has simply decided that the cost of the table scan is less than the cost of the nonclustered index for the larger range specified in the query.

Now let us place the query in a stored procedure:

```
CREATE PROCEDURE accounts_per_range_proc (@minbal MONEY, @maxbal
   MONEY)
AS
SET STATISTICS IO ON
SELECT account_no, balance FROM accounts
       WHERE balance BETWEEN @minbal AND @maxbal
RETURN
```

Let us execute it with the following EXEC statement:

```
exec accounts_per_range_proc @minbal=8000, @maxbal = 8100

account_no   balance
----------   --------
7880         8,000.43
12053        8,000.43
:
:
Table: accounts scan count 1, logical reads: 256, physical reads:
   0, read ahead reads: 0
```

This is exactly the same number of logical reads as before. The query optimizer has chosen a query plan that uses the nonclustered index as it did for the standalone query.

Now let us execute the stored procedure with the following EXEC statement:

```
exec accounts_per_range_proc @minbal=8000, @maxbal = 9000

account_no   balance
----------   ----------
7880         8,000.43
12053        8,000.43
:
:
Table: accounts scan count 1, logical reads: 2533, physical reads:
   0, read ahead reads: 0
```

The number of logical I/Os has increased from 400 executing the query as a standalone statement to 2,533 executing the query in a stored procedure. Why is this?

The problem is caused by the fact that the query plan was created and loaded into procedure cache by the first execution. The query optimizer created the query plan based on the parameters passed to it so in this case it created a query plan for the SELECT statement:

```
SELECT account_no, balance FROM accounts
   WHERE balance BETWEEN 8000 AND 8100
```

The next time the stored procedure was executed no query optimization was done and the query plan utilizing the nonclustered index was used. This is not the most efficient query plan for the range as can be seen from the logical I/Os.

In its worst manifestation we can imagine that the first stored procedure execution happens to use a query plan that is not efficient for all subsequent stored procedure executions. So how can we deal with this situation?

One mechanism available to us is to make sure that the stored procedure always creates and uses a new query plan. We can force a stored procedure to create and use a new query plan but there are also times when a stored procedure is automatically recompiled.

For example, if an index is deleted from a table used in the stored procedure or if the ALTER TABLE statement is used to change the table, perhaps by adding a column, the stored procedure will be recompiled. How does SQL Server know that these changes have taken place? It knows because two columns in the *sysobjects* system table keep track of changes to the table. These columns are *indexdel* and *schema_ver*. The *indexdel* column is incremented if an index is deleted and the *schema_ver* column is incremented when a table is altered with ALTER TABLE or a rule or default is bound or unbound.

Note that neither the CREATE INDEX statement nor the UPDATE STATISTICS statement cause a stored procedure to be recompiled, however the SET SHOWPLAN ON does. If showplan output is enabled, every execution of a stored procedure will cause a new plan to be created in the procedure cache. So be careful when attempting to look at the query plan used by a stored procedure!

How can we manually cause a stored procedure to be recompiled? There are a number of mechanisms:

▶ The *sp_recompile* stored procedure

▶ CREATE PROCEDURE WITH RECOMPILE

▶ EXECUTE WITH RECOMPILE

The *sp_recompile* system stored procedure ensures that each stored procedure and trigger that uses the specified table are recompiled the next time the stored procedure and triggers are run:

```
sp_recompile accounts

Each stored procedure and trigger that uses table accounts
will be recompiled the next time it is executed.
```

The *sp_recompile* system stored procedure actually increments the *schema_ver* column in the *sysobjects* system table. Note the mention of triggers. Triggers are just a special kind of stored procedure that gets automatically executed when inserts, updates and deletes happen to a table. As such, they have their query plans stored in procedure cache like any other stored procedure.

When we create a procedure we can use the *WITH RECOMPILE* option. This means that every execution of a stored procedure causes a new query plan to be created. Using this option means that we do not have the problem that a query plan is resident in cache that is inefficient for various parameter combinations. However, because we generate a new query plan for each execution of the stored procedure, the performance benefit of stored procedures is negated.

A less severe option is to execute a stored procedure with the *WITH RECOMPILE* option. This causes a new query plan to be created for just that execution.

These options will help us to avoid the problem described previously with an inefficient query plan loaded into procedure cache but they do mean that new query plans get created. Another option is to break the stored procedure up into smaller pieces:

```
CREATE PROC few_accounts_per_range_proc (@minbal MONEY, @maxbal
    MONEY)
AS
SET STATISTICS IO ON
SELECT account_no, balance FROM accounts
    WHERE balance BETWEEN @minbal AND @maxbal
RETURN

CREATE PROC many_accounts_per_range_proc (@minbal MONEY, @maxbal
    MONEY)
AS
SET STATISTICS IO ON
SELECT account_no, balance FROM accounts
    WHERE balance BETWEEN @minbal AND @maxbal
RETURN

CREATE PROC accounts_per_range_proc (@minbal MONEY, @maxbal MONEY)
```

```
AS
IF (@maxbal - @minbal) <= 100
    EXEC few_accounts_per_range_proc @minbal, @maxbal
ELSE
    EXEC many_accounts_per_range_proc @minbal, @maxbal
RETURN
```

The stored procedure *accounts_per_range_proc* is executed passing the minimum and maximum balance. It tests to see if the difference between the minimum and maximum balance is less than or equal to 100 and if it is it executes the stored procedure *few_accounts_per_range_proc*. If the difference is greater than 100 it executes the stored procedure *many_accounts_per_range_proc*. In this way the two stored procedures that access the data are compiled with their own execution plan. In this example the stored procedure *few_accounts_per_range_proc* gets a query plan that uses a nonclustered index whereas the query plan for *many_accounts_per_range_proc* uses a table scan. This method can work well but it does require the developer writing the stored procedures to know that a balance range greater than 100 is best dealt with by a table scan and, of course, this distribution can change over time.

Another approach is not to recompile the whole stored procedure but only the troublesome statement. This can be brought about by using the EXECUTE statement with a character string. For example:

```
CREATE PROC example_proc (@bal MONEY)
AS
declare @balstr varchar(10)
select @balstr = convert(varchar(10), @bal)
:
EXECUTE ("SELECT account_no, balance FROM accounts WHERE balance >
    " + @balstr)
:
RETURN
```

The Transact-SQL statement inside the EXECUTE statement goes through the same phases that any standalone Transact-SQL statement goes through, that is, parsing through to query compilation. This does not happen until the EXECUTE statement is actioned. Other Transact-SQL statements in the stored procedure are compiled just once.

We have already seen optimizer hints and how they can be used to force the query optimizer to use a particular index. Optimizer hints can also be used with queries in stored procedures to ensure that a particular query plan is always used.

How do you make sure that the procedure cache is large enough to hold your stored procedures? This will be discussed in Chapter 5.

4.3 The Query Optimizer and the Update Statement

One might be excused in thinking that an update is a simple operation, the contents of one or more columns are changed and that is the end of it. Unfortunately, this is not so. An update to a row may result in a number of different scenarios occurring. Which scenario occurs depends on many factors, some of which we will now investigate. The performance of the update statement will be governed by which scenario takes place.

The first question to consider when investigating updates is when will the update actually happen? This is governed by which of the two *update modes* known as *direct* and *deferred* are used. The direct update mode takes place at once with log records being written once to the transaction log. In contrast, the deferred update mode first writes any modifications that are to be made to the transaction log and flags them as NO-OPs. These transaction log records are then read again, written to the transaction log as real actions and the changes to the data made. Why is this deferred update mechanism used? We shall see shortly. However, the initial decision as to whether a deferred or direct update is used is made by the query optimizer and, thus, the topic is part of this chapter.

If the direct update mode is used the next question to consider relates to where is the update performed? There are three possible *methods* of update and these are known as *update-in-place, on-page delete/insert* and *full delete/ insert*. These will all be considered shortly but first of all let us explore why deferred updates are necessary.

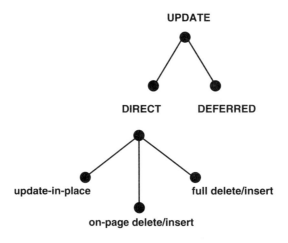

Figure 4.16
*Update Modes
And Update
Methods*

Suppose we have the following table of parts:

```
CREATE TABLE parts
    (
    partno INT PRIMARY KEY,
    partdesc VARCHAR(20)
    )
```

This table contains the following rows:

```
partno    partdesc
-------   --------------
0         assorted nails
1         electric drill
2         electric lathe
3         electric torch
4         electric light
5         assorted tacks
6         soldering iron

:

:
```

Imagine we were to issue the following statement:

```
UPDATE parts SET partno = partno + 1
```

We can imagine that this update takes the first *partno* value which is 1, adds 1 to it and produces a *partno* value of 2. But we already have a *partno* value of 2 in the database and we have a primary key constraint on the *partno* column so why does a primary key constraint violation not occur?

A violation does not occur because of the way that SQL Server handles the update. It uses the deferred mode which is an update mode that uses multiple steps. In the first step all the changes that need to happen are written to the transaction log and are marked as a NO-OP. The transaction log will now contain deletes to remove the existing values and inserts to add the new values. The transaction log is then re-read and all the deletes and inserts are applied. Note that in deferred mode updates are implemented as a delete operation followed by an insert operation.

The query optimizer can decide that a deferred mode will be required, but it is not until execution time that the decision as to whether an individual row update will be actioned as an update-in-place, on-page delete/insert or a full delete/insert is made. Even if the query optimizer decided that a direct mode would suffice this may be overridden at run time.

SQL Server will choose to use the direct mode to update tables if possible because it is quicker and requires less log records to be created than the deferred mode.

If the direct mode is used SQL Server might use an update-in-place, on-page delete/insert or a full delete/insert. Let us look at these different update methods.

4.3.0.1 Update-in-place

The update-in-place is the least costly update method. With an update-in-place, the row that is updated does not change position. No shuffling of rows occurs on the page and no index pointers referencing the row need to be adjusted. A single MODIFY transaction log record is created that contains the difference between the old and new value.

There are a number of restrictions that must be satisfied for SQL Server to be able to action an update-in-place and these restrictions depend on whether the update modifies a single row or multiple rows.

For updates that modify a single row:

▶ The column (or columns) that are modified must not result in a change of row size; however, they may be variable length columns.

▶ There must not be an update trigger present on the table.

▶ The table must not be marked for replication.

▶ Updated columns cannot form part of the clustered index.

▶ The new value of the column or columns cannot differ from the old value such that the variance is greater than 50% of the total row size.

For updates that modify multiple rows the restrictions are more severe:

▶ Any columns updated cannot be variable length, they must be fixed length.

▶ A nonclustered index that is used to access the rows to be updated cannot contain updated columns.

▶ The columns to be updated can be contained in a non-unique nonclustered index if the column is fixed length.

There are some other more subtle restrictions but these are the main ones. We will look at some examples of these restrictions shortly.

4.3.0.2 On-Page Delete/Insert

An on-page delete/insert is more costly than an update-in-place but less costly than other methods and is used when an update-in-place cannot be used because of the above restrictions. As the name implies, an on-page delete/insert is a delete followed by an insert but the row is re-inserted on the same page in such a way that it keeps its original row id. This is very important as a change in the row id would mean that every nonclustered index that references the row would have to be modified which could be a costly operation, both in terms of system resource and lock contention.

An on-page delete/insert is typically used when the row length changes. Update triggers and replication need to see the deleted and inserted rows and so an on-page delete/insert is used when the table is marked for replication or there is an update trigger present on the table. For example, the *inserted* and *deleted* trigger test tables must be visible to an update trigger.

4.3.0.3 Full Delete/Insert

A full delete/insert is actioned when there simply is not enough space on the page to accommodate the growth of the updated row. In this case it is removed from its home page with a delete operation and it is then re-inserted onto another page. Where is it re-inserted? If there is no clustered index present on the table it will be inserted into the last page of the table.

The original row id will now have changed. This change now means that every nonclustered index that references the row has to be modified, using system resource and increasing the chance of lock conflict with other users.

The full delete/insert may be actioned using the direct mode or the deferred mode depending on whether we are dealing with a row size increase or avoiding a key violation.

4.3.0.4 Checking the Update Mode and Method

There are various mechanisms that can be used to observe the mechanism SQL Server uses to update a row. There is some indication in the showplan output and the transaction log can be checked by counting the number of transaction log rows created by an update or by selecting from the transaction log and checking the op codes to see if an update was deferred.

A much better technique is to use the SQL Server trace flag 323. With SQL Server 6.5 this can be set with the DBCC TRACEON statement like other trace flags or by specifying the trace flag with the T option using the *sqlservr* command-line executable. The output, I find, is slightly different and as a personal preference I prefer using the the *sqlservr* command-line executable option.

Here are some examples of various update methods, again using the example table of parts:

```
CREATE TABLE parts
    (
    partno     INT          PRIMARY KEY,
    partdesc   VARCHAR(20)
    )
```

There is no update trigger present on the table and it is not marked for replication. No other indexes are present except the clustered index created by the primary key constraint. The table contains the following rows:

```
partno    partdesc
-------   ---------------
0         assorted nails
1         electric drill
2         electric lathe
3         electric torch
4         electric light
5         assorted tacks
6         soldering iron
:
:
```

Update 1: Update the part description from *electric light* to *electric meter*.

This update will not change the size of the column and the new value of the column does not differ from the old value such that the variance is greater than 50% of the total row size.

```
update parts set partdesc = 'electric meter' where partno = 4

update_mode: varct=2,rgcursor=0,rgtable=1,res-
    var=0,cstat=0x4,crows=1
Update: in-place, clust, safeind[0]=0x1
```

The output trace shows that the update is performed as an update-in-place as we expect.

Update 2: Update the part description from *assorted tacks* to *assorted screws*.

Although the new value of the column does not differ from the old value such that the variance is greater than 50% of the total row size, the update changes the size of the column from 14 to 15 characters.

```
update parts set partdesc = 'assorted screws' where partno = 5

update_mode: varct=2,rgcursor=0,rgtable=1,res-
    var=0,cstat=0x4,crows=1
Update: on-page delete/insert, clust, safeind[0]=0x1
```

The output trace shows that the update is performed as an on-page delete/insert as we expect if there is room on the page to fit the row.

Update 3: Update the part description from *electric torch* to *battery tester*.

This update will not change the size of the column, but the new value of the column does differ from the old value such that the variance is greater than 50% of the total row size.

```
update parts set partdesc = 'battery tester' where partno = 3

update_mode: varct=2,rgcursor=0,rgtable=1,res-
    var=0,cstat=0x4,crows=1
Update: on-page delete/insert, clust, safeind[0]=0x1
```

The output trace shows that the update is performed as an on-page delete/insert as we expect if there is room on the page to fit the row.

```
Update 4: Update the part number from 3 to 7.
```

This update is a single row update that updates the clustered index.

```
update parts set partno = 7 where partno = 3

update_mode: varct=2,rgcursor=0,rgtable=1,res-
    var=0,cstat=0x4,crows=1
Update: full delete/insert, clustered index unsafe, clust,
    safeind[0]=
```

The output trace shows that the update is performed as an full delete/insert as we expect.

```
Update 5: Update the part number by adding 1 to it.
```

This update is a multiple row update that updates the clustered index. As we discussed earlier, this would cause a key violation if performed as a direct mode update so the update mode chosen is deferred.

```
update parts set partno = partno + 1

Update: full delete/insert, deferred mode, clust, safeind[0]=0xfe
```

We can see that the amount of work performed during an update can vary dramatically depending on the type of update performed. It is worth seriously considering this when designing your database. It may be worth, perhaps, sacrificing some disk space and using fixed length character strings where you might have previously used variable length ones for those columns that are updated frequently, if doing so gives you a good performance boost.

5

SQL Server and Windows NT

5.1 SQL Server and CPU

5.1.1 Introduction

The first resource on a Windows NT server that is usually monitored is the CPU. CPUs have been gaining in power dramatically over the last few years and Windows NT supports a number of different processor architectures that are also supported by SQL Server 6.5. These are Intel, DEC Alpha AXP, MIPS and PowerPC.

As well as investing in the increasing power of a single processor system, more and more companies are purchasing Symmetric Multiprocessor (SMP) systems. Although a multiprocessor system may not reduce CPU bottlenecks when a single threaded process is consuming the CPU, multi-threaded processes such as SQL Server will benefit greatly.

CPU is a system resource. The more CPU power available the better the system is likely to perform. Windows NT schedules CPU time to the threads of a process and, if more threads require CPU time than there is CPU time available, a queue of waiting threads will develop. Sometimes a processor bottleneck is actually masking another bottleneck such as memory so it is important to look at CPU usage in conjunction with other resource usage on the system. This chapter provides an overview of CPU usage and looks at how SQL Server makes use of the CPU. It then looks at how CPU bottlenecks can be observed.

5.1.2 An Overview of Windows NT and CPU Utilization

To understand the way that Windows NT uses the CPU we first need to consider the difference between a process and a thread. A process can be considered to be an object that contains executable code and data, an address space which is a set of virtual addresses and any other resources allocated to the code as it runs. It also must contain a minimum of one thread of execution.

A thread is the item inside a process that is scheduled to run, not the process itself like in some older operating systems. A Windows NT process can contain any number of threads and a process that contains more than one thread is known as a multi-threaded process. Windows NT is able to simultaneously schedule a number of threads across multiple CPUs. These can be threads belonging to many processes or threads belonging to just one process.

SQL Server is a multi-threaded process and so it is able to schedule a number of threads simultaneously across multiple processors to perform a multitude of functions. SQL Server may have threads concurrently executing across multiple processors with one servicing a user connection, one performing a dump and one writing pages from cache to disk. Although SQL Server can be executing threads concurrently across multiple processors, it can be restricted to only using a subset of the available processors on the server.

The order in which threads are scheduled is governed by a priority associated with those threads. Windows NT always schedules the highest priority thread to run that is waiting for processor time to make sure that the highest priority work gets done first. Each process is allocated to one of four *base priority* classes:

▶ Idle

▶ Normal

▶ High

▶ Real-time

The *base priority* of a process can change within its base priority class. The base priority of a process *thread* varies within the base priority of its parent process. As a general rule, the base priority of a thread varies only within a range of two greater than or two less than the base priority of its process. The *dynamic priority* of a thread governs when it will be scheduled. The dynamic priority of a thread is being constantly adjusted by Windows NT. For example, the dynamic priority of a thread is typically increased when an I/O operation it has been waiting for completes and the thread now needs processor time. The dynamic priority of a thread can equal or grow beyond its base priority, but it can never drop below it.

By default, SQL Server runs at *Normal* priority.

5.1.3 How SQL Server Uses CPU

There are various ways that SQL Server can be configured with respect to how it makes use of the CPU. These can be grouped into the following categories:

▶ Priority

▶ Use of Symmetric Multiprocessing systems

▶ Thread usage

Let us consider these in turn.

5.1.3.1 Priority

On the Windows NT server running SQL Server it is likely that little interactive use will take place. The server will communicate with client workstations. Usually, when there is interactive use made of a workstation it is preferable to increase the priority of the foreground application, that is, the application running in the window that is currently displayed at the top of the other windows.

This can be done using the *System* icon in the *Control Panel* and choosing the *Performance* tab. This is shown in Figure 5.1.

SQL Server is never a foreground application and so, on the server, the performance boost selected should be *None*. On the client workstation, however, boosting the foreground priority makes sense. Of course, using ISQL/w, for example, on the server directly will not benefit from any priority boost so you might find that you do not get great performance. This does not mean that SQL Server is running slowly, just that ISQL/w is not priority boosted and so will be contending equally with it for the CPU.

Another method of changing the priority of SQL Server is to change the advanced server configuration option *priority boost*. This governs whether or not SQL Server should run at a higher priority than other processes on the same server.

Setting priority boost to 1 causes SQL Server to execute at a higher priority and to be scheduled more often. This will have a negative impact on other applications running on the server and so this parameter should be used with care unless the server has been designated as being dedicated to SQL Server. To use our example above, using ISQL/w directly on a server that has priority boost set to 1 would result in degraded ISQL/w performance.

Figure 5.1
Changing Fore-
ground Priority

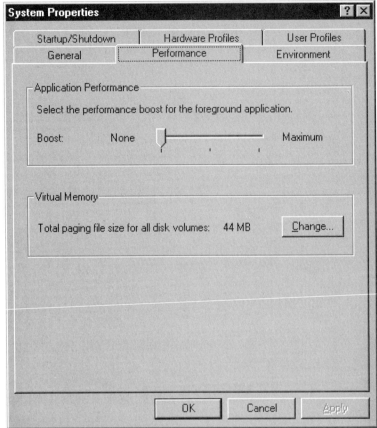

5.1.3.2 Use of Symmetric Multiprocessing Systems

With respect to symmetric multiprocessing systems, SQL Server can be configured to use anything from all of the processors through to just one by setting the advanced server configuration option *SMP concurrency.* The SMP concurrency option governs the number of threads that SQL Server will release to Windows NT for execution which limits the number of CPUs used by SQL Server.

Leaving the default value to be 0 means that SQL Server will auto configure. In auto configure mode, the limit is set to $N - 1$ processors, where N is the number of processors detected at SQL Server startup. On a uniprocessor machine this value will be set to 1.

If the SMP concurrency option is set to -1 we get what is known as *Dedicated SMP Support.* This means that SQL Server will use all the processors. If a value other than 0 or -1 is used then SQL Server will use that many processors.

For example, if the SMP concurrency option is set to 2 on a 4 processor system, the maximum number of processors that SQL Server can use will be 2.

Which processors on a multiprocessor system can SQL Server use? Generally, Windows NT does not guarantee that any thread in a process will run on a given processor. A thread may migrate from processor to processor, which causes reloading of the processor's cache. Under heavy system loads, specifying the processor that should run which thread can boost performance by reducing the reloading of processor cache. This is likely to only make much of a difference with four or more processors under load.

The association between a processor and a thread is called *processor affinity*. SQL Server 6.5 enables a processor affinity mask to be specified as a server configuration option. By setting bits in the mask, the system administrator can decide which processors SQL Server runs on. The number of the bit set represents the processor. For example, setting the mask to the value 126 (hexadecimal 0x7E) sets the bits 01111110 or 1, 2, 3, 4, 5 and 6. This means that SQL Server threads should run on processors 1, 2, 3, 4, 5 and 6. On an 8 processor system this means that SQL Server threads should not run on processors 0 and 7. Avoiding these processors is reasonable as Windows NT allocates all I/O handling to processor 0 and work associated with the network interface card to the highest numbered processor available, in our example, processor 7.

5.1.3.3 Thread Usage

When an SQL Server client executes a request, the network handler places the command in a queue and the next usable thread from the *worker pool* of threads acquires the request and handles it. If no free worker thread is available when a request arrives, SQL Server creates a new thread dynamically, until it reaches the server configuration option *maximum worker threads*.

The default value for maximum worker threads is 255 which is usually greater than the server configuration option *User Connections*. However, when there are a large number of connections (typically hundreds), using a thread for every user connection may deplete operating system resource. To avoid this SQL Server can use a technique called *thread pooling*. With thread pooling a pool of worker threads will handle a larger number of user connections.

If the maximum worker threads value has not been exceeded a new thread is created for each user connection. Once the maximum worker threads value has been exceeded user connections will share the pool of worker threads. A new client request will be handled by the first thread in the pool that becomes free.

The priority of the SQL Server process, the use of SMP systems and thread usage are the various ways that SQL Server can be configured with respect to how it makes use of the CPU.

Let us now look at how we can detect processor bottlenecks.

5.1.4 Investigating CPU Bottlenecks

The tools used to observe CPU bottlenecks are typically the Performance Monitor and the Task Manager. There are also a number of tools on the Windows NT Resource Kit 4.0 CD. We will focus on using the Performance Monitor in this section although the *Processes* and *Performance* tabs in the Task Manager are also quite useful. These are shown later in Figures 5.10 and 5.11 when we investigate memory. The *System*, *Processor* and *Process* objects are a useful place to start and it is worth looking at some of their counters as shown below in Table 5.1.

In Figure 5.2 the Performance Monitor is being used to monitor the following counters:

▶ Processor: % Processor Time

▶ System: Processor Queue Length

Table 5.1 *Selected Counters For The System, Processor And Process Objects*

CPU Related Counters	Explanation
System: % Total Processor Time	The percentage that all of the processors are busy in the sampling interval. Represents one or more processors.
System: Processor Queue Length	How many threads need CPU time but are having to wait. This counts only waiting threads, not those being handled. This counter belongs to the System object because there is only one queue even when there are multiple processors on the server.
Processor: % Processor Time	The percentage that a processor is busy. There is an instance of this counter for every processor on the server.
Processor: % User Time	The percentage that a processor is busy in User Mode. User Mode means application code and subsystem code.
Processor: % Privileged Time	The percentage that a processor is busy in Privileged Mode. Privileged Mode means operating system services.
Process: % Processor Time	The percentage of CPU time that a process is busy.

Figure 5.2

A Busy Processor

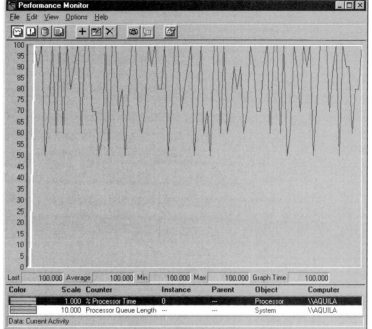

The counter Processor: % Processor Time is highlighted. We can see that the processor appears to be 100% utilized. This in itself is not necessarily going to cause a bottleneck. However, we can see that the Processor Queue Length averages around 8 (note the scale factor of 10 so it can be seen on the display). This means that 8 threads are waiting for the CPU and this is a clear indication that we have a processor bottleneck.

So what is causing the bottleneck? Is it one process or many processes? We can monitor the processor usage of each process to get a feel for the answer. In Figure 5.3 the Performance Monitor is being used to monitor the Process: % Processor Time counter.

It is pretty clear that one process is monopolizing the processor. It is the highlighted process which we can see is SQL Server. We need to further investigate why this is and if it is not a database or application design problem, consider perhaps moving SQL Server onto its own server. If no process stands out in this display this might be an indication that the processor is just too slow.

Can we drill down further into SQL Server? We can look at the individual threads. In Figure 5.4 the Performance Monitor is being used to monitor the

Figure 5.3
Monitoring
Processor Time
For Individual
Processes

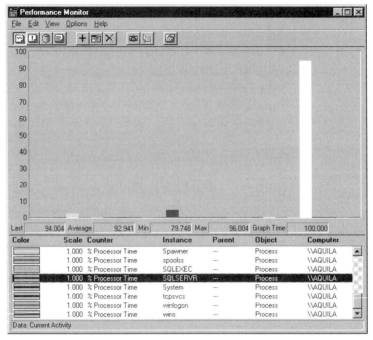

Figure 5.4
Monitoring CPU
Usage At The
Thread Level

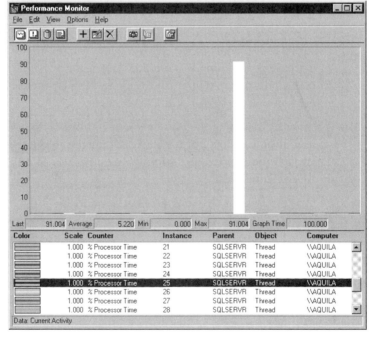

Figure 5.5
SQL Server
Instances Versus
Thread ID

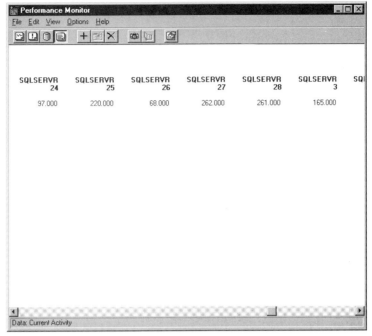

Thread: % Processor Time counter for all the SQLSERVR instances. We can clearly see that the thread with thread instance number 25 is using most of the CPU. How do we relate this to an SQL Server server process id (*spid*)? If we choose *View* and then *Report* we are taken into the Report display.

We can then add the *Thread: ID Thread* counter. This gives us a display as shown in Figure 5.5. We can see the SQL Server instances and the corresponding Windows NT thread ID. In our example we have thread instance number 25 mapping to thread ID 220. Now all we have to do is map this to a spid. One way of doing this is to execute the following SQL statement against the *sysprocesses* system table:

```
SELECT spid, kpid, status, program_name, cpu, physical_io,
   memusage
FROM master..sysprocesses
```

spid	kpid	status	program_name	cpu	physical_io	memusage
1	0	sleeping		0	0	1
2	0	sleeping		0	0	0
3	0	sleeping		0	41	0
4	0	sleeping		0	22	0
10	232	sleeping	SQLEXEC -Alert Engine	150	60	1

```
11    97     sleeping  SQLEXEC         481  13           1
                       -Task Refresher
12    97     sleeping  SQL PerfMon     1692 77           1
13    220    runnable  Microsoft       150122            2
                       ISQL/w
```

The *kpid* column is the Windows NT thread ID. We can look down this column for our thread ID 220 and find the spid, in this case 13. Once we know the spid we can obtain information such as the program being run, in this case, Microsoft ISQL/w. Note that other columns represent system resource usage and these can be helpful in themselves.

An alternative to using the above SELECT statement is to use *DBCC SQLPERF (THREADS)*.

```
DBCC SQLPERF (THREADS)

Spid   Thread ID   Status    LoginName   I/Os   CPU   MemUsage
----   ---------   --------   ---------   ----   ---   --------
1                  sleeping   (null)      0      0     1
2                  sleeping   (null)      0      0     0
3                  sleeping   (null)      41     0     0
4                  sleeping   (null)      22     0     0
5                  sleeping   (null)      0      0     0
6                  sleeping   (null)      0      0     0
7                  sleeping   (null)      0      0     0
8                  sleeping   (null)      0      0     0
9                  sleeping   (null)      0      0     0
10     232(0xe8)   sleeping   sa          60     150   1
11     97(0x61)    sleeping   sa          13     561   1
12     97(0x61)    sleeping   probe       77     1692  1
13     220(0xdc)   runnable   sa          2      25717 1
```

Hint: If thread pooling is taking place many different Windows NT threads will service a single SQL Server spid over time so the Windows NT thread ID will not be meaningful in these circumstances.

5.1.5 Solving Problems with CPU

Having determined that there is indeed a CPU bottleneck and that there is a queue of threads waiting for processor time the next step is to find out what is using up the CPU. Other bottlenecks should be investigated such as memory to ensure that they are not manifesting themselves as a CPU bottleneck. If there is no particular candidate process to home in on then the CPU is probably too slow and either a faster CPU can be purchased or another additional CPU. If it is obvious which application is monopolizing the CPU and it is not SQL Server then it might be an idea to move that application to another server.

If SQL Server is monopolizing the CPU then it may be possible to track down the actual thread and then spid. In this case it might then be possible to track down why this thread is using so much CPU. If there is no particular candidate thread to home in on then the CPU is probably too slow and another additional CPU might be the most cost effective solution.

Another consumer of CPU is the network interface card. Replacing 8- or 16-bit cards with 32-bit cards will save some CPU. Network interface cards that use bus-mastering direct memory access (DMA) are less of a burden on the CPU.

5.2 SQL Server and Memory

5.2.1 Introduction

Another important resource on the Windows NT server is memory. Over the last few years the amount of memory found on servers and workstations has rapidly increased and while, not long ago, 8 Mb seemed an enormous amount of memory many of my customers are running Windows NT servers with anything from 256 Mb to two Gigabytes.

Having large amounts of physical memory is not enough in itself. The software running on the server must be able to benefit from it and it is there-fore vital that the server operating system manages memory in an efficient and intelligent fashion. Windows NT employs a virtual memory manager to do just that and it can provide excellent memory management on a wide range of memory configurations with multiple users.

SQL Server uses the virtual memory management features of Windows NT to enable it and other processes to share the physical memory on the server and to hold memory pages on disk in a page file.

Physical memory is a system resource. The more physical memory the bet-ter the system is likely to perform. If there is not enough physical memory on the server then performance will be degraded as processes fight for memory. This section on memory provides an overview of the Windows NT virtual memory model and looks at how SQL Server uses memory. It then looks at how memory bottlenecks can be observed.

5.2.2 An Overview of Windows NT Virtual Memory Management

Like a number of modern server operating systems Windows NT uses a flat, linear 32-bit memory model. Each process is able to address 4 Gigabytes of virtual memory. The upper 2Gb of virtual memory is reserved for system code and data that is accessible to the process only when it is running in privileged mode. The lower 2Gb is available to the process when it is running in user mode.

Information held in physical memory can usually be categorized as either code or data. Windows NT divides the code and data into 4Kb *pages* (8Kb on the DEC Alpha platform).

The pages given to a Windows NT process by the virtual memory manager are known as the *working set* of the process and this working set holds pages containing any code and data recently used by the process. The working set of a process can grow or shrink as the virtual memory manager transfers pages of code and data between hard disk and physical memory. This is known as *paging*. All virtual memory operating systems page and the secret is to make sure that the amount of physical memory and the memory requirements of processes is such that paging does not become a burden on the system. In this situation, paging can cause disk bottlenecks and start to consume the processor.

If a page of code or data is required by a process and it is not present in the working set of the process a *page fault* results. The page is then brought into its working set. Whether the working set of the process then grows is determined by the availability of free memory on the server. If there is an abundance of free memory the working set of the process will grow as the new page is added. If there is a lack of free memory, pages in the working set that have not been used for a while will be removed. This is known as working set *trimming*. If pages are continually being taken out of the working set of a process to make room for new pages it is likely that the removed pages will be needed again soon. The process will again page fault and the cycle is repeated.

We can see that, if memory is running low, code and data pages will be continually removed from and added to the working set of the process resulting in many page faults. This can lead to a disk bottleneck and wasted CPU as the system spends more time paging than doing useful work on behalf of the user.

There are in fact two types of page fault. A *hard* page fault happens when the code or data page needs to be retrieved from disk. A *soft* page fault happens when it is discovered elsewhere in physical memory. Soft faults use CPU but hard faults cause disk reads and writes to occur.

When a page is removed from the working set it may need to be written to disk if it has been changed. If it has not been changed this need not happen. The area on disk that pages are read from and written to is known as the page file. The file name of the page file is *pagefile.sys* and its default size is the size of physical memory plus 12 Mb. If memory is *committed* to a process (known as committed memory) space will be reserved for it in the page file.

5.2.3 How SQL Server Uses Memory

SQL Server is a single Windows NT process as is the SQL Executive process that manages components such as the replication and alert subsystems. The amount of memory you can give to SQL Server really depends upon the amount of memory available on your Windows NT server and the memory requirements of other processes running on the server. Ideally, if it is possible, dedicate a single Windows NT server to run SQL Server and then SQL Server will not compete for memory resources with anything else. Of course, it can compete with Windows NT itself for memory but this will degrade performance and so when the memory requirements of SQL Server are configured it is best to leave ample for Windows NT.

The *SQL Server 6.0 Administrator's Companion* provides a useful table that gives a rough guideline on how much memory to allocate to SQL Server and Windows NT for various values of physical memory if no other processes are running. This is shown in Table 5.2.

Of course, the fact that you can give 28Mb to SQL Server on a 48Mb server does not mean that SQL Server will benefit from having 28Mb nor

Table 5.2 *Allocation Memory To SQL Server and Windows NT*

Physical Memory in (Mb) on Server	Approximate SQL Server Memory Allocation (Mb)
16	4
24	8
32	16
48	28
64	40
128	100
256	216
512	464

does it mean that it will be all that it requires. Only by investigating the cache hit ratio can we know if the data cache is large enough or too large and wasting memory and only by investigating paging activity can we tell if SQL Server has been given too much memory and Windows NT insufficient.

5.2.4 Configuring Memory for SQL Server

The maximum amount of memory that SQL Server is allowed to use is specified with the SQL Server configuration option *memory*. It is stated as a number of 2Kb pages. The system stored procedure *sp_configure* or the SQL Enterprise Manager can be used to configure memory. In the SQL Enterprise Manager the server to be configured can be right mouse clicked in the *Server Manager* window and *Configure...* chosen. The *Server Configurations/Options* dialog box then appears. The *Configuration* tab can then be selected as shown in Figure 5.6.

The change in memory configuration will not be actioned until SQL Server is restarted. This raises an interesting point. What happens if you make

Figure 5.6
Configuring
Memory With The
SQL Enterprise
Manager

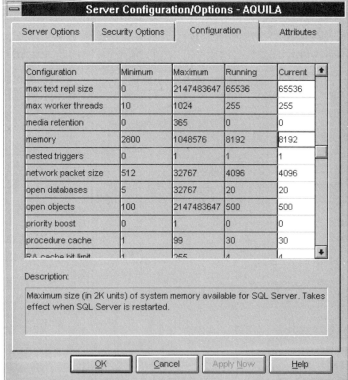

a mistake and configure SQL Server to have more memory than is present on the server? In this case SQL Server will fail to start. You cannot reconfigure the memory value to your original intention as you need to start SQL Server to do this. This looks like a catch-22 but there is a way around the problem.

It is possible to start SQL Server with a *minimal configuration* by specifying the *f* option. This is usually done with the *sqlservr* command-line executable:

```
sqlservr -f
```

Starting SQL Server with this option results in the following:

Memory usage is temporarily changed. User connections, open databases, locks, open objects, language information in cache and asynchronous I/O are all set to their minimum values. The procedure cache is set to 50% with minimal total procedure and buffer cache. Only one user can connect to SQL Server as it starts in single user mode and the checkpoint mechanism, read ahead and remote access is disabled. The configuration option *Tempdb_in_ram* is temporarily set to 2Mb. Any auto-execution stored procedures are not executed.

Once the server has been started with the minimal configuration option, the memory configuration parameter can be changed using the *sp_configure* system stored procedure and then SQL Server can be restarted normally.

Once we have specified that SQL Server will have a number of megabytes of memory it is useful to be able to see how this is apportioned. This is shown graphically in Figure 5.7.

Some memory is used for SQL Server's own code and data structures which we cannot configure. Some memory is used for user connections, locks, open databases and open objects. These are all configurable parameters and so the amount of memory used for these depends on their current values. The memory left is divided between the procedure cache and the data cache. This is achieved with the *procedure cache* configuration parameter which by default is set to 30% meaning that 30% of the SQL Server memory left is given to the procedure cache and 70% to the data cache.

If more physical memory is added to a server and the SQL Server memory configuration parameter increased as per Table 5.2, the procedure cache and the data cache will grow in proportion. It may be that sufficient memory is already available for the procedure cache in which case it may be more beneficial to use this memory for the data cache by lowering the *procedure cache* configuration parameter.

Figure 5.7
*How Memory Is
Apportioned By
SQL Server*

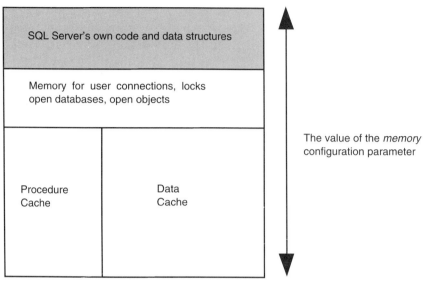

The DBCC statement DBCC MEMUSAGE lets us see how SQL Server memory has been distributed:

```
DBCC MEMUSAGE

Memory Usage:

                            Meg.   2K Blks       Bytes
     Configured Memory:  16.0000      8192    16777216
            Code size:    1.7166       879     1800000
    Static Structures:    0.2489       128      261040
               Locks:    0.2480       127      260000
         Open Objects:    0.1068        55      112000
       Open Databases:    0.0031         2        3220
    User Context Areas:    0.7447       382      780912
           Page Cache:    8.9682      4592     9403792
         Proc Headers:    0.2161       111      226554
      Proc Cache Bufs:    3.6289      1858     3805184

Buffer Cache, Top 20:

    DB Id    Object Id    Index Id    2K Buffers
        5            5           0            27
        1            5           0            25
        1            1           0            13
        1    544004969           0            11
        1           36           0             8
        1           99           0             7
        1            1           2             5
        1            2           0             5
        1            3           0             5
        1            5           1             3
        .
```

```
             5              2              0              3
             1              6              0              2
             1              6              1              2
             1             45            255              2
             2              2              0              2
             2             99              0              2
             3              2              0              2
             4              2              0              2
             5              1              0              2
             5              3              0              2

Procedure Cache, Top 20:

Procedure Name: sp_MSdbuserprofile
Database Id: 1
Object Id: 837578022
Version: 1
Uid: 1
Type: stored procedure
Number of trees: 0
Size of trees: 0.000000 Mb, 0.000000 bytes, 0 pages
Number of plans: 2
Size of plans: 0.171600 Mb, 179936.000000 bytes, 90 pages

Procedure Name: sp_helpconstraint
Database Id: 1
Object Id: 437576597
Version: 1
Uid: 1
Type: stored procedure
Number of trees: 0
Size of trees: 0.000000 Mb, 0.000000 bytes, 0 pages
Number of plans: 1
Size of plans: 0.111692 Mb, 117118.000000 bytes, 58 pages
:
:
```

The first section shows the allocation of the memory. In this example the *configured memory* is 16 Mb. Within this 16 Mb, static structures use 0.2489 Mb and the SQL Server *code size* takes 1.7166 Mb. The data cache, represented as the *page cache* is configured to have 8.9682 Mb. The procedure cache is configured to have 3.6289 + 0.2161 Mb.

The second section displays information about the data cache and shows the number of 2 Kb buffers allocated to the top twenty objects in it.

The third section displays information about the procedure cache and shows the cache usage of the top twenty compiled objects in it.

5.2.5 Configuring Memory for the Procedure Cache

So how do we know if we are allowing enough memory for the procedure cache? To calculate the size of the procedure cache needed, try taking the size of the largest plan in your server, as shown by DBCC MEMUSAGE, and multiply it by the maximum number of concurrent users on the system. Now multiply this figure by a factor of 1.25 to allow for other structures and you will have a first cut procedure cache sizing.

The size of the largest plan in your server can be checked using DBCC MEMUSAGE. Looking at the DBCC MEMUSAGE output above, the system stored procedure *sp_MSdbuserprofile* appears to be taking up the most space in the procedure cache at 90 pages. There are in fact two plans so we can estimate the size of a plan to be about 45 pages. In a system that supports 200 concurrent users maximum we can estimate our procedure cache usage to be:

```
45 × 200 × 1.25 = 11,250 2 Kb pages
```

We can monitor procedure cache usage in SQL Server 6.5 by means of the Performance Monitor. The Performance Monitor has an object *SQLServer - Procedure Cache* that has a number of associated counters. The counter *Procedure Cache Used %* gives us an indication of the amount of procedure cache being used. We want this to be high so we are not wasting memory but at the same time not so high as to cause us problems with insufficient procedure cache to load stored procedures. Monitoring this counter closely over a period of time is advised.

5.2.6 Placing Tempdb in Memory

The *tempdb* system database is used as scratch workspace by SQL Server. We have already seen how the query optimizer can choose query plans that use worktables and these use space in tempdb. If temporary tables are created in Transact-SQL code then these too use space in tempdb. It follows that the tempdb database can, in some systems, experience sustained high disk I/O rates.

One option provided by SQL Server to help us out is that of allowing us to place tempdb in memory. Instead of the tempdb database residing on disk it resides on an in-memory device. This is accomplished by setting the server configuration option *tempdb in ram (mb)* to the size of tempdb required in megabytes.

At first this sounds like a good idea but there are some points that we need to consider. Placing tempdb in memory obviously uses up memory but where does this memory come from? It does not come from SQL Server's memory allocation but rather it comes from the memory that is left, usually for Windows NT. Stealing memory from Windows NT is rarely a good idea unless you have plenty of it. As we have discussed, starving Windows NT of memory so that the available free memory is reduced will cause paging to occur which is likely to eventually lead to a performance problem which defeats the object of putting tempdb in memory in the first place.

Another option is to reduce the memory used by SQL Server by the amount required by tempdb so that the memory used by Windows NT remains constant. In this case we are reducing the memory available for the procedure cache and data cache. Assuming that we have sized the procedure cache so that memory is not wasted we cannot reduce it so we will have to take the memory away from the data cache.

Now, the data cache is used for *all* the databases on the server *including* tempdb but placing tempdb in memory only benefits tempdb. It follows, therefore, that placing tempdb in memory is likely to adversely affect all the databases on the server.

For this reason, usually it is not a good idea to place tempdb in memory unless the server has large amounts of physical memory and tempdb constantly experiences a high disk I/O rate. A possible alternative may be to place tempdb on your fastest disk device.

5.2.7 Investigating Memory Bottlenecks

If memory starts to get tight on the server performance will start to suffer. This is most likely to happen on a server that is running applications other than just SQL Server as they will contend for memory.

Before we investigate memory bottlenecks we need to look at the tools that we can use to do so. The first piece of information that we will want to know is likely to be how much physical memory does the server have. We can easily check this by choosing *About Windows NT* from the *Help* menu in Windows Explorer as shown in Figure 5.8.

Another handy tool is the *Task Manager* that is present in Windows NT 4.0. There are a number of tabs that can be chosen and these are *Applications*, *Processes* and *Performance*. The Applications tab is shown in Figure 5.9. This tab shows the status of programs that are running on the system. SQL Server is not shown as it is running as a service. The Processes tab displays information about processes that are running on the system as shown in Figure 5.10. Information such as the *memory usage* and the *page faults* are shown for each process. Columns can be added or removed from this tab. The Performance tab, shown in Figure 5.11, displays a graph of CPU and Memory usage history as well as a textual display.

Figure 5.8
Memory Available
As Shown By The
Windows Explorer

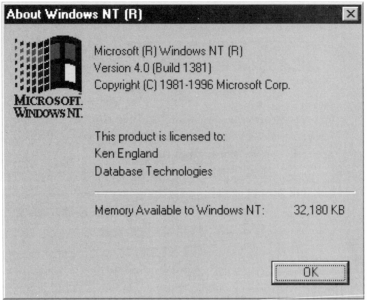

Figure 5.9
The Windows NT
Task Manager
Applications Tab

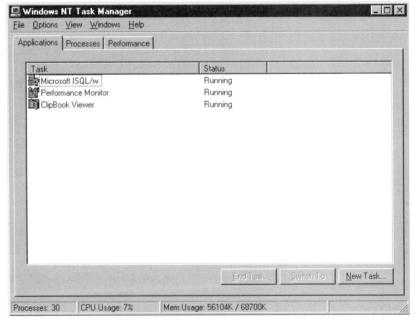

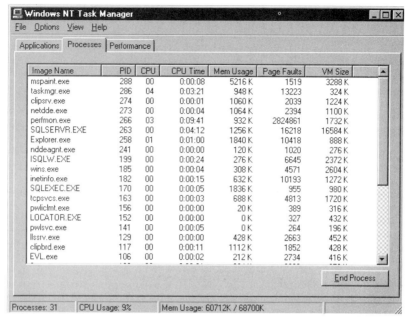

Figure 5.10
The Windows NT Task Manager Processes Tab

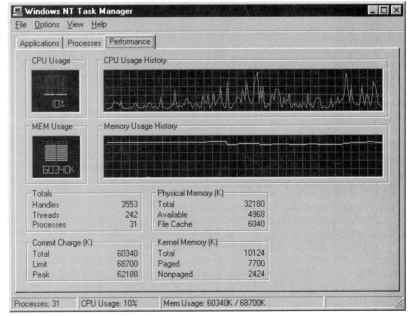

Figure 5.11
The Windows NT Task Manager Performance Tab

The most useful tool is the Performance Monitor which have already met. There are a number of useful Performance Monitor objects concerning memory and these are Memory, Paging File and Process.

There are also a number of tools on the Windows NT Resource Kit 4.0 CD.

Let us now focus on using the Performance Monitor to investigate memory bottlenecks. The Memory object is a useful place to start and it's worth a look at some of the Memory objects' counters as shown in Table 5.3.

In Figure 5.12 the Performance Monitor is being used to monitor the following counters:

▶ Memory: Page Reads/sec

▶ Memory: Pages Input/sec

▶ Memory: Page Faults/sec

Table 5.3 *Selected Counters For The Memory Object*

Memory Object Counter	*Explanation*
Page Faults/sec	This counter includes both hard page faults and soft page faults. Hard page faults result in disk I/O. Soft page faults mean pages are found elsewhere in memory.
Pages Input/sec	This is a measure of the number of pages brought in from disk every second. The difference between this value and Page Faults/sec represents soft page faults.
Pages Output/sec	This is a measure of the number of pages written to disk every second to make room in the working set of the process for newly faulted in pages. If the process modifies pages they must be written out. They cannot be discarded.
Pages/sec	Total of Pages Input/sec plus Pages Output/sec.
Page Reads/sec	The reads from disk per second to satisfy page faults. This is an important counter. As a rule of thumb, if this counter exceeds 5 pages per second there is a memory shortage. A single read operation can actually bring in more than one page.
Page Writes/sec	The writes to disk per second to satisfy page faults. This is another important counter as it measures real disk I/O work being done by the system because of page faulting. A single write operation can actually write out more than one page
Available bytes	How much memory remains that can be given to processes.

Figure 5.12
*Memory Pages
Being Read In
From Disk*

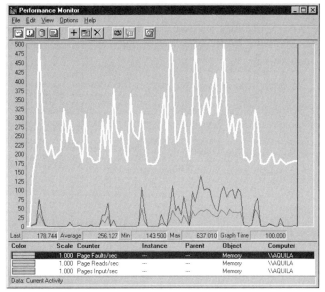

The scales of the counters have been adjusted where necessary to make them all 1.000 to facilitate comparison. The vertical maximum on the chart has been consequently adjusted to 500. The line that peaks the highest is Page Faults/sec and the line at the bottom of the chart is Page Reads/sec. The middle line is Pages Input/sec.

The averages for these counters is as follows:

Counter	Average
Page Reads/sec	18
Pages Input/Sec	30
Page Faults/sec	256

The Page Faults/sec counter represents the sum of hard and soft page faults. The Pages Input/Sec counter represents hard faults so about 12% of the faults are hard faults. The 30 pages that are input per second are brought in by 18 page reads per second so approximately 1.7 pages are being brought in by every disk read. Although the majority of page faults are soft, 18 I/Os per second are hitting the disk to retrieve pages.

It is useful to also examine the disk activity to see how hard paging is hitting the disks. Some useful counters are

▶ % Disk Read Time

▶ Avg. Disk Queue Length

▶ Disk Reads/sec

The % Disk Read Time is the percentage of elapsed time that the selected disk drives are busy servicing read requests. Avg. Disk Queue Length is the average number of read and write requests queued on the selected disks. Disk Reads/sec is the rate of read operations on the disk.

These are shown in Figure 5.13. The averages for these counters is as follows:

Counter	Average
Page Reads/sec	8.4
Pages Input/Sec	17.1
Page Faults/sec	219
% Disk Read Time	25.1
Avg. Disk Queue Length	0.7
Disk Reads/sec	13

We can immediately compare Page Reads/sec with Disk Reads/sec. This shows us that more than 64% of our disk activity is caused by paging. The disk is busy about 25% of the time. The Avg. Disk Queue Length is small at about 0.7.

Figure 5.13
Memory Counters With Disk Counters

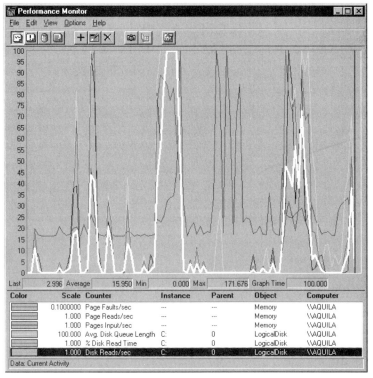

A similar investigation can be performed for page writes. It is also worth looking at which individual processes are faulting heavily. This can be done by monitoring the Page Faults/sec counter on the Process object for all the Process instances. If this is viewed in histogram format on the Chart display, processes that are page faulting heavily immediately stand out as shown in Figure 5.14.

Another area worth monitoring is the page file to see if it is filling. Ensure that there is enough free space to let it expand if it needs to.

5.2.8 Solving Problems with Memory

The main two approaches to solving memory problems are making best use of available memory and adding more physical memory to the server.

To make more use of available memory remove anything that is not needed but is consuming memory resource. For example, Windows NT services, drivers and network protocols that are not used. As was mentioned earlier, if possible dedicate the server to SQL Server.

Increasing the size of the paging file and adding another paging file may help. The addition of extra memory should be also accompanied by an increase in paging file size and, if possible, an increase in secondary cache size.

Figure 5.14
Monitoring Page Faults For Individual Processes

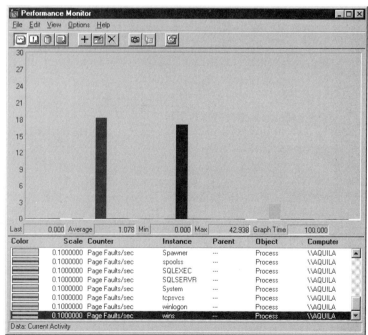

5.3 SQL Server and Disk I/O

5.3.1 Introduction

A bottleneck that is often experienced with database management systems concerns the disk subsystem. By definition a database is a shared repository of information and consequently many users are likely to be reading and writing to the database. Depending on whether the database supports an Online Transaction Processing (OLTP) system or a Decision Support System (DSS) users may update small amounts of data or may perform read only queries on large amounts of data.

The disks themselves are different from most other components in the server in that they typically have moving parts. The disk surface rotates and the disk heads move in and out across the disk surface. Relative to memory access this takes a long time and so SQL Server uses many techniques to help it minimize disk access. In fact, as we have seen, the query optimizer attempts to choose an access strategy that limits the number of disk I/Os performed.

Care should be taken when investigating disk I/O bottlenecks as there can be many causes. A very common cause is a memory bottleneck that results in high levels of paging to disk as was described in the last section.

5.3.2 An Overview of Windows NT and Disk I/O

To perform its disk I/O SQL Server issues reads and writes to Windows NT and lets Windows NT deal with the business of reading and writing to the underlying disk subsystem. To provide high levels of disk I/O throughput Windows NT provides various levels of RAID (Redundant Arrays of Inexpensive Disks) and SQL Server can make use of this capability. Various vendors also provide hardware based RAID solutions. These increase the cost of the system but tend to provide better performance and are becoming increasingly popular.

Windows NT supports the following RAID levels:

▶ RAID 0 - disk striping

▶ RAID 1 - disk mirroring (sometimes known as volume shadowing)

▶ RAID 5 - disk striping with parity

In a RAID 0 stripe set data is spread across all the drives in the set. If you were to create a file or database device on a RAID 0 stripe set Windows NT would actually break the file into 64 Kb pieces (known as chunks) as you created it putting each new 64 Kb piece on the next disk in the set circling round when it moved off the last one. We can imagine a three disk stripe set now providing three sets of heads to access the file or database device and this is the bonus of RAID 0—performance. RAID 0 provides very good performance for both reading and writing. The downside of RAID 0 is that the loss of a single disk will affect the whole stripe set.

In RAID 1 data is duplicated on a mirror disk drive (some RAID implementations allow more than one mirror). Writes are performed to both members of the stripe set. This configuration gains us redundancy. We can lose one of the members and still continue working with the other one. There is no performance advantage using RAID 1 for writing; in fact it can be slower but it may well give some performance boost to reading. A downside of RAID 1 is that twice as much disk space is necessary.

RAID 5 is very similar to RAID 0. However, as well as writing data onto a disk drive in the stripe set, parity information is written to another stripe set member. As well as striping data we stripe parity information. This gives us a level of redundancy. We can lose one disk and the data information on that disk can be recreated from the parity on other disks when a request for data on the failed disk is made. The downside of RAID 5 is that, although read performance is good, write performance is worse than RAID 0 as two disks must be written to. Hardware based implementations of RAID 5 can help to absorb this write performance degradation. Table 5.4 summarizes the different RAID levels.

Table 5.4   *RAID Levels 0, 1 and 5*

RAID Type	*Characteristics*	*Number of Disks*	*Reliability*	*Performance*
RAID 0: disk striping	Data is spread over all the disks in the stripe set with no redundancy	N	Less than a single disk	High for read and write
RAID 1: disk mirroring	Data duplicated on each member	2N	Higher than RAID 0 or 5 or single disk	Good for read but less than a single disk for write
RAID 5: disk striping with parity	As RAID 0 but parity information stored with data for redundancy	N+1	Higher than RAID 0 or single disk	As RAID 0 for read but less than a single disk for write

What happened to RAID levels 2, 3 and 4? These are not supported by Windows NT and are considered to be evolutionary steps towards RAID 5.

Another aspect of Windows NT disk I/O that we should mention here is that of synchronous I/O versus asynchronous I/O as SQL Server uses both. When a synchronous I/O is issued the application issuing the I/O waits until it has completed before doing anything else. When an asynchronous I/O is issued the application issuing the I/O carries on working and does not wait for the I/O to complete. SQL Server makes use of asynchronous I/O in many areas, in particular, the checkpoint and lazy writer processes as we shall see later.

5.3.3 How SQL Server Uses Disk I/O

SQL Server uses a cache known as the *data cache* to help minimize disk I/Os. There is a single data cache per SQL Server which all databases share. In this section we will look at the data cache and the various techniques used to make reading from it and writing to it more efficient.

5.3.3.1 An Overview of the Data Cache

As we discussed earlier, when SQL Server memory is distributed a portion of it goes to the procedure cache and the data cache. The procedure cache has already been covered so in this section we will discuss the data cache and how it can help to reduce disk I/Os.

The data cache is a collection of 2Kb buffers used to hold databases pages. By database pages we mean, for example, data pages, index pages and distribution pages. The idea behind the data cache is simple. If a user connection requests a row SQL Server will translate this into a page request and it will then look for the page in the data cache to see if any other user connection has previously retrieved it. This request for a page represents a logical I/O.

If the page cannot be found it must be retrieved from the database on disk and this disk I/O represents a physical I/O. The page is read into a free buffer and the data requested by the connection obtained. The page is now in cache and, assuming that it does not leave the cache for any reason, it will be available for any connection requesting it. The next connection requesting that page will issue a logical I/O that will be satisfied from the data cache. This is a memory access as opposed to a disk access and is consequently much faster than the original request that brought in the page from disk.

We can envisage a situation where a whole database gets brought into the cache and this is quite feasible, the only limiting factor being the size of the data cache. In reality 20% of most databases get accessed 80% of the time so we find that the most accessed pages in the database find themselves in data cache. Note that increasing the size of the data cache does not bring us a linear performance increase. Once we can hold the most accessed pages in a database or group of databases in the data cache, the allocation of more memory to the data cache brings us little gain.

An empty data cache is created when SQL Server is started. At this point most database page requests end up as physical I/Os. After a while a steady state is reached with the data cache holding the most frequently used pages as shown in Figure 5.15. The percentage of time a requested database page is found in the data cache is known as the *cache hit ratio*. The cache hit ratio is defined as:

```
cache hit ratio (%) = ((logical I/O - physical I/O)/ logical I/O)
     * 100
```

What happens if we fill the data cache and then we need to read in a new page? We will discuss the mechanisms employed shortly but SQL Server will have to make room in the data cache for the new page. If the new page has been changed by a user connection then it is known as a *dirty* page and it cannot be discarded because it reflects the latest state or version of that page. It must be written back to the database on disk. However, if the page has not been changed it can be discarded. SQL Server keeps track of which pages have not been used for the longest period of time. This is important because this is taken into account when SQL Server jettisons pages from the cache. It is said to use a *least recently used* or *LRU* algorithm.

Figure 5.15
A Steady State Reached In The Data Cache

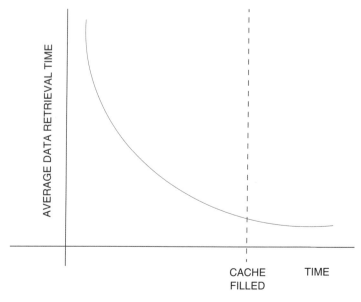

Chapter 5

How does SQL Server find out if a page is resident in the data cache? It could look at every used buffer in the data cache but this would be very expensive for large data caches consisting of tens of thousands of buffers. Instead it uses an internal hashing scheme to quickly locate buffers. The number of hash buckets used to support this mechanism can be changed by using the server configuration option *hash buckets*. The default value is normally sufficient for most systems.

What happens if we change pages in the data cache? How do they get to disk? To explain this we need to look at two system processes:

▶ The checkpoint process

▶ The lazy writer process

5.3.3.2 The Checkpoint Process

To understand how the checkpoint process functions we need first to understand what happens when a transaction is committed. Once a commit is issued SQL Server will flush all the changes to the transaction log so that they are now in safe storage on disk. Note that the changes are written to the transaction log not the database. The latest version of the changed pages remains in the data cache unless it is removed to make space for new pages.

Suppose the server now crashes. When SQL Server restarts it will initiate automatic recovery during which any incomplete transactions are rolled back. The old data cache is now gone as it was in volatile memory so the only location that the latest versions of the changed pages reside is in the transaction log. Before allowing any users onto the database SQL Server must roll forward the completed transactions present in the transaction log to it.

One can imagine that the transaction log could contain many changes that need to be applied to the database and this could take a long period of time. To avoid this situation SQL Server has a system process called a checkpoint process. The checkpoint process wakes up frequently and checks the transaction log of each database on the server. It decides whether a roll forward of the transaction log would take longer than the server configuration option *recovery interval*. If it would, the checkpoint process flushes all dirty pages to the database and writes a checkpoint record in the transaction log of that database so it knows how far back down the transaction log it would have to go in order to process a roll forward in the event of an SQL Server restart.

The checkpoint process uses asynchronous I/O which means that a number of disk I/Os are issued in parallel. This is known as a *batch write* because a batch of pages are written in one go. Figure 5.16 shows the batch writes that occur as part of a checkpoint process.

Looking at the highlighted *SQLServer: I/O - Batch Writes/sec* counter we can see that over 90 batch writes per second have occurred, that is, over 90 pages have been written per second. The counter *SQLServer: I/O - Outstanding Writes* peaks at about 10 during the checkpoint process. This is the number of physical writes pending and is a measure of how the disk subsystem is keeping up.

Finally, the *SQLServer: I/O - Log Writes/sec* counter can be seen to peak at about 40 just as the checkpoint starts. This is the number of transaction log records physically written to disk per second. SQL Server always writes changes to the transaction log before it writes changes to the database and so any dirty pages not already in the transaction log must be written to it before they are written to the database. Why does this counter also peak some time before the checkpoint kicks in? This is due to the lazy writer as we shall see shortly. As well as a checkpoint being issued automatically, the database owner can also issue a checkpoint using the Transact-SQL statement *CHECKPOINT.*

Figure 5.16
Batch Writes Per Second During A Checkpoint

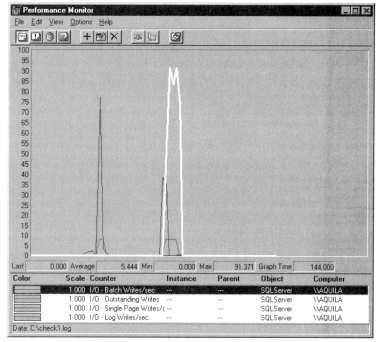

So how many pages are asynchronously written in a batch write? The default value is 8 but this can be changed using the advanced server configuration option *max async IO*. Usually this value is adequate but performance may be improved by increasing it on systems with databases defined on multiple physical database devices that reside on separate physical disks or on databases using disk striping. A value too large will cause the disk subsystem to become swamped which may result in poorer performance. If in doubt, test with a benchmark. The best performance is usually seen on systems using disk striping with intelligent controllers that can issue disk I/O operations in parallel to multiple disk drives.

5.3.3.3 The Lazy Writer Process

The lazy writer is a system process that helps to maintain a threshold of free buffers. To understand why the lazy writer process is beneficial it is useful to first of all imagine a scenario without it.

Suppose we have filled the data cache with dirty pages. A user connection wants to retrieve a page that is not in the data cache. SQL Server must find a free buffer to place it in. It checks the buffer pool for a free buffer and finds that there are none and so it must perform a single page write to disk of a dirty buffer to free it. This results in disk I/O to the transaction log and the database. Meanwhile, the connection that only wanted to retrieve a page is still waiting.

This stalling of connections while SQL Server frees up space in the buffer pool is not efficient and hence we have the lazy writer process. The lazy writer process writes out dirty pages to the transaction log and the database when a threshold value has been crossed. This threshold value represents a number of free buffers as specified by the *free buffers* advanced server configuration option. This option is automatically changed by the system whenever the memory option is changed and is equal to 5 percent of the available memory.

Figure 5.17 shows the Performance Monitor display shown in Figure 5.16 but with the *SQLServer: Cache - Number of Free Buffers* and *SQLServer: I/O - Lazy Writes/sec* counter added. We can see the highlighted counter *SQLServer: I/O - Lazy Writes/sec* rise rapidly just as the *SQLServer: Cache - Number of Free Buffers* counter drops to about 50 (note the scale factor). Peaking with the *SQLServer: I/O - Lazy Writes/sec* counter is the counter *SQLServer: I/O - Log Writes/sec*. This is because all the dirty pages the lazy writer process is writing to disk must have their changes recorded in the transaction log first.

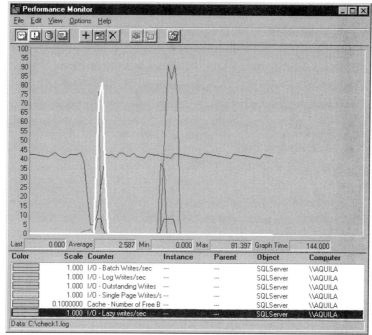

Figure 5.17
*Lazy Writes Per
Second As Free
Buffers Become
Low*

Like the checkpoint process, the lazy writer process writes a batch of pages. The size of the batch is governed by the advanced server option *max lazywrite I/O*. The default value is 8 and the maximum value is *max async I/O*. Increasing this value adheres to the same guidelines as increasing max async I/O. Note that the lazy writer eliminates the need to checkpoint frequently for the purpose of creating free buffers.

Note that if a free buffer is needed and none are free a dirty buffer is written to the transaction log and database to free one up. This uses a single page write as measured by the *SQLServer: I/O - Single Page Writes/sec* counter. This often can be seen to take a non-zero value during a checkpoint but if it is greater than one between checkpoints this is indicative of the fact that the lazy writer is not freeing buffers quickly enough. Maybe increasing the number of free buffers or *max lazywrite I/O* may help.

5.3.3.4 Keeping Tables and Indexes in Cache

Usually tables and indexes that are accessed frequently stay in the data cache because other least recently used pages are flushed out first. In this way the pages that are often required are the pages that connections get fast access to.

However, it is possible that fast access is required to tables and indexes that are not accessed frequently enough to keep them in the data cache. In this situation two techniques can be used to keep these objects in cache.

To keep a table and its indexes in data cache the *sp_tableoption* system stored procedure can be used:

```
sp_tableoption 'branches', 'pintable', true
```

Note that the table name can use wildcard characters. This statement does not load pages from the table into the data cache but once they are read into data cache by normal activity, they stay there and are not removed. This can result in little data cache being left for other tables and indexes so table pinning should be used with care.

To turn the option off just use the *false* keyword:

```
sp_tableoption 'branches', 'pintable', false
```

Another mechanism that can be used to lengthen the stay of index pages in the data cache is use of the trace flag 1081. This trace flag effectively gives index pages one extra life. If an index page is about to be removed from the data cache by the LRU mechanism it is left in until the next time the LRU mechanism tries to remove it, at which point it leaves the data cache if it still has not been used. The net result is that index pages stay in the data cache a while longer than they normally would.

5.3.3.5 Parallel Data Scan

Parallel Data Scan (PDS) or *read ahead processing* as it is sometimes known is a mechanism that is used by SQL Server to reduce the number of stalls a thread experiences waiting for a disk I/O to complete and to also reduce the number of actual physical I/Os performed. It is a similar concept to instruction pre-fetch in a CPU. If SQL Server realizes that a table scan or an index scan is taking place, in other words sequential scanning of pages, it can start to pre-fetch pages into the data cache before the thread requests those pages. This means that when the thread requests a page it is found in the data cache and so the thread does not stall waiting for a physical I/O to disk to complete.

If a read ahead mechanism was not employed a thread issuing many disk I/Os while executing a table scan or index scan would spend a large amount of time waiting for the disk I/O to complete as shown in Figure 5.18.

We know that disk I/O takes a long time relative to memory access and this is represented by "*t*" in Figure 5.18. If we employ a read ahead mechanism which can read the pages into cache using another thread before the

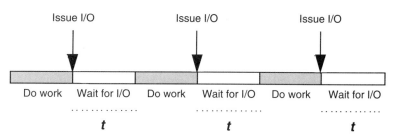

Figure 5.18
Performing A Table Scan With No Read Ahead

user's thread requests them we have eliminated the stall caused by the physical read and only the data cache access is required as shown in Figure 5.19.

The read ahead mechanism also reads in units of extents so it reads in 8 pages in one disk I/O which clearly is more efficient than reading 8 pages with 8 single page reads. So what can benefit from the read ahead capability? Basically, anything that performs a sequential scan of data pages, including:

► Table scans

► Nonclustered index leaf scans

► DBCC statements such as DBCC CHECKTABLE

► Transact-SQL statements such as UPDATE STATISTICS

How does SQL Server know that, for example, a table scan is taking place? It knows because that was the decision that the query optimizer made.

SQL Server must make some decisions when considering using the read ahead mechanism. When should the read ahead mechanism cut in? If it cuts in too soon it might read pages into data cache that are not needed because they are already there. Better to get some confirmation that a few requests by the user connection are not found in data cache before starting. Similarly, there is no point in the read ahead thread continuing to retrieve pages, once started, if it starts to find that pages are already in the data cache. Another consideration is how far in front of the user connection should the read ahead be reading?

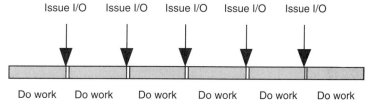

Figure 5.19
Performing A Table Scan With Read Ahead

SQL Server makes these decisions based on a set of server configuration options specific to the read ahead mechanism all of which begin with the prefix *RA*. These are:

▶ RA cache hit limit

▶ RA cache miss limit

▶ RA delay

▶ RA pre-fetches

▶ RA worker threads

▶ RA slots per thread

With the exception of *RA worker threads* these are all advanced server configuration options and with the exception of *RA slots per thread* and *RA worker threads* these are all dynamic options, that is, the change takes effect immediately.

The *RA cache miss limit* option initiates read ahead. When an operation performing a sequential scan does not find a page in the data cache *RA cache miss limit* times, a read ahead thread will start to asynchronously pre-fetch pages into the data cache by reading the next few extents. The default value of this option is 3.

The *RA cache hit limit* option terminates read ahead. When the read ahead mechanism finds that a page is already in the data cache *RA cache hit limit* times, read ahead stops until the next time a page is not found in the data cache at which point it continues. The idea of the read ahead mechanism is to pre-fetch pages into the data cache. If it finds that they are already there, read ahead activity would just be an overhead with no gain. The default value of this option is 4.

The *RA delay* option causes the user connection executing the query to stall when read ahead is initiated to give the read ahead mechanism time to get started. The default value is 15 milliseconds.

The *RA pre-fetches* option specifies the number of extents the read ahead mechanism should pre-fetch ahead of the query. The default value of this option is 3.

The *RA worker threads* option specifies the number of threads used to service read-ahead requests. Each thread will manage a number of *slots*. Each slot equates to a distinct range scan. This option should be set to the maximum number of concurrent users on the system. The default value of this option is 3.

Note that a warning will be logged in the SQL Server error log if the number of user connections requesting read ahead scans exceeds the number of configured slots (see next option):

```
97/01/17 14:59:37.57 spid6 WARNING: no read ahead slots available.
    Use sp_configure to increase the number of slots ('RA worker
    threads' or 'RA slots per thread').
```

The *RA slots per thread* option is the number of parallel requests each read ahead worker thread will manage. The value of *RA worker threads* multiplied by the value of *RA slots per thread* gives the total number of parallel read ahead scans that SQL Server will support. The default value of this option is 5 so the product of the values *RA worker threads* and *RA slots per thread* is by default 15.

It is often useful to be able to disable the read ahead capability when undergoing certain types of performance testing. For example, with read ahead enabled a query will experience an excellent cache hit ratio because read ahead has pre-fetched the pages required by the query into the data cache. When investigating the most efficient size for the data cache it might be worthwhile disabling read ahead to avoid a skew of results.

A number of mechanisms can be used to disable read ahead. Firstly, the RA server configuration options can be adjusted to effectively disable read ahead. The usual, but not only, option to modify is *RA worker threads* which can be set to zero. This will disable read ahead. Alternatively, two trace flags can be use. Trace flag 652 disables read ahead for the whole server whereas trace flag 653 disables read ahead for the current connection.

To measure the impact of read ahead the SET STATISTICS I/O statement can be used or DBCC SQLPERF (RASTATS).

```
DBCC SQLPERF (RASTATS)

Statistic                   Value
-----------------------     -----
RA Pages Found in Cache      63.0
RA Pages Placed in Cache     24.0
RA Physical I/Os             7.0
Used Slots                   0.0

SELECT * FROM accounts

account_no     customer_no     branch_no     balance
----------     -----------     ---------     --------
6400           103200          1000          2,132.33
12800          106400          1000          1,515.24
:
:
12799          106400          1099          7,482.22
19199          109600          1099          1,457.26
```

```
(25000 row(s) affected)

Table: accounts scan count 1, logical reads: 400, physical reads:
  5, read ahead reads: 395

DBCC SQLPERF (RASTATS)

Statistic                    Value
----------------------       -----
RA Pages Found in Cache       76.0
RA Pages Placed in Cache     419.0
RA Physical I/Os              57.0
Used Slots                     0.0
```

In the above example we have performed a table scan of the *Accounts* table which contains 25,000 rows in 400 pages. Prior to executing the Transact-SQL SELECT statement we have run a DBCC SQLPERF (RASTATS) statement which we repeat after the SELECT statement finishes. The SQL Server has just started so there are no pages from the *Accounts* table in the data cache.

The line of output displayed by SET STATISTICS IO ON shows that 400 logical reads were required to perform the table scan but only 5 physical reads. The number of read ahead reads performed was 395. This means that 395 pages were read into the data cache by the read ahead mechanism. The low value of physical reads performed by this query is due to read ahead. We can see that the 400 logical I/Os correspond to 5 physical I/Os issued by the query plus access to the 395 pages in data cache brought in by the read ahead mechanism.

If we compare the RASTATS results from DBCC we can see that the new *RA Pages Placed in Cache* value of 419 minus the previous value of 24 gives us our 395 pages placed in data cache.

Note that it took ($57 - 7 = 50$) *RA Physical I/Os* to bring these pages in. This equates closely with the fact that read ahead fetches extents, that is, 395/8 = 49.4 extents. The read ahead mechanism does not read part extents so it reads 50, hence, 50 *RA Physical I/Os*.

This last value is the best figure we could have hoped for. Suppose we have a badly fragmented table with many page splits. We saw the cause of this in Chapter 3. The read ahead mechanism follows the page chain and so, in a badly fragmented table, extents will be read in that may only contain one useful page. In this case the *RA Physical I/Os* value would increase and efficiency would drop. As was discussed in Chapter 3, use DBCC SHOWCONTIG to examine page fragmentation and to remove it rebuild clustered indexes, perhaps using a fillfactor.

Note what happens if we issue the query again immediately:

```
SELECT * FROM accounts

account_no      customer_no      branch_no      balance
----------      -----------      ----------     --------
6400            103200           1000           2,132.33
12800           106400           1000           1,515.24
:
:
12799           106400           1099           7,482.22
19199           109600           1099           1,457.26

(25000 row(s) affected)

Table: accounts scan count 1, logical reads: 400, physical reads:
    0, read ahead reads: 0
```

In this case the pages are all in data cache already. The *RA cache miss limit* value is never reached and read ahead is never initiated.

5.3.4 Investigating Disk I/O Bottlenecks

The tool used to observe disk I/O bottlenecks is typically the Performance Monitor. The Task Manager displays little useful information as far as disk I/O is concerned. There are also a number of tools on the Windows NT Resource Kit 4.0 CD to enable you to measure, for example, disk efficiency. We will focus on using the Performance Monitor as it is the most comprehensive tool.

Before we look at Performance Monitor counters we need to make sure that we run the *diskperf* command and reboot Windows NT. This will activate statistics collection for the Performance Monitor counters associated with disk activity. If we do not do this Performance Monitor will display zeros for all disk counter values. Once we have run the diskperf command we will not have to run it again until we want to turn statistics collection for the disk counters off.

To activate statistics collection for the counters associated with disk activity:

```
diskperf -y
```

To deactivate statistics collection:

```
diskperf -n
```

To check whether statistics collection is enabled or disabled:

```
diskperf
```

If the fault tolerant disk driver *Ftdisk* is being used to support, for example, mirror sets and stripe sets with or without parity:

```
diskperf -ye
```

Table 5.5 *Logical And Physical Disk Counters*

Logical/Physical Disk Object Counter	Explanation
% Disk Time	How busy is the disk? This is the percentage of elapsed time that the selected disk is busy handling read and write requests.
% Disk Read Time	This is the percentage of elapsed time that the selected disk is busy handling read requests.
% Disk Write Time	This is the percentage of elapsed time that the selected disk is busy handling write requests.
Disk Reads/sec	The rate of read operations on the disk.
Disk Writes/sec	The rate of write operations on the disk.
Avg. Disk Queue Length	The average number of read and write requests for the disk in the sample interval. If disk queue length is greater than two and the %Disk Time is high this may indicate a disk bottleneck. Affected by *max async IO* and *max lazywrite IO*.
Current Disk Queue Length	This is an instantaneous value at the point of sample. It includes the requests being serviced.

Let us look at some of the more useful counters associated with disk activity.

The *Logical Disk*, *Physical Disk* and *SQLServer* objects are a useful place to start and it is worth a look at some of their counters. Again, note that often it is a memory bottleneck that manifests itself as a disk bottleneck and so the counters associated with the *Memory* object, as described earlier, should be monitored also. The Logical And Physical Disk counters are shown in Table 5.5. The SQLServer counters are shown in Table 5.6.

In the Performance Monitor chart in Figure 5.20 we can see that the highlighted counter *Logical Disk: Disk Writes/sec* peaks at about 92. The other counter *Logical Disk: Current Disk Queue Length* peaks at the same time at about 9 (note the scale factor). From the chart we can see that the D: partition has experienced a large burst of activity. This is not continuous so we do not have a bottleneck but it is interesting to see what is causing the high disk activity.

Table 5.6 *SQLServer Counters*

SQLServer Object Counter	Explanation
Cache - Number of Free Buffers	The number of buffers currently free. If this drops below the threshold specified by *free buffers* the lazy writer will cut in. If it continually drops low increase free buffers.
Cache Hit Ratio	The percentage of time that a page was found in the data cache. Usually 95% plus on a server in steady state with a large cache.
I/O - Batch Average Size	Governed by *max async IO*. The average number of 2K pages written to disk during a batch I/O operation. The checkpoint process is the main user of batch I/O.
I/O - Batch Max Size	Governed by *max async IO*. The maximum number of 2K pages written to disk during a batch I/O operation.
I/O - Batch Writes/sec	The number of 2K pages written to disk per second using batch I/O, often high.
I/O - Lazy Writes/sec	The number of 2K pages written out to disk per second by the lazy writer. This cleans buffers and returns them to the free buffer pool.
I/O - Log Writes/sec	The number of transaction log pages physically written to disk per second. Any changes must be recorded in the log before they can be written to the database. The log experiences high disk I/O so it can easily become a disk I/O bottleneck.
I/O - Outstanding Reads	The number of physical reads waiting to be serviced. A sustained value here can indicate a disk bottleneck.
I/O - Outstanding Writes	The number of physical writes waiting to be serviced. A sustained value here can indicate a disk bottleneck.
I/O - Page Reads/sec	The number of physical page reads per second. This is what we try and minimize with indexes and data cache for example.
I/O - Single Page Writes/sec	The number of single page writes performed per second by logging and cache flushes. Can happen if there are no buffers left in the free buffer pool and a single page is flushed.
I/O - Trans. per Log Record	The number of transactions that were crammed into a log record before it was written to disk. This can help to reduce disk I/Os to the transaction log.

Table 5.6 *SQLServer Counters (continued)*

SQLServer Object Counter	Explanation
I/O - Transactions/sec	The number of Transact-SQL command batches executed per second (note that this is not transactions per second).
RA - Pages Fetched into Cache/sec	Pages brought into the data cache by the read ahead mechanism.
RA - Pages Found in Cache/sec	Pages found to be already in cache.
RA - Physical Reads/sec	Physical extent reads performed by the read ahead mechanism.
RA - Slots Used	How many RA slots are being used. This is a measure of the number of parallel data scans happening at a given time.

In Figure 5.21 we have added the counter *SQLServer: I/O - Batch Writes/ sec*. This peaks (completes) as the disk write activity drops off and it is in fact this checkpoint activity that contributes to the disk write activity. If we add the counter *SQLServer: I/O - Log Writes/sec* while keeping the counter *SQLServer: I/O - Batch Writes/sec* highlighted we can see that, as shown in

Figure 5.20
Investigating Disk Activity

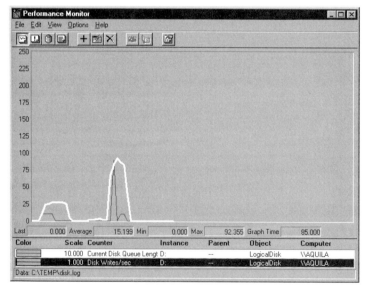

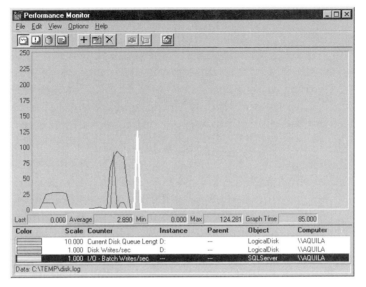

Figure 5.21
Investigating Disk Activity—Adding Batch Writes/sec

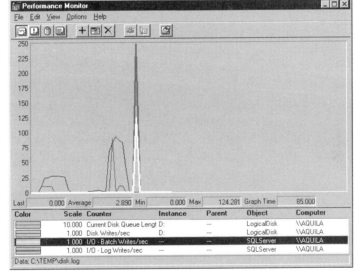

Figure 5.22
Investigating Disk Activity—Adding Log Writes/sec

Figure 5.22, there is high write activity to the transaction log at the same time as to the database. This is the other contributor to the disk writes.

5.3.5 Solving Problems with Disk I/O

Having determined that there is indeed a disk I/O bottleneck and that there is a sustained queue of requests the next step is to eliminate causes other than

SQL Server such as a memory bottleneck causing high levels of paging to disk.

If the disk bottleneck proves to be SQL Server it could be a specific set of queries in which case it is possible that they can be made more efficient by rewriting or by a change in index design. However, if the workload on the SQL Server as a whole is generating more disk I/O than the I/O subsystem can handle it may be time to invest in a RAID approach.

There are a number of RAID topologies that can be used. The fastest implementation of RAID, however, is usually hardware based. One suggestion would be to place the database on a RAID 0 disk stripe set to get the best read and write performance. Redundancy could then be achieved by mirroring this stripe set. The transaction log needs to be mirrored but as the transaction log tends to be written sequentially a single mirrored disk should give good performance as long as no other application is writing to the disk, in other words, the transaction log has the disk to itself.

6

Transactions and Locking

6.1 Introduction

I once visited a customer to sanity check the physical design for a new database. In the course of checking the design I happened to notice that there were some people in an adjoining room entering data into forms on their PCs. Every so often one of these people would raise their hands in the air for a few seconds. After a while my curiosity got the better of me and I asked the person who had invited me to do the sanity check what was happening.

It transpired that the people in the next room where entering trades into a financial system but the lock conflict caused by the action of entering two trades simultaneously was so bad that they found it easier to raise their hands just before they pressed *Enter* on the keyboard to signal to their colleagues not to do the same. Ironically, what they were doing was implementing a locking protocol that single threaded the insertion of a trade. This is an example of a multi-user system where two users are one user too many!

Unfortunately, there are many multi-user systems out there that suffer from locking problems. Whether you design a system with locking in mind tends, like most things in life, to depend on your previous experiences. While I was working for the Digital Equipment Corporation I was involved in the design of many multi-user online transaction processing systems (OLTP). I came to learn very quickly that if I did not constantly keep asking the question "Is this transaction likely to be the cause of a locking bottleneck?" then I would run into trouble. If your background is single user systems or read only databases, this question might not be the first one on your mind.

This chapter introduces the concepts of transactions and locking, perhaps two of the most important features provided by a modern database management system and, perhaps, also two of the features whose correct implementation by a database designer are most critical to database performance. The default SQL Server locking protocol provided by SQL Server 4.2 was, on the whole, not modifiable by the developer. However, with the advent of SQL Server 6.0 and SQL Server 6.5, the default locking protocol provided by SQL Server can be easily changed to behave in a number of different ways. The locking protocol has also become much more sophisticated. These capabilities will be covered in this chapter.

6.2 Why a Locking Protocol?

Single user access to a database does not require a locking protocol nor does single or multi-user access to a read only database. Database management systems in reality must support more that one user concurrently changing information and it is this multi-user access that requires the database management system to provide a protocol to ensure that the changes being made to the database data by one user are not corrupted by another. Locking is not a luxury in a multi-user environment, it is a necessity.

Locking protocols are not all or nothing. Some protocols are more stringent than others with different database management systems adopting their own unique approaches. Locking is the natural enemy of performance and so a more stringent locking protocol is more likely to adversely affect performance than a less stringent one. However, a more stringent locking protocol is also likely to provide a more consistent view of the data.

To provide a taste as to why a locking protocol is necessary let us consider some multi-user scenarios:

Scenario 1   In this scenario Mike modifies a stock level by subtracting one thousand from it, leaving 100 items. Katy reads the stock level and sees that there are only 100 items in stock. Immediately after Katy has read this value and acted upon it, Mike's transaction fails and is rolled back returning the stock level to its original value of 1100. This is shown graphically in Figure 6.1.

This scenario highlights a classic problem. Katy has been allowed to read changes made by Mike before Mike has committed the changes, in other words, before Mike has irrevocably changed the data by ending the transaction with a commit. Until the transaction ends, Mike can choose to rollback the transaction, change the value again or commit the transaction. In our example, Mike's transaction actually fails before it completes causing the database management system to rollback the change. Katy is said to have read *uncommitted* or *dirty* data.

Scenario 2   In this scenario Mike's transaction sums a list of debts in a table and checks the result against a total debt value held elsewhere in the database.

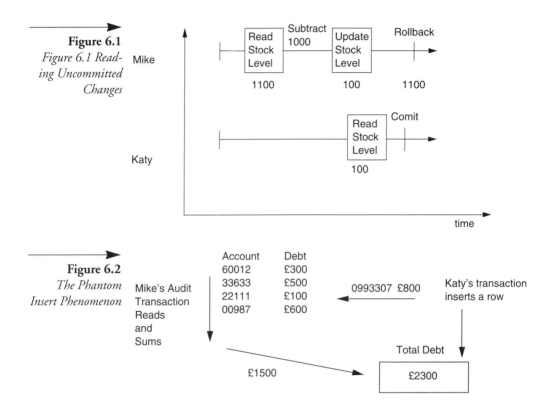

Figure 6.1

Figure 6.1 Reading Uncommitted Changes

Figure 6.2

The Phantom Insert Phenomenon

While Mike's transaction is summing the values in the list, Katy's transaction inserts a new row into the debt table after Mike's transaction has passed by and updates the total debt value. When Mike finishes summing the list and compares the calculated sum with the total debt value it reports a discrepancy where in fact there is no discrepancy at all. This is called the *phantom insert* phenomenon. This is shown graphically in Figure 6.2.

These are only two examples of a number of possibilities that can occur if locking protocols are not used or the locking protocol used is not stringent enough and we shall revisit some of these scenarios later. We have said that SQL Server uses a locking protocol so let us now investigate how this works.

6.3 The SQL Server Locking Protocol

The locking protocol adopted by SQL Server consists of placing different types of lock on different database objects. In SQL Server 6.0 these objects were a complete table or a database page. As we have seen, a database page is 2 Kb in size and any object resident within this 2 Kb is locked implicitly when the database page is locked so, if a database page is locked, every row held on that page is effectively locked. Typically a database page will be a data page or an index page.

SQL Server 6.5, however, introduced row level locking for insert operations. As we shall see, this means that individual rows on a page may be locked. We will now look in detail at the types of lock used, what objects can be locked and the duration of these locks.

6.3.1 Shared and Exclusive Locks

To generalize, SQL Server applies a write lock when it writes information onto a page or a read lock when it reads information off a page. Writing information usually refers to inserting, updating or deleting rows whereas reading information usually refers to retrieving rows with, for example, a SELECT statement. There are some simple rules that we can make at this point.

▶ If a user has placed a read lock on a page, another user can also place a read lock on that page. In other words, both users can read the same page simultaneously. In fact any number of users can place a read lock on a page at the same time.

▶ If a user has placed a write lock on a page, another user cannot also place a write lock on that page. Also, another user cannot place a read lock on that page. In other words, once a user has placed a write lock on a page, other users cannot place read or write locks on the same page simultaneously.

Because many users can place read locks on the same page concurrently these read locks are usually referred to as *shared* locks. Write locks, on the other hand, are normally referred to as *exclusive* locks. Table 6.1 shows the compatibility between shared and exclusive locks. As can be seen, only shared locks are compatible

Once a lock has been placed on a database page it has a lifetime. Suppose the Transact-SQL statement that caused the lock to be taken out was executed inside

Table 6.1 *Compatibility Between Shared And Exclusive Locks*

Mode of Currently Granted Lock	Mode of Requested Lock	
	exclusive	shared
exclusive	✗	✗
shared	✗	✔

a user defined transaction. In the default case, shared locks live for the time it takes for the SQL statement to read the page or table whereas exclusive locks live for the length of the user defined transaction. This is shown graphically in figure 6.3. This behavior can be overridden with the use of the *holdlock* keyword as we shall see later in this chapter.

Hint: Beware of the *set implicit_transactions on* statement. It will automatically start a transaction when Transact-SQL statements such as SELECT, INSERT, UPDATE and DELETE are used. The transaction will not be committed and its locks released until an explicit COMMIT TRANSACTION statement is executed. To see if it is set use DBCC USEROPTIONS (see later).

SQL Server also uses locks other than shared or exclusive. It uses update locks as an optimization to avoid deadlocks. We will look at update locks when we investigate deadlocks later.

6.3.2 Page, Table, and Row Level Locking

As mentioned above, SQL Server 6.5 now supports row level locking for insert operations. I suspect that Microsoft provided row level locking for two reasons. Firstly, it is technically an important capability *in some circumstances* and secondly, because not having row level locking was a marketing poison arrow. Some database vendors who do provide row level locking and have done so for a while used to make the row level locking subject a key issue. If you do not provide it then you should not get on the Invitation to Tender!

I sometimes get annoyed at the great emphasis placed on row level locking as this misses an important point which is that applications require different

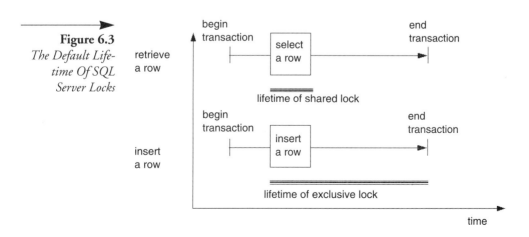

Figure 6.3
The Default Lifetime Of SQL Server Locks

levels of locking granularity. One application may benefit from page level locking while another application may benefit from row level locking. Why is this? To investigate it is useful to consider the different granularity of lock that could be taken out by some theoretical database management system.

Figure 6.4 shows the database concurrency for different lock granularity. By lock granularity we mean the object that is locked from, on one side of the spectrum an individual column in a row to the other side of the spectrum, a whole database. As can be observed from the graph, locking individual columns provides the highest level of concurrency. By this we mean that multiple users could be updating different columns in the same row simultaneously. They would not be involved in lock conflict.

If the lock granularity is implemented at the database level, the lowest level of concurrency is achieved. Multiple users could not simultaneously change anything at all in the database. If they tried, they would be involved in lock conflict.

So if locking individual columns provides the highest level of concurrency, why do SQL Server and databases in general not lock at the column level? To explain this we need to add some more information to our graph.

In Figure 6.5 we have added system resource usage to our graph. It can be seen that an increase in system resource usage parallels an increase in lock granularity. The finer the granularity, the more system resource used.

This is why SQL Server and databases in general do not lock at the column level. The system resource usage in terms of the number of locks

Figure 6.4
*Concurrency
Vs Locking
Granularity*

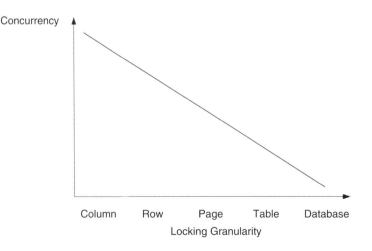

Figure 6.5
System Resource
Vs Locking
Granularity

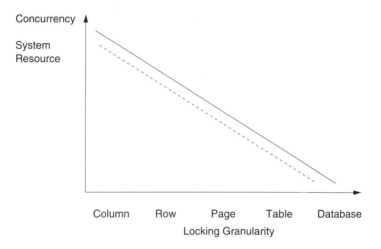

required and their management would be too great. Locks are supposed to be 32 bytes each in SQL Server 6.5; however, if you look at their memory usage via DBCC MEMUSAGE it looks more like 60 bytes. Using 60 bytes of memory to lock a 10 byte column seems a little over the top. To lock at the column level would probably use tens of thousands of locks in a medium sized database which could equate to many megabytes of memory. The CPU resource needed to manage these locks would be massive.

Consequently, SQL Server 6.5 locks rows, pages and tables which, depending on the application, is a reasonable approach. The database itself can, of course, be set to single user mode which effectively provides locking at the database level.

6.3.2.1 When are Page Level Locks Used?

Locking at the database page level can be considered to be the default situation. Usually, unless you have changed the default behavior, SQL Server will take shared and exclusive locks out on database pages. As previously mentioned, any object resident within a database page, be it a data page or an index page, is locked implicitly when the database page is locked.

As Figure 6.6 shows, when page level locking is being used, many pages in a table can become locked. As different users access data pages, typically via an index, these data pages will become locked. If a table scan is being used to read data, page locks will be taken out and released in a sequential fashion. So at a given point in time, during a table scan, a data page somewhere in the table will be locked.

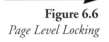

Figure 6.6
Page Level Locking

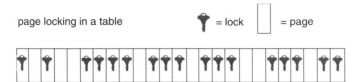

6.3.2.2 When are Table Level Locks Used?

SQL Server can and will lock at the table level in certain situations. If SQL Server decides that an SQL statement is likely to lock the majority of pages in a table it will lock at the table level. By default, this occurs when SQL Server finds it is holding more than 200 page locks. This attempted lock escalation of page locks to a table lock may or may not succeed depending on the locks held by other users in the table. If it does succeed, the page locks will be released and the table lock acquired.

The advantage to holding a single table lock is down to system resource. Managing a single table lock is less resource intensive than managing multiple page locks and saving locks will save memory. However, locking at the table level may reduce concurrency; for example, an exclusive lock held at the table level will block all other users from accessing rows within that table whether they wish to acquire shared or exclusive locks.

Prior to SQL Server 6.0, the database administrator had no control over when SQL Server escalated page locks to table locks. At the point when greater than 200 page locks were acquired, SQL Server would attempt to replace the page locks with a table lock. The value of 200 was hard-wired into SQL Server.

From SQL Server 6.0 the database administrator can now specify when *lock escalation* occurs. Using the SQL Enterprise Manager *Configuration* tab in the *Server Configuration/ Options* dialog box or sp_configure, three configuration options pertaining to lock escalation may be set:

▶ LE threshold percent

▶ LE threshold minimum

▶ LE threshold maximum

Figure 6.7
Table Level Locking

Note that to display all three options, the server configuration parameter *Show Advanced Options* must be set as *LE threshold minimum* is considered to be an advanced configuration option.

The *LE threshold percent* option allows the database administrator to choose the percentage of pages locked in the table before SQL Server attempts to acquire a table lock. A value of 10, for example, means that once 10% of the pages in the table have page locks, SQL Server attempts to acquire a table lock.

Obviously, this percentage will equate to very different numbers of pages depending on the table size. For this reason the two other options are provided. The *LE threshold minimum* option places a minimum value on the number of pages locked before SQL Server attempts to acquire a table lock. For example, if the *LE threshold percent* is set to 10% and the *LE threshold minimum* is set to 50, SQL Server would not attempt to acquire a table lock if 10% of the pages in a 100 page table were locked. SQL Server, however, would attempt to acquire a table lock if 10% of the pages in a 1000 page table were locked as 10% of the pages is greater than the *LE threshold minimum* value of 50 pages.

The *LE threshold maximum* option is used in a similar way and it places a maximum value on the number of pages locked before SQL Server attempts to acquire a table lock. If, for example, a table consists of 10,000 pages and the *LE threshold percent* is set to 10%, SQL Server will attempt to acquire a table lock when 1000 pages are locked. If, however, the *LE threshold maximum* is set to 500, SQL Server would attempt to acquire a table lock when only 500 pages are locked.

The *LE threshold minimum* option is in place to minimize frequent lock escalation in small tables and the *LE threshold maximum* option is in place to allow the database administrator to keep the number of locks below a reasonable limit for large tables. If *LE threshold percent* is set to 0 then a table lock is acquired only when the number of locked pages reaches *LE threshold maximum*. An *LE threshold percent* value of 0 is the default value as is an *LE threshold maximum* value of 200. Using these default values, SQL Server 6.5 effectively mimics the SQL Server 4.2 behavior.

Note that we previously stated that if a table scan is being used to read data, page locks will be taken out and released in a sequential fashion. If we choose to use the holdlock keyword, discussed later, we are requesting not to release page locks when we have finished with the page. In this circumstance, when performing a table scan, SQL Server will immediately attempt to take out a table lock as it correctly realizes that if it is going to end up holding a shared lock on every page in the table, it may as well take out a table lock straight away.

6.3.2.3 When are Row Level Locks Used?

SQL Server 6.5 introduced support for row level locking. Row level locking, in this release, is not used for operations other than inserts and even then it is optional. Because row level locking is only used for insert operations it is known as *Insert Row-level Locking* or IRL.

IRL is specified at the table level and by default is turned off. To turn IRL on or off the *sp_tableoption* system stored procedure is used:

```
sp_tableoption 'accounts', 'insert row lock', 'true'

sp_tableoption 'customers', 'insert row lock', 'false'
```

Note that the table name can contain wildcard characters. To turn on IRL for all the tables in the current database:

```
sp_tableoption '%.%', 'insert row lock', 'true'
```

To turn on IRL for all tables in the current database beginning with 'a':

```
sp_tableoption 'a%', 'insert row lock', 'true'
```

To see which tables have an IRL active:

```
sp_tableoption '%.%', 'insert row lock'

Option Status       Table Name     Owner Name
-------------       ----------     ----------
False               branches       dbo
True                accounts       dbo
```

If a database name is specified the database name must be the name of the current database or *sp_tableoption* will fail. This means that wildcarding the database name will not work:

```
sp_tableoption '%.%.%', 'insert row lock', 'true'

Msg 15387, Level 11, State 1
If the qualified object name specifies a database, that database
   must be current database.
```

This is desirable behavior as otherwise it would be too easy to turn on IRL for all tables resident on the server by mistake.

So when is IRL beneficial? As we discussed in Chapter 3, if there is no clustered index on a table or there is a clustered index but it is created on a monotonically increasing key a hotspot will occur at the end of the table. IRL will help us to eliminate this locking hot spot. Imagine the default scenario using page locking. The first user to insert a row into the table will immediately take out an exclusive page lock on the last page.

Other users will also attempt to take out an exclusive page lock on the last page so that they can insert their rows. As exclusive locks are not compatible, the first user will cause the other users to wait in a queue until he or she releases the exclusive lock when their transaction ends. This will clearly cause a performance bottleneck as shown in Figure 6.8.

Suppose we enable IRL for the table. The first user to insert a row into the table will immediately take out an *Insert_page* lock on the last page. Other users will also attempt to take out an *Insert_page* lock on the last page so that they can insert their rows. However, *Insert_page* locks are compatible with one another so the first user will not cause the other users to wait in a queue. As shown in Figure 6.9, all the users will be able to insert their rows. Their *Insert_page* locks will be released when their transactions complete.

Hint: An Insert_page lock is compatible only with other Insert_page locks.

This is not the complete story, however, as there is another type of lock associated with IRL. Taking the above example of multiple users inserting into a page, eventually the page will fill and a new page will be acquired. A *Link_page* lock is obtained by the first transaction that discovers that the current page no longer has empty space and that a new page needs to be allocated and linked to the current page. In this situation, the *Insert_page* lock held by the transaction is promoted to a *Link_page* lock. Any new attempts to acquire an *Insert_page* lock are blocked until the transaction holding the *Link_page*

Figure 6.8
Lock Contention Caused By Page Level Locking

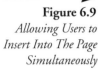

Figure 6.9
Allowing Users to Insert Into The Page Simultaneously

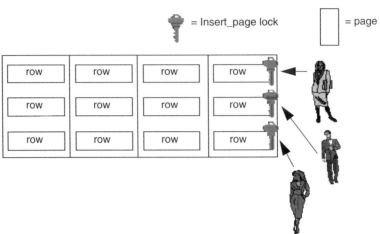

lock finishes. Table 6.2 shows the compatibility between *Insert_page* and *Link_page* locks..

Is IRL only beneficial for locking bottlenecks on data pages? It can be beneficial for index pages also. Consider our *Accounts* table:

```
CREATE TABLE accounts (
                        account_no      INT       NOT NULL,
                        customer_no     INT       NOT NULL,
                        branch_no       INT       NOT NULL,
                        balance         MONEY     NOT NULL
                        )
```

Let us assume that IRL is not enabled for this table. Suppose we have created a clustered index on the *branch_no* column and a unique nonclustered index on the *account_no* column. Imagine that the *account_no* column is a monotonically increasing key. When multiple users simultaneously insert rows into this table the *branch_no* value will represent any one of many branches and the clustered index will insert the new rows throughout the

Table 6.2   *Compatibility Between Insert_page And Link_page Locks*

Mode of Currently Granted Lock	Mode of Requested Lock	
	Insert_page	Link_page
Insert_page	✔	✔
Link_page	✘	✘

table. As the rows will not be inserted at the end of the table there will be no hotspot.

However, if we consider the unique nonclustered index on *account_no*, we can see that the key values being simultaneously inserted are close to one another in value and are highly likely to reside on the same index page. In fact, the last page in the index leaf level (the index page containing the highest key values) will become a hotspot due to page level locking on that page.

What happens if we enable IRL? In this case the users will take out *Insert_page* locks on the index page and will be able to simultaneously insert index entries. The index page will no longer be a locking hotspot.

Hint: The acquisition of a new index page will cause a blocking *Link_page* lock to be taken out causing users to wait for the *Link_page* lock to be released.

What about the clustered index? In this example, the clustered index pages will undergo page level locking. The clustered index will not use IRL as it is not a unique clustered index. If the *Accounts* table had used a unique clustered index on *account_no* then IRL would have been used.

Are there any pitfalls with IRL? There are some considerations to be made. First, more transaction log records are generated when IRL is used causing the transaction log to fill more quickly. Increasing the size of the transaction log in conjunction with transaction log space monitoring should help to avoid any problems. Second, *Insert_page* locks are not compatible with shared or exclusive locks. If an attempt is made to update a row after it has been inserted SQL Server will attempt to take out a page level lock. The page level lock is incompatible with the *Insert_page* locks held on the table by other users and the update will be forced to wait until the *Insert_page* locks are released. Unfortunately, if other users are also performing inserts followed by updates, deadlocks are likely to occur. Deadlocks will be discussed in the next section.

So we have introduced shared and exclusive locks and page, table and row level locking. We need to introduce more types of lock before we can give examples of the SQL Server locking protocol in action, but first let us look at a phenomenon known as a *deadlock* or a *deadly embrace*.

6.3.3 Deadlocks

A deadlock situation can occur in SQL Server when a user holds a lock on a resource needed by a fellow user who holds a lock on a resource needed by the first user. This is a deadly embrace and the users would wait forever if SQL Server did not intervene. This is shown graphically in Figure 6.10.

SQL Server chooses one of the deadlocked users as a victim and issues a rollback for their transaction. They will receive an error message similar to the one below:

```
Msg 1205, Level 13, State 2
Your server command (process id 4) was deadlocked with another
    process and has been chosen as deadlock victim. Re-run your
    command
```

In the application code, this error should be trapped and dealt with cleanly. The application might retry a number of times before giving up and informing the user that there is a problem.

A connection can set its deadlock priority such that, in the event of it being involved in a deadlock, it will be chosen as the victim:

```
SET DEADLOCK_PRIORITY LOW
```

To return to the default deadlock handling mechanism:

```
SET DEADLOCK_PRIORITY NORMAL
```

Generally, the transaction involved in the deadlock that has accumulated the least amount of CPU time is usually chosen as the victim.

6.3.4 Update Locks

As well as placing shared and exclusive locks on database pages SQL Server also makes use of a type of lock known as an *update* lock. These locks are associated with SQL statements that perform update and delete operations which need to initially read in database pages. These pages have update locks placed on them which are compatible with shared read locks but are not compatible with other update locks or exclusive locks. If the data on the page must subsequently be updated or deleted SQL Server attempts to promote the update locks to exclusive locks. If any other shared locks are associated with the database page SQL Server will not be able to promote the update locks until these

Figure 6.10
A Deadlock Between Two Users

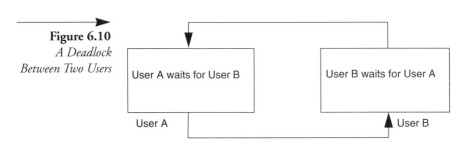

are released. In reality the update lock is not promoted but a second lock is taken out which is in fact an exclusive lock.

Why bother with update locks? Update locks are really an optimization to minimise the possibility of deadlocks. Consider two users, Mike and Katy, who are about to update rows on the same page. Without update locks, each user will take out a shared lock on the page. Shared locks are compatible so both users will acquire the lock successfully. Mike's UPDATE statement, finding a row that meets the criteria in its WHERE clause attempts to take out an exclusive lock on the page. Mike's UPDATE statement will now have to wait as it is blocked by Katy's shared lock.

Katy's UPDATE statement, finding a row that meets the criteria in its WHERE clause attempts to take out an exclusive lock on the page. Katy's UPDATE statement cannot take out the exclusive lock as it is blocked by Mike's shared lock. Her update statement would also be forced to wait except this is clearly a deadlock. SQL Server will choose a victim and their transaction will be rolled back. This is shown graphically in Figure 6.11.

Now let us take the same example but this time we will make use of update locks. This is exactly what SQL Server does.

When Mike issues his UPDATE statement he now takes out an update lock on the page instead of a shared lock. Katy's UPDATE statement also attempt to take out an update lock on the page but update locks are not compatible so she will be forced to wait. Mike's UPDATE statement, finding a row that meets the criteria in its WHERE clause attempts to take out an exclusive lock on the page. As Katy does not have any locks on the page,

Figure 6.11
A Deadlock Caused By Two Users Updating The Same Page

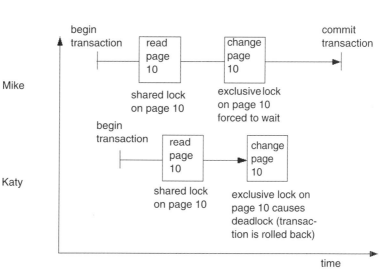

Mike's UPDATE statement successfully acquires the exclusive lock on the page and completes. Mike now commits his transaction and releases his locks. Katy's UPDATE statement which has been waiting can now proceed. This is shown graphically in Figure 6.12.

Clearly, this is a cleaner mechanism. No transactions are deadlock victims which means no transactions are cancelled and rolled back. Transactions that are rolled back have their work done so far effectively thrown away. Using update locks, Katy's update statement merely suffers a short delay.

6.3.5 Intent Locks

As well as placing shared and exclusive locks on database tables SQL Server also makes use of a type of lock known as an *intent* lock. Intent locks are placed on the table when a user locks pages in the table and stay in place for the life of the page locks. These locks are used primarily to ensure that a user cannot take out locks on a table that would conflict with another user's page locks. For example, if SQL Server decided that a user was holding many page locks and an escalation to a table lock was desirable, the page locks held by others users would not be overlooked when attempting the escalation.

6.3.6 Modifying the Default Locking Behaviour

There are two ways in which SQL Server's default locking behavior can be modified. Individual SQL statements can be qualified with a keyword to modify the locking behavior for that particular statement or a default envi-

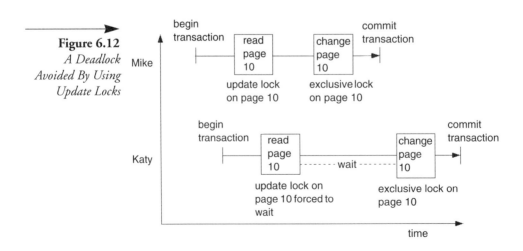

Figure 6.12
A Deadlock Avoided By Using Update Locks

ronment can be set with the SET TRANSACTION ISOLATION LEVEL statement. Apart from the HOLDLOCK keyword, all the keywords mentioned in this section and the SET TRANSACTION ISOLATION LEVEL statement are newly introduced with SQL Server 6.0. The keywords used to modify the locking behavior for a particular SELECT statement are classified in SQL Server 6.0 as *optimizer hints.*

Hint: SQL Server 6.5 allows optimizer hints on the UPDATE statement as well as the SELECT statement.

6.3.6.1 Optimizer Hints

The keywords available as optimizer hints for modifying locking behavior are:

► HOLDLOCK

► NOLOCK

► PAGLOCK

► TABLOCK

► TABLOCKX

► UPDLOCK

They are used on a SELECT statement, for example:

```
SELECT * FROM titles (HOLDLOCK)

SELECT price FROM titles (NOLOCK) WHERE title_id = 'MC2222'
```

The effect of these optimizer hints is described below:

Holdlock   The HOLDLOCK keyword forces a shared lock on a table to stay until the transaction completes. This will increase data consistency as it will enforce *repeatable reads.* This means that a data value that is read on more than one occasion within a transaction is guaranteed to be the same value, that is, it cannot have been changed by any *other* transaction.

Using the HOLDLOCK keyword may, and usually will, degrade performance as lock contention may increase. An example of using the HOLDLOCK keyword is given later in this chapter.

Nolock   The NOLOCK keyword allows a *dirty read* to take place, that is, a transaction can read the uncommitted changes made by another transaction.

Paglock   The PAGLOCK keyword forces shared page locks to be taken where otherwise SQL Server may have used a table lock. For example, consider the following statement:

```
SELECT * FROM accounts (HOLDLOCK)
```

As discussed previously, the query optimizer will choose a table scan as the strategy used to execute the query. The lock manager will, by default, immediately take out a table lock. By using PAGLOCK, the lock manager will use page locking instead of table locking. Note that once the relevant LE threshold has been reached, SQL Server will attempt to escalate the page locks to a table lock. This is shown graphically in the Performance Monitor chart display in Figure 6.13. Page locks (highlighted) can be seen increasing until they are escalated to a table lock. This chart monitored the following Transact-SQL statement execution:

```
SELECT * FROM accounts (HOLDLOCK PAGLOCK)
```

Tablock   The TABLOCK keyword forces a shared table lock to be taken where otherwise SQL Server may have used page locks. This keyword essentially overrides the *LE threshold* configuration options for the specific SELECT statement.

Tablockx   The TABLOCKX keyword forces an exclusive table lock to be taken.

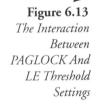

Figure 6.13
The Interaction Between PAGLOCK And LE Threshold Settings

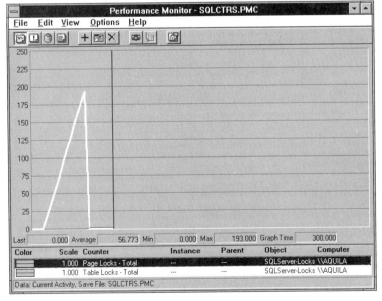

Updlock The UPDLOCK keyword forces SQL Server to take update locks where otherwise SQL Server would have used shared locks.

6.3.6.2 Transaction Isolation Level

SQL Server allows the *transaction isolation level* to be set for a connection. This sets a default locking behavior.

Levels of transaction isolation are specified by the ANSI standard with each one defining the type of phenomenon not permitted while concurrent transactions are running. The higher the isolation level, the more stringent the locking protocol with the higher levels being a superset of the lower levels. The transaction isolation levels that can be set in SQL Server 6.5 are:

► Read Uncommitted

► Read Committed

► Repeatable Read

► Serializable

The locking behavior that corresponds with *read uncommitted* provides the least integrity but potentially the best performance. The *read committed* isolation level provides more integrity than *read uncommitted* and the *repeatable read* isolation level more so still. The greatest integrity is provided by the *serializable* isolation level. We have already met repeatable reads and the phantom phenomena. Table 6.3 shows whether the repeatable read and the phantom phenomena are allowed by the various isolation levels.

It can be seen that only the *serializable* isolation level prevents all these phenomena from occurring. However, in SQL Server 6.5 the *serializable* and *repeatable read* isolation levels are identical in that they prevent all the phenomena, hence, the *repeatable read* isolation level also prevents phantoms.

Table 6.3 *Isolation Levels And Allowed Locking Phenomena*

Isolation Level	*Dirty Reads*	*Nonrepeatable Reads Allowed*	*Phantoms Allowed*
Serializable	No	No	No
Repeatable Read	No	No	Yes (see text)
Read Committed	No	Yes	Yes
Read Uncommitted	Yes	Yes	Yes

By default, SQL Server runs at transaction isolation level read committed.

The transaction isolation level is set for the connection with the following syntax:

```
SET TRANSACTION ISOLATION LEVEL READ UNCOMMITTED

SET TRANSACTION ISOLATION LEVEL READ COMMITTED

SET TRANSACTION ISOLATION LEVEL REPEATABLE READ

SET TRANSACTION ISOLATION LEVEL SERIALIZABLE
```

The DBCC utility with the USEROPTIONS parameter can be used to check the current isolation level of the connection:

```
DBCC USEROPTIONS

Set Option          Value
----------          ---------
textsize            64512
language            us_english
dateformat          mdy
datefirst           7
isolation level     repeatable read
```

6.3.7 Locking in System Tables

Transact-SQL statements such as CREATE TABLE manipulate system tables. For example, when a table is created rows are inserted into the *sysobjects, sysindexes and syscolumns* system tables. Prior to SQL Server 6.5, statements such as CREATE TABLE were not allowed in user defined transactions and so locking was not an issue as locks were held for the duration of the CREATE statement. With SQL Server 6.5, however, the following Data Definition Language (DDL) statements can appear in user defined transactions:

ALTER TABLE	DROP PROCEDURE
CREATE DEFAULT	DROP RULE
CREATE INDEX	DROP TABLE
CREATE PROCEDURE	DROP TRIGGER
CREATE RULE	DROP VIEW
CREATE TABLE	GRANT
CREATE TRIGGER	REVOKE
CREATE VIEW	SELECT INTO
DROP DEFAULT	TRUNCATE TABLE
DROP INDEX	

Because these statements can now appear in user defined transactions it is possible that a long-lived user defined transaction can cause locking problems in the system tables. If a table is created in a user defined transaction SQL Server takes out exclusive page locks in the *sysobjects, sysindexes* and *syscolumns* system tables. Even if the transaction is not committed, a SELECT statement issued in another connection can see the new row in these tables. It follows, therefore, that a dirty read has taken place and it is possible that the transaction in which the table was created subsequently issues a rollback removing it.

More importantly though, two user defined transactions that create tables or other system objects at the same time will probably be involved in a lock conflict. It is important, therefore, that these transactions are committed quickly.

6.3.8 Monitoring Locks

Finally, we need to introduce the means by which we can observe SQL Server lock management in action and then we can look at some examples of the SQL Server locking protocol. There are a number of ways to find information about the locking that is happening within SQL Server:

▶ Use the *sp_lock* system stored procedure

▶ Use the *SQL Enterprise Manager*

▶ Use the Performance Monitor

▶ Interrogate the system table *syslocks* directly

Additionally, the *sp_who* system stored procedure is useful in finding blocked and blocking processes and the DBCC utility can be used to set trace flags to record lock and deadlock information.

6.3.8.1 Using sp_lock

The *sp_lock* system stored procedure displays information about the locks held by processes using the server. It can be entered as a standalone statement in which case it will display all locks managed by the server or can take an SQL Server process identifier (spid) as a parameter. Some example output from the *sp_lock* system stored procedure is shown below:

```
sp_lock

spid      locktype      table_id      page      dbname
----      ----------    ---------     ----      -------
4         Sh_intent     496004798     0         master
4         Ex_extent     0             40        tempdb
6         Sh_intent     3             0         banking
6         Sh_intent     176003658     0         banking
```

```
6          Sh_page        176003658    368      banking
7          Sh_intent      3            0        banking
7          Sh_table       48003202     0        banking
9          Ex_intent      112003430    0        banking
9          Ex_page        112003430    136      banking
9          Update_page    112003430    136      banking
```

Hint: To translate the table_id to a table name use the built-in system function OBJECT_NAME. For example:

```
select object_name (176003658)
--------
branches
```

The above output from *sp_lock* shows a number of locks held on various objects. SQL Server process identification number (spid) 6 has requested and been granted a shared intent lock on the *Branches* table and a shared page lock on database page number 368 allocated to the *Branches* table.

```
6 Sh_intent    176003658    0      banking
6 Sh_page      176003658    368    banking
```

Spid 7 has requested and been granted a shared table lock on the *Customers* table.

```
7 Sh_table     48003202     0      banking
```

Note that spid 6 had performed an indexed access on the table to retrieve the row whereas spid 7 had performed a table scan of the table using the HOLDLOCK keyword.

Spid 9 has requested and been granted an exclusive intent lock on the table *Accounts* and an exclusive page and update page lock on database page number 136 allocated to the *Accounts* table.

```
9 Ex_intent    112003430    0      banking
9 Ex_page      112003430    136    banking
9 Update_page  112003430    136    banking
```

Note that shared intent locks can be seen held on table id 3. This table is the *syscolumns* table and is locked because we are seeing processes reading metadata.

6.3.8.2 Using the SQL Enterprise Manager

The SQL Enterprise Manager allows the database administrator to monitor current locking activity in a graphical fashion. If *Server…Current Activity* is selected from the menu the *Current Activity* window is displayed as shown in Figure 6.14 with the *User Activity* tab in the foreground.

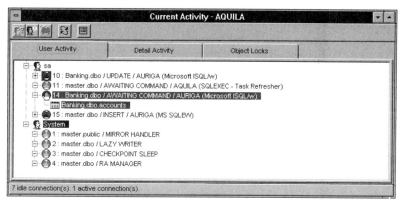

Figure 6.14
The SQL Enterprise Manager User Activity Tab

The current active connections are shown grouped by login ID. As the legend in Figure 6.15 shows, some processes are *sleeping*, and some processes are *runnable*. The process with spid 10 is blocked by the process with spid 14. A red background indicates a blocking lock.

This blocking can often be seen more clearly if the *Detail Activity* tab is selected as shown in Figure 6.16.

To see more information about what a process is doing the entry in the list can be double-clicked which displays the *Process Details* window as shown in Figure 6.17. As can be seen, the last Transact-SQL statement executed is displayed.

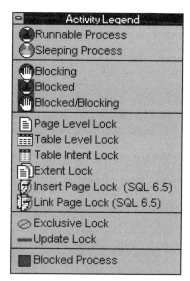

Figure 6.15
The Activity Legend

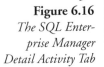

Figure 6.16
*The SQL Enter-
prise Manager
Detail Activity Tab*

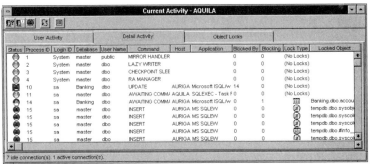

Figure 6.17
*The SQL Enter-
prise Manager
Process Information
Window*

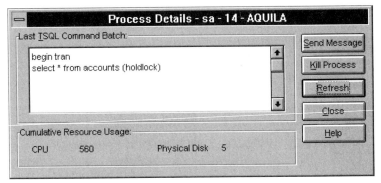

Lastly, the *Object Locks* tab can be selected which provides information on the objects a process has locked. For example, spid 14 (the blocker) has a shared table lock on the *Accounts* table in the *Banking* database, as shown in Figure 6.18.

These SQL Enterprise Manager displays take a little getting use to but once you are familiar with them they are a real help in resolving lock contention problems.

Figure 6.18
*The SQL Enter-
prise Manager
Object Locks Tab*

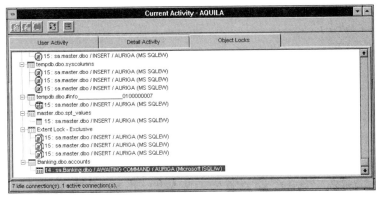

6.3.8.3 Using the Performance Monitor

The Performance Monitor is a Windows NT utility that enables system managers and database administrators to monitor the many objects within a Windows NT system. There are many counters that can be monitored for many objects but here we are interested in those counters specific to the SQL Server object. There are counters associated with I/O, cache and the network but, in this chapter, our concern is with the counters associated with locking. These counters can be grouped under the categories shown in Table 6.4.

As we have already seen, there are many ways in which data can be displayed with the Performance Monitor. Data can be displayed in a customizable chart from which lock activity can be continuously monitored or data can be collected to a log file and then later replayed. An alert window can be used to display information about counters whose values have exceeded a user definable maximum and optionally a program can be executed when this happens. A program supplied with SQL Server named *SQLALRTR.EXE* can be invoked to place an error in the Windows NT Application Event Log with a source of SQL Server. The SQL Server Alert Subsystem can then act on this error. The values of counters can also be displayed in a simple, but easy to read, report format. The best mode of display is down to user preference and the actual monitoring task that is being performed.

Figure 6.19 and Figure 6.20 show two chart displays. Figure 6.19 shows a graphical display and Figure 6.20 shows a histogram display. The top half of each display shows the chosen chart format and the bottom half shows the counters that have been chosen as targets for monitoring. For example, one of the counters being monitored is *Total Locks*. When one of these counters is selected, the *last, average, minimum* and *maximum* values for that counter is displayed.

Table 6.4 *Data Values Monitored For The SQL Server Object*

SQL Server-Locks Object Counters	Explanation
Total	total exclusive, shared, blocking and total for server
Table	total exclusive table locks, shared table locks and total table locks
Extent	total exclusive, previous and next extent locks and total extent locks
Intent	total exclusive intent locks, shared intent locks and total intent locks
Page	total exclusive page locks, shared, update page locks and total page lock
Users	maximum users blocked, users blocked

Figure 6.19
Example Performance Monitor Output Using A Graphical Display

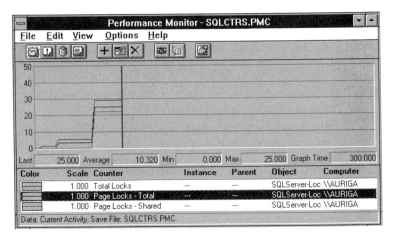

Figure 6.20
Example Performance Monitor Output Using A Histogram Display

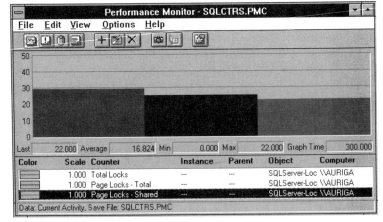

6.3.8.4 Interrogating the Syslocks Table

The *syslocks* system table can be interrogated in the same way that any other system table can be interrogated. It is only found in the master database where it holds information concerning the locks held in the SQL Server. Unlike most other system tables it is materialized when a query is executed that accesses it, otherwise it does not exist physically. A query issued against the *syslocks* table produces output such as that shown below:

```
SELECT * FROM syslocks

id      dbid    page    type    spid
--      ----    ----    ----    ----
3       1       0       4       4
0       2       128     8       4
```

The *id* and *dbid* columns are the id of the table and the database respectively. The page column is the page number and the spid is the SQL Server process identifier of the process holding the lock. Perhaps the most interesting column is the lock type column. This column holds a value that refers to the kind of lock. This is shown in Table 6.5. Note that some of these locks, for example extent locks, are used by SQL Server to internally manage the allocation and deallocation of 16 Kb extents.

Note that if 256 is added to any of the above values it means that the lock is blocking another user, for example, 257 means that an exclusive table lock is blocking another user.

6.3.8.5 Using sp_who

The system procedure *sp_who* can be used to obtain information on the processes active within an SQL Server. It can be entered as a standalone statement in which case it will display information on all users and processes. It can take an SQL Server process identifier (*spid*) or alternatively an SQL Server

Table 6.5 *The Meaning Of Lock Type Values In Syslocks*

Value	Lock Type
1	table lock (exclusive)
2	table lock (shared)
3	intent lock (exclusive)
4	intent lock (shared)
5	page lock (exclusive)
6	page lock (shared)
7	update page lock
8	extent lock (exclusive)
9	extent lock (update)
10	ShTab_ExIntent
11	next extent lock
12	previous extent lock
13	insert page
14	link page

login name as a parameter. Some example output from the *sp_who* system stored procedure is shown below:

```
spid status    loginame hostname blk dbname   cmd
---- ------    -------- -------- --- ------   ---------------
1    sleeping  sa                0   master   MIRROR HANDLER
2    sleeping  sa                0   master   CHECKPOINT SLEEP
3    sleeping  sa                0   master   LAZY WRITER
4    runnable  england  AURIGA   0   master   SELECT
5    sleeping  england  AURIGA   0   banking  AWAITING COMMAND
6    sleeping  stanley  AURIGA   5   banking  SELECT
```

Note that the process with spid 6 has a 5 in the blk column whereas other processes have 0. This is because the process with spid 6 is being blocked by another user—in fact the user with spid 5. If we were to issue an *sp_lock* as shown below we would see an entry for spid 5. In this case we can see that spid 5 is holding an exclusive table lock. The fact that it is blocking another process can be seen from the -blk suffix.

```
spid     locktype      table_id   page   dbname
-----    -----------   --------   ----   -------
5        Ex_table-blk  1600308    0      banking
```

Note that using *sp_lock* alone does not provide information on which process is being blocked, the database administrator must also use *sp_who*.

6.3.8.6 Using Trace Flags with DBCC

As previously mentioned the SQL Server documentation states that *trace flags are not part of the supported feature set.* It is worth mentioning them here though as they can be used to provide some lock trace information. The database consistency checker, more usually referred to as DBCC, can be used to set trace flags or they can be set if SQL Server is started at the command line. Trace information can be sent to destinations such as the errorlog (using trace flag 3605) or the client (using trace flag 3604). Locking information can be generated by setting the trace flags to 1200 or 1204 and 1205 for deadlock information. Some example trace output is shown below:

6.3.8.7 Trace Flag 1200

```
DBCC TRACEON (3604,1200)
SELECT account_no FROM accounts
Process 14 requesting table lock of type SH_INT on 6 3
chaining lock onto PSS chain
Process 14 requesting page lock of type SH_PAGE on 6 315
chaining lock onto PSS chain
Process 14 releasing page lock of type SH_PAGE on 6 315
Process 14 requesting page lock of type SH_PAGE on 6 315
```

```
chaining lock onto PSS chain
Process 14 releasing page lock of type SH_PAGE on 6 315
Process 14 releasing table lock of type SH_INT on 6 3
Process 14 requesting page lock of type SH_PAGE on 6 25
chaining lock onto PSS chain
Process 14 releasing page lock of type SH_PAGE on 6 25
Process 14 requesting page lock of type SH_PAGE on 6 27
chaining lock onto PSS chain
Process 14 releasing page lock of type SH_PAGE on 6 27
Process 14 requesting table lock of type SH_INT on 6 112003430
Process 8 releasing page lock of type SH_PAGE on 4 368
Process 8 releasing table lock of type SH_INT on 4 176003658
:
:
Process 14 requesting page lock of type SH_PAGE on 6 2280
chaining lock onto PSS chain
account_no
-----------
1
2
:
182
183
Process 14 releasing page lock of type SH_PAGE on 6 2280
Process 14 requesting page lock of type SH_PAGE on 6 2281
chaining lock onto PSS chain
184
185
:
```

The output can be somewhat cryptic but with a little effort a database administrator can follow what is happening. In the example above spid 14 is performing a table scan and, after some initial reading of the system tables, is sequentially reading pages. When it wants to read a page it requests and acquires a page lock and when it has read a page it releases the page lock. Note that page locks refer to page numbers whereas table locks refer to the object id of the table. As we have seen, the OBJECT_NAME() function may be used to find the table name:

```
SELECT OBJECT_NAME (112003430)
-------------------------------
accounts
```

Whether tables or pages are being referenced, the number preceding the object id or page number is the database id. The *DB_NAME()* function may be used to find the database name:

```
SELECT DB_NAME(6)
------------------
Banking
```

To find to which object a page belongs, use the *DBCC PAGE* statement:

```
DBCC TRACEON (3604)
DBCC PAGE (6, 2280)
PAGE:
Page found in cache.
BUFFER:
Buffer header for buffer 0x91e1e0
page=0x1062800 bdnew=0x91e1e0 bdold=0x91e1e0 bhash=0x8da860
bnew=0x91e240
bold=0x91c740 bvirtpg=16779496 bdbid=6 bpinproc=0 bkeep=0
bspid=0
bstat=0x1004 bpageno=2280
PAGE HEADER:
Page header for page 0x1062800
pageno=2280 nextpg=2281 prevpg=0 objid=112003430 timestamp=0001
0002e822
nextrno=2034 level=0 indid=2 freeoff=2045 minlen=11
page status bits: 0x80,0x2
```

The next example shows Trace Flag (1200) output when page locks are escalated to a table lock:

```
DBCC TRACEON (3604,1200)
BEGIN TRAN
SELECT account_no FROM accounts (HOLDLOCK PAGLOCK)
:
:
7136
7137
Process 14 requesting page lock of type SH_PAGE on 6 2351
chaining lock onto PSS chain
Process 14 requesting table lock of type SH_TAB on 6 112003430
chaining lock onto PSS chain
Checking the Pss chain for page locks
freeing page lock for page 2351, dbid 6 and objid 112003430 after
promotion to table lock
:
:
```

The promotion of page locks to a table lock and the subsequent releasing of the page locks can clearly be seen.

6.3.8.8 Trace Flag 1204

This trace flag returns the type of locks participating in a deadlock and the current commands involved.

```
96/10/01 20:58:33.62 spid14 *** DEADLOCK DETECTED with spid 13 ***
spid 14 requesting EX_PAGE (waittype 0x5), blocked by:
SH_PAGE: spid 13, dbid 6, page 0xab8, table 0x6ad0966, indid 0
UP_PAGE: spid 14, dbid 6, page 0xab8, table 0x6ad0966, indid 0
```

```
pcurcmd UPDATE(0xc5), input buffer: update accounts set balance =
    10 where account_no = 20000
spid 13 waiting for EX_PAGE (waittype 0x5), blocked by:
SH_PAGE: spid 14, dbid 6, page 0xaba, table 0x6ad0966, indid 0
UP_PAGE: spid 13, dbid 6, page 0xaba, table 0x6ad0966, indid 0
pcurcmd UPDATE(0xc5), input buffer: update accounts set balance =
    10 where account_no = 1000
VICTIM: spid 14, pstat 0x0000 , cputime 10
```

In the above example spid 13 and spid 14 are involved in a deadlock. The database id is specified as 6, which DB_NAME() translates to the *Banking* database. The deadlock is caused by activity in table 0x6ad0966 which in decimal is 112003430 (the scientific calculator in the Accessories Program Group is useful here). The OBJECT_NAME function translates this value to the *Accounts* table. The database pages involved in the deadlock are 0xab8 and 0xaba which translate to 2744 and 2746 respectively.

The output shows what is blocking each SPID and the blocked Transact-SQL statement. Finally the output shows which SPID is the victim, in this case, SPID 14.

6.3.8.9 Trace Flag 1205

This trace flag returns detailed information about the commands being executed at the time of a deadlock. You will need to set trace flag 1204 to get information out of trace flag 1205 but, to be honest, the extra information is probably only likely to be useful (and understandable) by Microsoft Support.

6.4 SQL Server Locking in Action

Now that we understand how SQL Server uses its locking protocol we can look at some examples. In order to keep the output as clear as possible, the actual results of the SELECT statements are not shown.

Our examples will use the *Accounts* table in the *Banking* database. In these examples, all indexes have been removed from this table unless otherwise specified.

```
Mike                      Katy

SELECT * FROM accounts    SELECT * FROM accounts
*** OK ***                *** OK ***
```

In the above example, Mike retrieves all the rows in the *Accounts* table. Katy attempts to concurrently retrieve all the rows in the *Accounts* table and is successful. This is because Mike places and releases shared locks on the pages in the *Accounts* table as he scans through it. Katy also attempts to place shared locks on the pages in the *Accounts* table and, as shared locks are compatible, her attempt is also successful.

In the next example, Mike updates all the rows in the *Accounts* table. He performs this operation within a transaction which he does not end. Katy attempts to retrieve rows from the *Accounts* table.

```
Mike                                      Katy

BEGIN TRANSACTION
UPDATE accounts SET balance = 0
                                          SELECT * FROM accounts
*** OK ***
                                          *** wait ***
```

In this example, Katy again attempts to place a shared lock on pages in the *Accounts* table. This time, however, these shared page locks she attempts to place on the *Accounts* table are incompatible with Mike's exclusive table lock and so her attempt is unsuccessful. She will be forced to wait until Mike finishes his transaction. SQL Server took out an exclusive table lock as an optimization. Mike's UPDATE statement had no WHERE clause and so every page would have been locked until escalation to a table lock occurred so it is more efficient to take out the table lock straight away.

This example serves to illustrate a very important point, which is, transactions should be kept as short as possible. If they are not, then they could block another transaction for an unacceptable length of time.

If we were to issue an *sp_lock* at this point we would see the following fragment of output:

```
spid       locktype        table_id       page      dbname
----       ------------    ---------       ----      ------
6          Ex_table-blk    112003430       0         Banking
```

Mike, spid 6, is holding an exclusive table lock with a -blk suffix that denotes that this lock is blocking another. An *sp_who* issued at this point would show:

```
spid   status     loginame  hostname   blk   dbname    cmd
----   ------     --------  --------   ----  ------    ---------------
5      sleeping   katy      AURIGA     6     Banking   SELECT
6      sleeping   mike      AURIGA     0     Banking   AWAITING COMMAND
```

In the next example, Mike again updates all the rows in the *Accounts* table. Again, he performs this operation within a transaction which he does not end. This time Katy attempts to delete the rows in the *Accounts* table.

```
Mike                                Katy

BEGIN TRANSACTION
UPDATE accounts SET balance = 0     BEGIN TRANSACTION
                                    DELETE accounts
*** OK ***
                                    *** wait ***
```

In this example, Katy attempts to place an exclusive lock on the *Accounts* table. The exclusive table lock she attempts to place on the *Accounts* table is incompatible with Mike's exclusive table lock and so her attempt is unsuccessful. Again, she will be forced to wait until Mike finishes his transaction.

In the next example Mike will again update rows in the *Accounts* table and Katy will retrieve them. This is the same as the second example except that now Katy will issue her SELECT statement first. We will use BEGIN TRANSACTION for both users.

```
Mike                                Katy

                                    BEGIN TRANSACTION
BEGIN TRANSACTION                   SELECT * FROM accounts
UPDATE accounts SET balance = 0
                                    *** OK ***
*** OK ***
```

In this example, Katy attempts to place shared locks on pages in the *Accounts* table. She is successful as Mike has not issued his update yet. Mike then issues his update which is also successful. Mike's exclusive table lock is not blocked by Katy's shared page locks because SQL Server will have released the shared locks when the SELECT statement completed. Katy's locks have been and gone before Mike issues his update. The fact that Katy issues her SELECT statement within a transaction is irrelevant.

We can now introduce a *holdlock* example. As previously mentioned, the HOLDLOCK keyword forces a shared lock on a table to stay until the transaction completes. This will increase data consistency (it will provide repeatable reads as we shall see shortly) but possibly at the expense of concurrency. The previous example is repeated below but Katy now uses the HOLDLOCK keyword.

```
Mike                                Katy

                                    BEGIN TRANSACTION
BEGIN TRANSACTION                   SELECT * FROM accounts (HOLDLOCK)
UPDATE accounts SET balance = 0
*** wait ***                        *** OK ***
```

Now Mike is forced to wait. The HOLDLOCK keyword forces SQL Server to not release the shared page locks until the transaction completes and so SQL Server takes out a table lock as an optimization. Katy's shared table lock blocks Mike's exclusive table lock. If we were to issue an *sp_lock* at this point we would see the following fragment of output:

```
spid    locktype        table_id        page    dbname
-----   -----------     --------        ----    --------
5       Sh_intent       3               0       Accounts
5       Sh_table-blk    112003430       0       Accounts
```

Katy, spid 5, is holding a shared table lock and the -blk suffix can be seen that denotes that this lock is blocking another.

In the next example, Mike and Katy both attempt to update different rows.

```
Mike                                    Katy

BEGIN TRANSACTION
UPDATE accounts SET balance = 0
   WHERE account_no = 1000              BEGIN TRANSACTION
                                        UPDATE accounts SET balance = 0
                                           WHERE account_no = 20000

*** OK ***
                                        *** wait ***
```

Even though both Mike and Katy are updating different rows, because there is no index defined on the *account_no* column resulting in a table scan, table locks will be used. Concurrency is therefore low and Katy must wait for Mike to complete his transaction before her update can execute.

Let us now create some indexes on the *Accounts* table:

```
CREATE UNIQUE NONCLUSTERED INDEX accounts_account_no_idx ON
   accounts
(account_no)

CREATE CLUSTERED INDEX accounts_branch_no_idx ON accounts
(branch_no)
```

If we repeat the last example we see a different result. This time Katy is not blocked.

```
Mike                                    Katy

BEGIN TRANSACTION
UPDATE accounts SET balance = 0
WHERE account_no = 1000                 BEGIN TRANSACTION
                                        UPDATE accounts SET balance = 0
                                        WHERE account_no = 20000

*** OK ***
                                        *** OK ***
```

This is because indexed access can now be used and consequently page level locks can be taken out. If we were to issue an *sp_lock* at this point we would see the following fragment of output:

```
spid   locktype      table_id      page   dbname
----   --------      ---------      ----   -------
5      Ex_intent     112003430     0      Banking
5      Ex_page       112003430     304    Banking
5      Update_page   112003430     304    Banking
6      Ex_intent     112003430     0      Banking
6      Ex_page       112003430     305    Banking
6      Update_page   112003430     305    Banking
```

Katy has placed an update and an exclusive page level lock on page 304 and Mike has placed an update and an exclusive page level lock on page 305. Note that they have both placed exclusive intent locks. The update transactions have not locked any index pages as the column updated (*balance*) is not involved in either index.

Suppose Mike had issued the following update statement:

```
UPDATE accounts SET branch_no = 2000 WHERE account_no = 20000
```

If we were to issue an *sp_lock* at this point we would now see the following fragment of output:

```
spid   locktype      table_id      page   dbname
-----  -----------   ---------      ----   -------
5      Ex_intent     112003430     0      Banking
5      Ex_page       112003430     304    Banking
6      Ex_page       112003430     320    Banking
5      Update_page   112003430     304    Banking
6      Ex_intent     112003430     0      Banking
6      Ex_page       112003430     305    Banking
6      Update_page   112003430     305    Banking
```

We can see that an exclusive page lock is now also held on page 320. This is because an index page is now being written to as the *branch_no* column is part of the *accounts_branch_no_idx* index.

Suppose Mike and Katy insert rows into the *Accounts* table. Let us assume that there are no indexes on the *Accounts* table.

```
Mike                                    Katy

BEGIN TRANSACTION
INSERT INTO accounts
VALUES (26001, 120000, 1000, 156)
                                        BEGIN TRANSACTION
                                        INSERT INTO accounts
                                        VALUES (26002, 123345, 9000, 4456)
*** wait ***                            *** OK ***
```

If we were to issue an *sp_lock* at this point we would now see the following fragment of output:

```
spid   locktype     table_id    page    dbname
----   --------     --------    ----    -------
6      Ex_intent    112003430   0       Banking
6      Ex_page-blk  112003430   2743    Banking
5      Ex_intent    112003430   0       Banking
```

We can see that an exclusive page lock is held on page 2743. This is because Mike has taken out this page lock in order to insert his row into the *Accounts* table. Because there is no index on the table, all rows will be inserted at the end, that is, the last page. Consequently, Katy also tries to take out an exclusive lock on the last page (page 2743) in the table and is blocked.

Now let us enable IRL on the *Accounts* table and repeat the scenario:

```
sp_tableoption 'accounts', 'insert row lock', 'true'
```

Mike	Katy
BEGIN TRANSACTION	
INSERT INTO accounts	
VALUES (26001, 120000, 1000, 156)	
	BEGIN TRANSACTION
	INSERT INTO accounts
	VALUES (26002, 123345, 9000, 4456)
*** OK ***	
	*** OK ***

Mike does not block Katy and both insertions are allowed to complete.

If we were to issue an *sp_lock* at this point we would now see the following fragment of output:

```
spid   locktype      table_id     page    dbname
-----  --------      ---------    ----    -------
6      Ex_intent     112003430    0       Banking
6      Insert_page   112003430    2743    Banking
5      Ex_intent     112003430    0       Banking
5      Insert_page   112003430    2743    Banking
```

Both Mike and Katy have taken out *Insert_page* locks out on page 2743.

6.5 Uncommitted Data, Repeatable Reads, Phantoms, and More

With our knowledge of locking protocols we can now investigate how SQL Server deals with the reading of uncommitted data, non-repeatable reads and phantoms.

6.5.1 Reading Uncommitted Data

Figure 6.1 illustrated the problems with reading uncommitted data. As should already be clear, SQL Server forbids this by virtue of the fact that any row that has been changed cannot be read by another user as an exclusive page or table level lock will prevent the row being retrieved until the write transaction ends.

SQL Server 6.0 onwards, however, allows the default behavior to be over-ridden. A query is allowed to read uncommitted data with the use of the NOLOCK keyword, introduced earlier in this chapter. For example, the following SELECT statement would read the row from the *Accounts* table regardless of whether another transaction had the page or table locked with an exclusive lock:

```
SELECT balance FROM accounts (NOLOCK) WHERE account_no = 15000
```

Suppose Mike updates a row in the *Accounts* table. He performs this operation within a transaction which he does not end. Katy attempts to retrieve rows from the titles table.

```
Mike                              Katy

BEGIN TRANSACTION
UPDATE accounts SET balance = 500  SELECT price FROM accounts
   WHERE account_no = 15000           (NOLOCK)
                                    WHERE account_no = 15000
*** OK ***
                                  *** OK ***
```

In this example, Katy does not attempt to place a shared lock and she can read the row that Mike has updated. She will read a balance of 500. Mike may well ultimately choose to roll back his change leaving Katy with incorrect balance information.

6.5.2 Non-Repeatable Reads

In the case of a non-repeatable read, a transaction is allowed to read a data item on more than one occasion and retrieve different values each time. This is shown graphically in Figure 6.21. By default, SQL Server allows non-repeatable reads. It is sometimes desirable, however, to guarantee repeatable reads, that is, each read of the same data item while in the same transaction returns the same value. The means of guaranteeing repeatable reads in SQL Server is by the use of the HOLDLOCK keyword.

If the HOLDLOCK keyword is used, when the page is read the first time a shared lock is taken out as usual. This then remains until the end of the transaction. This blocks any other transaction from changing the data item.

Figure 6.21
Non-Repeatable Reads

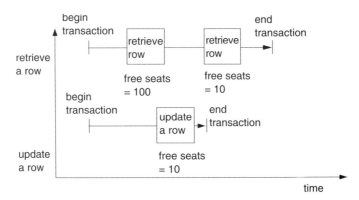

```
            Mike                           Katy

                                           BEGIN TRANSACTION
                                             SELECT balance FROM accounts
                                             (HOLDLOCK)
                                             WHERE account_no = 15000

                                           *** OK ***

            BEGIN TRANSACTION
            UPDATE accounts SET
              balance = 50.00
              WHERE account_no = 15000

            *** wait ***
                                           select balance from accounts (holdlock)
                                           where account_no = 15000
                                           *** OK ***
```

Now Mike is forced to wait. Katy's shared locks block Mike's exclusive table lock and when Katy repeats her read she will receive the same value, hence, the use of the HOLDLOCK keyword has provided repeatable reads. Again, this is at the expense of concurrency.

With SQL Server 6.0 onwards, setting the isolation level to repeatable read (or serializable) will also provide repeatable reads.

```
            Mike                           Katy

                                           SET TRANSACTION
                                           ISOLATION LEVEL REPEATABLE READ

                                           BEGIN TRANSACTION
                                           SELECT balance FROM accounts
                                           WHERE account_no = 15000
                                           *** OK ***

            BEGIN TRANSACTION
            UPDATE accounts SET
```

```
                    balance = 50.00
                    WHERE account_no = 15000
                    *** wait ***
                                          SELECT balance FROM accounts
                                          WHERE account_no = 15000
                                          *** OK ***
```

Again, Mike is forced to wait. Katy's shared locks block Mike's exclusive table lock and when Katy repeats her read she will receive the same value. The use of the HOLDLOCK keyword is not required as the *set transaction isolation level repeatable read* statement has provided repeatable reads.

6.5.3 Phantoms

The phantom problem was illustrated in Figure 6.2. By default, SQL Server does not forbid phantoms but the use of the HOLDLOCK keyword will prevent them as the following examples show:

```
Mike                                    Katy

BEGIN TRANSACTION
SELECT SUM(balance) FROM accounts
125,195,935.31
*** OK ***
                                        INSERT INTO accounts VALUES
                                        (27000,122456,1200, 1000)
                                        *** OK ***
SELECT SUM(balance) FROM accounts
125,196,935.31
*** OK ***
```

In the example above, phantoms are allowed to occur. The two sums of the same list of values give different results. In the next example, Katy's transaction is blocked and the phantom phenomenon is not allowed to occur.

```
Mike                                    Katy

BEGIN TRANSACTION
SELECT SUM(balance)
   FROM accounts (HOLDLOCK)
125,195,935.31
*** OK ***
                                        INSERT INTO accounts VALUES
                                           (27000,122456,1200, 1000)
                                        *** wait ***
SELECT SUM(balance) FROM accounts
125,195,935.31
*** OK ***
```

The use of the HOLDLOCK keyword is not required if the *set transaction isolation level serializable (or repeatable read statement)* is used.

```
Mike                                Katy

SET TRANSACTION
ISOLATION LEVEL SERIALIZABLE

BEGIN TRANSACTION
SELECT SUM(balance) FROM accounts
125,195,935.31

*** OK ***
                                    INSERT INTO accounts VALUES
                                    (27000,122456,1200, 1000)

                                    *** wait ***
SELECT SUM(balance) FROM accounts
125,195,935.31

*** OK ***
```

6.5.4 More Modified Locking Behavior

While showing examples of how the HOLDLOCK keyword and transaction isolation levels can modify the default locking behavior, it's also worth looking at examples of some of the other keywords introduced earlier in this chapter. We have already seen an example of NOLOCK so let us look at TABLOCKX, for example. The TABLOCKX keyword forces an exclusive table lock to be taken on a table which means that no other user, regardless of their Transact-SQL statement, can access rows in the table.

```
Mike                    Katy

BEGIN TRANSACTION
SELECT SUM(balance) FROM
accounts (TABLOCKX)

*** OK ***              BEGIN TRANSACTION
                        SELECT SUM(balance) FROM accounts

                        *** wait ***
```

Even though the two transactions are only reading the table, Katy is forced to wait.

The PAGLOCK keyword forces shared page locks to be taken where otherwise SQL Server may have used a table lock.

Suppose we execute the following SELECT statement within a transaction:

```
SELECT balance FROM accounts (HOLDLOCK) WHERE balance = 10000
```

We would see the following output from *sp_lock*:

```
spid  locktype   table_id   page  dbname
----  --------   ------     ----  -------
11    Sh_table   112003430  0     Banking
12    Sh_intent  544004969  0     master
12    Ex_extent  0          352   tempdb
```

However, suppose we execute the SELECT statement within a transaction using the PAGLOCK keyword:

```
SELECT balance FROM accounts (HOLDLOCK PAGLOCK) WHERE balance =
    10000
```

We would see the following output from *sp_lock*:

```
spid  locktype   table_id   page  dbname
-----  --------   ---------  ----  -------
11    Sh_intent  112003430  0     Banking
11    Sh_page    112003430  408   Banking
11    Sh_page    112003430  409   Banking
11    Sh_page    112003430  410   Banking
:
:
12    Sh_intent  544004969  0     master
12    Ex_extent  0          352   tempdb
```

As can be seen, the first SELECT statement uses a single shared table lock whereas the second SELECT statement uses a number of shared page locks (this assumes no lock escalation has taken place).

6.6 A Summary of Lock Compatibility

We have seen a number of scenarios involving locks and it is worth now summarizing the compatibility between different locks. Page level locks are either shared, exclusive or update, and these interact as shown in Table 6.6.

A cross denotes incompatibility, that is, one lock will block the other. A tick denotes compatibility, that is, the locks can happily exist with each other.

Table locks are a little more involved as intent locks must also be considered as shown in Table 6.7.

As discussed earlier, intent locks are used to flag the fact that page locks are being held in a table. If Mike is holding shared page locks on a table, SQL Server will place a shared intent lock on the table and, if Katy is holding exclusive page locks on the table, SQL Server will place an exclusive intent lock on the table. From Table 6.7 it can be seen that these intent locks are compatible. However, if an attempt is made to escalate the page locks,

Table 6.6 *Page Level Lock Compatibility*

Mode of Currently Granted Lock	Mode of Requested Lock				
	exclusive	insert_page	link_page	shared	update
exclusive	✗	✗	✗	✗	✗
insert_page	✗	✔	✔	✗	✗
link_page	✗	✗	✗	✗	✗
shared	✗	✗	✗	✔	✔
update	✗	✗	✗	✔	✗

Table 6.7 *Table Level Lock Compatibility*

Mode of Currently Granted Lock	Mode of Requested Lock			
	exclusive	shared	exclusive intent	shared intent
exclusive	✗	✗	✗	✗
shared	✗	✔	✗	✔
exclusive intent	✗	✗	✔	✔
shared intent	✗	✔	✔	✔

belonging to either Mike or Katy, to a table lock, it will not be allowed as incompatibility between the intent locks and the requested table locks will forbid it.

What about the locks that are placed when an index is created on a table? If we consider what is actually happening, in a non-clustered index the index leaf level is stored on separate pages from the actual data. This means that the leaf level index pages that are being written to during the non-clustered index creation are not the same pages as those holding the data rows. Therefore the pages holding the data rows need only be read by SQL Server in order to create the index and only a shared lock needs to be placed on the table.

The index leaf level of a clustered index, on the other hand, is essentially the data itself. This means that the leaf level index pages that are being written to during the clustered index creation are the same pages as those holding the data rows. Therefore the pages holding the data rows must be written to by SQL Server in order to create the index and an exclusive lock needs to be placed on the table.

Monitoring Performance

7.1 Introduction

As we have mentioned on a number of occasions, physical database design is not a static one-off process. Once the database has gone into production the user requirements are likely to change. Even if they do not, the database data is likely to be volatile and tables are likely to grow. Figure 7.1 shows a typical monitoring and tuning cycle.

Over the last few chapters we have seen a number of tools that can be used to monitor performance. There are also other tools that have hardly been mentioned. This chapter will look at the array of tools that the database administrator can use to monitor SQL Server performance in the form of system stored procedures, DBCC reports, the Windows NT Performance Monitor, the SQL Enterprise Manager and SQL Trace.

7.1.1 System Stored Procedures

There are a number of system stored procedures that can assist in performance monitoring, including:

▶ *sp_lock*

▶ *sp_who*

▶ *sp_monitor*

The system stored procedures *sp_lock* and *sp_who* provide information on locks and on blocked processes. Both these system stored procedures were described in Chapter 6 and so we will concentrate on *sp_monitor* here.

SQL Server writes resource usage information into a number of global variables and *sp_monitor* then formats and displays this information. In fact it

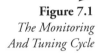

Figure 7.1
*The Monitoring
And Tuning Cycle*

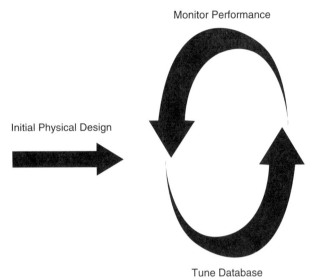

Monitor Performance

Initial Physical Design

Tune Database

displays the current values of the global variables and the difference between these current values and the values last time *sp_monitor* was run.

```
sp_monitor

last_run            current_run          seconds
----------          -----------          -------
4 Feb 1997 20:50    4 Feb 1997 20:52     116

cpu_busy            io_busy              idle
-------------       -----------          -------
4(3)-2%             1(0)-0%              4219(109)-93%

packets_received    packets_sent         packet_errors
----------------    -------------        -------------
189(8)                                   182(8)0(0)

total_read          total_write          total_errors    connections
-------------       -------------        -------------   -----------
438(153)            200(2)               0(0)5(0)
```

The *cpu_busy*, *io_busy* and *idle* values are measured in seconds. The value 4(3)-2% is decoded as 4 seconds of CPU use since SQL Server was started and (3) is decoded as 3 seconds of CPU use since *sp_monitor* was last executed. The CPU has been busy 2% of the time since *sp_monitor* was last executed. Similarly, for *total_write* the value 200(2) can be decoded as 200 writes since SQL Server was started and (2) is decoded as 2 writes since *sp_monitor* was last executed.

These global variables are available to be read by Transact-SQL statements if the database administrator prefers his or her own format. The *sp_monitor* Transact-SQL definition can easily be examined using the SQL Enterprise Manager.

Many database administrators use their own home-grown stored procedures to interrogate the system tables. Taking this approach means that the output is customized to individual preference and is fine-tuned for the application.

7.1.2 DBCC Reports

There are a number of DBCC reports that have been already mentioned in this and previous chapters that are useful for performance tuning, such as DBCC MEMUSAGE. Various performance statistics can also be obtained through the use of DBCC SQLPERF which takes a number of options:

▶ IOSTATS

▶ LRUSTATS

▶ NETSTATS

▶ RASTATS

▶ THREADS

▶ LOGSPACE

These options can be used to obtain I/O, cache and network statistics since the server was started and also information on Windows NT threads and transaction log space. Many of the counters are also found in the Performance Monitor. We have already met dbcc sqlperf (threads) in Chapter 5 so we will not show example output from it again.

```
dbcc sqlperf (iostats)

Statistic                 Value
----------------------    --------
Log Flush Requests        16.0
Log Logical Page I/Os     4854.0
Log Physical I/Os         622.0
Log Flush Average         0.0257235
Log Logical IO Average    7.80386
Batch Writes              537.0
Batch Average Size        537.0
Batch Max Size            8.0
Page Reads                864.0
Single Page Writes        1.0
Reads Outstanding         0.0
```

```
Writes Outstanding         0.0
Transactions               10.0
Transactions/Log Write     0.0160772
```

The above output shows I/O statistics concerning batch write activity, such as that generated by the checkpoint process, transaction log I/O and read and write queues.

```
dbcc sqlperf (lrustats)

Statistic                 Value
-------------------       -------
Cache Hit Ratio           99.7518
Cache Flushes             1278.0
Free Page Scan (Avg)      4.64177
Free Page Scan (Max)      1.0
Min Free Buffers          409.0
Cache Size                4050.0
Free Buffers              420.0
```

The above output shows statistics concerning the data cache, such as the cache hit ratio, the cache size and the number of free buffers in the cache. If the number of free buffers in the cache drops below the server configuration option *free buffers* the lazy writer process will start to flush dirty buffers to disk.

```
dbcc sqlperf (rastats)

Statistic                 Value
----------------------    -----
RA Pages Found in Cache   78.0
RA Pages Placed in Cache  950.0
RA Physical I/Os          127.0
Used Slots                0.0
```

The above output shows statistics concerning the read ahead mechanism, such as how many pages were brought into the cache, and how many 16 Kb reads were performed.

```
dbcc sqlperf (netstats)

Statistic                 Value
-----------------------   ------
Network Reads             0.0
Network Writes            2931.0
Command Queue Length      0.0
Max Command Queue Length  0.0
Worker Threads            5.0
Max Worker Threads        5.0
Network Threads           0.0
Max Network Threads       0.0
```

The above output shows statistics concerning the use of the network, such as the current number of worker threads servicing the command queue and the maximum and current command queue length which is a measure of how well SQL Server is servicing requests.

Hint: To easily display all the above three classes of statistics use dbcc perfmon.

```
dbcc sqlperf(logspace)

Database Name   Log Size (MB)   Log Space Used (%)   Status
------------    -------------   ------------------   ------
personnel       2.0             16.6992              0
Banking         50.0            99.4805              0
msdb            2.0             1.95313              0
pubs            0.0             0.0                  1
tempdb          0.0             0.0                  1
model           0.0             0.0                  1
master          0.0             0.0                  1
```

As long as the transaction log is on a separate device from the database, sqlperf(logspace) will display the percentage of the log used. In the display above, the *Banking* database has its transaction log on a separate device but the *Pubs* database does not.

If it is required to reset the statistics, the *clear* option can be used:

```
dbcc sqlperf (lrustats,clear)
LRU statistics have been cleared.
```

7.1.3 The Windows NT Performance Monitor

The Windows NT Performance Monitor is a tool provided with Windows NT to facilitate performance monitoring through a graphical interface. There are many *objects* that can be monitored for Windows NT, such as the *processor* object and the *memory* object and for each object *counters* can be monitored. The processor object has counters such as *%Processor Time.*

There are special objects for SQL Server such as:

▶ SQLServer

▶ SQLServer-Licensing

▶ SQLServer-Locks

▶ SQLServer-Log

▶ SQLServer-Procedure Cache

▶ SQLServer User Defined Counters

▶ SQLServer-Users

There are also objects to assist in monitoring replication. The *SQLServer* object has associated counters such as *Cache Hit Ratio*, the *SQLServer-Locks* object has associated counters such as *Total Locks*, the *SQLServer-Log* object has associated counters such as *Log Space Used (%)* and the *SQLServer-Users* object has associated counters such as each user's *Physical I/O*. A typical display, showing *Cache Hit Ratio* and four other counters, is shown in Figure 7.2.

Many counters can be displayed simultaneously and the display can be changed to be a histogram or a report. Alerts can also be set as shown in Figure 7.3. In this case when a counter reaches or drops below a value set by the database administrator an alert is recorded.

An object newly introduced in SQL Server 6.5 that is worthy of more discussion is the user-defined counters object. This object consists of 10 user-defined counters named *SQL User Counter 1* to *SQL User Counter 10*. The idea behind user-defined counters is that the database administrator can define his or her own counters by writing a stored procedure that retrieves the information to be monitored and returns the information in an integer.

Up to 10 stored procedures can be written by the database administrator and these must be named *sp_user_counter1* to *sp_user_counter10*. An example of one of these stored procedures is shown below:

```
CREATE PROCEDURE sp_user_counter1
AS SELECT COUNT(*) FROM bank_transfer_queue
```

Figure 7.2
The Performance Monitor Showing Cache Hit Ratio

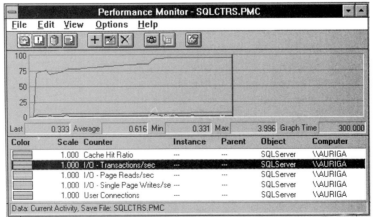

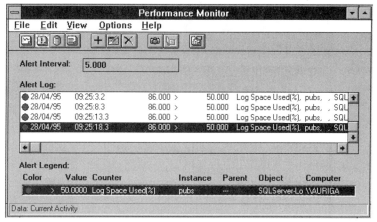

Figure 7.3
The Alert Log Showing A Log Space Alert

The SELECT statement counts the number of items outstanding in a table that represents a money transfer queue. The database administrator can then monitor the user-defined counter *SQL User Counter 1* in the Performance Monitor and if necessary define an alert.

The Performance Monitor can also log data into a monitor log file for playback later. This facility is very useful as it means that samples can be taken, say every few minutes, over a period of days. Performing monitoring over a long period makes it easier to spot trends and sustained bottlenecks. The Windows NT Performance Monitor is probably the key tool for monitoring SQL Server performance and all SQL Server database administrators should familiarize themselves with it.

7.1.4 The SQL Enterprise Manager

The SQL Enterprise Manager can be used to assist in performance monitoring. Figure 7.4 shows the *current activity* display which can be used to, among other things, display locking activity. Here spid 12 is blocking spid 14.

7.1.5 SQL Trace

SQL Trace is a utility that appeared in SQL Server 6.5. Once you have used SQL Trace it is hard to remember how you ever managed without it! SQL Trace runs on the server and displays in one or more windows information concerning the Transact-SQL statements sent to the server from any clients. No modification is necessary to the clients, all you have to do is create a filter on the server, set various options on the filter and run it.

Figure 7.4
*Monitoring Cur-
rent Activity In The
SQL Enterprise
Manager*

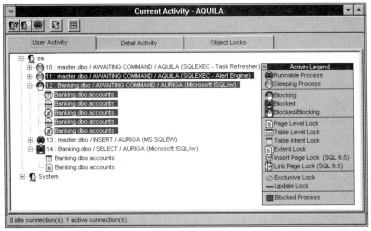

Various options are available to determine what is traced. The filter you define can trace Transact-SQL statements, connections, disconnections or remote procedure calls. All this activity can be traced or you can be more selective and filter by logins, applications and client workstations. A filter can also be set up to log any SQL statement that contains a particular string. This string can contain wildcard characters.

Performance information can be optionally captured such as start times, end times, durations, CPU usage, reads, and synchronous writes. Data can be logged to a script file or an activity log. The script file can be executed within ISQL/w as all captured information extraneous to the actual Transact-SQL statement is preceded by the ANSI SQL comment (--). This means that if a Transact-SQL statement is seen to take a long time, the script containing it can be executed with showplan on to investigate the query optimizer strategy. The activity log contains information in a format that can be easily loaded into a table using BCP for subsequent analysis and archiving.

If SQL Trace is to be used interactively it can be started from the SQL Server 6.5 Program Group where it has its own icon. To create a filter the *New Filter* dialog box must be used as shown in Figure 7.5.

After naming the filter, login ids, application names and client workstation names (host names) can be chosen if a subset of the activity is to be logged. It is possible to use a window per connection if required and to optionally record performance information. SQL Trace information can be viewed onscreen, captured to a script file or captured to a log file or any combination of these.

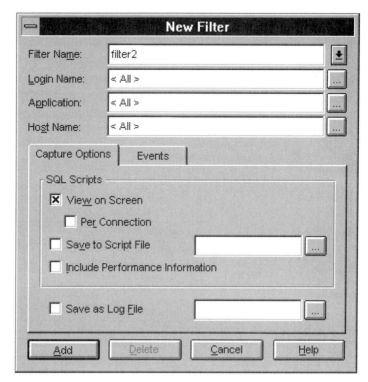

Figure 7.5
The SQL Trace New Filter Dialog Box—Capture Options Tab

As shown in Figure 7.6, the events to be captured can be set. These include all Transact-SQL statements or only a subset containing specified strings, connections, disconnections and remote procedure calls.

Once the filter has been defined it can be started. From that point on the recorded activity is displayed in a window or windows depending on the options chosen. An example is shown in Figure 7.7.

We can see the following Transact-SQL statement recorded:

```
SELECT branch_name, SUM(balance) FROM accounts, branches
WHERE accounts.branch_no = branches.branch_no
GROUP BY branch_name
```

SQL Trace has also recorded performance information for this statement. The statement execution started at 04/02/97 23:10:17.686, was of duration 19.926 seconds with CPU usage 0.972 seconds. It took 210 physical reads and 0 writes.

Figure 7.6
The SQL Trace
New Filter Dialog
Box—Events Tab

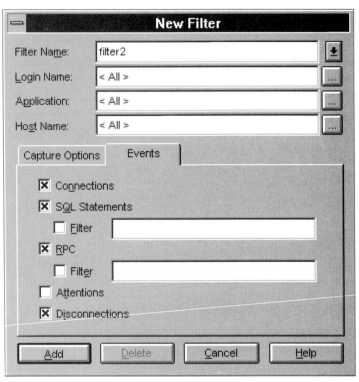

Figure 7.7
Activity Recorded
In A Filter
Window

As previously stated, the information captured in the log file can be loaded using BCP to a table. The format of the table is:

```
CREATE TABLE SQLTrace
(
Event            CHAR(12)         NOT NULL,
UserName         CHAR(30)         NOT NULL,
ID               INT              NOT NULL,
SPID             INT              NOT NULL,
```

```
StartTime         DATETIME          NULL,
EndTime           DATETIME          NULL,
Application       CHAR(30)          NOT NULL,
Data              VARCHAR(255)      NULL,
Duration          INT               NULL,
CPU               INT               NULL,
Reads             INT               NULL,
Writes            INT               NULL,
NT_Domain         VARCHAR(30)       NULL,
NT_User           VARCHAR(30)       NULL,
HostName          VARCHAR(30)       NULL,
HostProcess       INT               NULL
)
```

I find that I must sometimes change a NOT NULL to a NULL to avoid problems. For example, the column *Application* can receive a NULL value as some applications do not "announce" themselves.

A BCP statement used to load the table could be:

```
bcp PerfDB..SQLTrace in c:\sqltrace_logs\filter2.log /Usa /c /P
```

Once a mechanism has been set up to load activity information into a table various useful activities can be performed. For example, we can run a Transact-SQL statement similar to the one below to look for the Transact-SQL statements with the greatest duration:

```
SELECT
username,
application,
(duration/1000) AS 'Elapsed Time In Seconds',
(CPU/1000) AS 'CPU Time In Seconds',
reads,
writes,
hostname,
data
FROM SQLTrace WHERE
   duration > 2000 AND
   event = 'SQL'
ORDER BY duration
```

This gives the output shown below:

username	application	Elapsed Time In Seconds	CPU Time In Seconds
sa	Microsoft ISQL/w	2	1
sa	Microsoft ISQL/w	18	7
sa	Microsoft ISQL/w	52	2

reads	writes	hostname
138	0	AURIGA

```
148         0              AURIGA
1           0              AURIGA

data
------------------------------------------------------------------
SELECT branch_name, SUM(balance) FROM accounts, branches WHERE
    accounts.branch_no = branches.branch_no GROUP BY branch_name
SELECT customers.customer_no, balance FROM customers, accounts
    WHERE customers.customer_no = accounts.customer_no AND
    balance > 1000 ORDER BY balance
SELECT * FROM accounts ORDER BY balance
```

I have had to break the output into three parts so it is easily readable but it should be clear that this can quickly point to Transact-SQL statements that need further investigation. We can also obtain some simple performance statistics. We can easily find the average, minimum and maximum duration or the number of statements executed. There are many possibilities and simple statistics like this can help us spot trends.

SQL Trace can also be activated from the command line or by executing an extended stored procedure *xp_sqltrace*. With the new INSERT syntax in SQL Server 6.5, it is possible to log activity directly into a table:

```
INSERT INTO SQL Trace EXECUTE master..xp_sqltrace TRACE, @event-
    filter = 31
```

In this way, SQL Trace can be activated for a time period every day to log data straight into a table. While SQL Trace is logging to the table it can be read if the NO LOCK optimizer hint is used on the SELECT statement.

8

A Performance Tuning Checklist

Here follows a few thoughts that might be useful as an aide-mémoir when you are considering performance issues.

8.1 System Resource Usage

Establish trends. Use the Performance Monitor to monitor resources into a log file over a period of time. Get to know the normal ranges of the key counters.

When using the Performance Monitor interactively run the GUI on a machine other than the server being monitored to minimize the Performance Monitor impact.

Do not jump to conclusions. The performance problem may be caused by something you do not expect. It's easy to become convinced that something is causing a problem that isn't and to subconsciously twist the evidence to fit your theory.

Remember that system resource bottlenecks may be a symptom of something else. A classic is a disk I/O bottleneck that is caused by paging due to a memory shortage.

Do not forget that SQL Server does not automatically take advantage of the fact that you have added more physical memory. You will need to adjust the *memory* server configuration option.

Ensure that you have sufficient page file space.

Remember that, unless you have adjusted the *SMP concurrency* server configuration option, SQL Server will only release threads to one of your processors in a dual processor server.

Remove services and protocols you are not using from the server. Do not run a screen saver on the server.

Try and run SQL Server on a dedicated server with no other applications running. It is much easier to optimize SQL Server in this situation. Try and avoid installing SQL Server on a Primary Domain Controller (PDC).

Place tempdb on a fast device. In the majority of cases it is usually best not to place tempdb in memory.

Use RAID for your database and transaction log. One approach would be to use a RAID 0 stripe set for the database and mirror it. Use a dedicated disk for the transaction log and mirror it.

Hardware based RAID is faster than software based RAID. SQL Server based mirroring is likely to be discontinued at some point in the future according to the Microsoft SQL Server documentation.

Use a good quality network card. A 32-bit network card has better throughput than a 16-bit card.

8.2 Choosing Efficient Indexes

It is likely that for all but the smallest of tables the database designer will need to define indexes. These will probably consist of a clustered index with a number of nonclustered indexes. Queries benefit from lots of indexes but too many indexes will degrade the performance of Transact-SQL statements that change data such as INSERT, UPDATE and DELETE as all the indexes will need to be maintained which requires CPU and disk I/O. Even worse, many indexes being updated is likely to dramatically increase lock contention.

Consider using a clustered index when:

▶ It is desired to avoid hot spots caused by insertions into the last page of the table.

▶ The physical ordering supports the range retrievals of important queries, that is, queries that use BETWEEN and LIKE.

▶ Few duplicate values mean that an equality test (=) returns *few* rows.

▶ Many duplicate values mean that an equality test (=) returns *many* rows.

▶ The clustered index key is used in the ORDER BY clause of critical queries.

▶ The clustered index supports the GROUP BY clause of critical queries.

▶ For a given row in the outer table of a join, there are *few* rows that match in the inner table. A clustered index on the join column in the inner table will be beneficial.

For a given row in the outer table of a join, there are *many* rows that match in the inner table. A clustered index on the join column in the inner table will be beneficial.

Avoid using a clustered index on a volatile column, that is, a column that is updated frequently. This would result in the data row moving around the table repeatedly.

Consider using a nonclustered index when:

▶ Few duplicate values mean that an equality test (=) returns *few* rows.

▶ The nonclustered index key is used in the ORDER BY clause of critical queries.

▶ The nonclustered index supports the GROUP BY clause of critical queries.

▶ For a given row in the outer table of a join, there are *few* rows that match in the inner table. A nonclustered index on the join column in the inner table will be beneficial.

▶ A critical query can be efficiently covered.

Avoid using a nonclustered index when a query returns many rows, such as a range retrieval or there are many duplicate values returned by an equality test. Also, if for a given row in the outer table of a join, there are many rows that match in the inner table, a nonclustered index on the join column in the inner table will not be beneficial.

Avoid using a nonclustered index on a volatile column. The result may not be as unfavorable as using a clustered index as the data row will not move but the index will still have to be maintained.

Also consider that many applications will require the selection of a row by its primary key. This is a single row selection and therefore would normally benefit from the creation of an index containing the same columns as the primary key. As it is not common to request ranges of primary keys a nonclustered index is probably the best option. Also, rows are often inserted in ascending primary key order, especially if the primary key value is system generated, such as an invoice number or sales number. In this case, a clustered index would not eliminate the hot spot on the last page as rows would be added to the *end* of the clustered index.

Do not create an index on a column that is not very selective. An example of this would be a column that contained a status flag that contained two or three values. It is unlikely that such an index would be used by the query optimizer.

Be careful creating indexes with large keys. Fewer keys can be held in an index page resulting in many index pages and so deeper indexes. Also, if the index key is large or the first column of a composite index key is large, few steps can be held in the distribution page which reduces its efficiency.

Regularly check the levels of internal and external page fragmentation with DBCC SHOWCONTIG. Clean up by rebuilding indexes with DBCC DBREINDEX. Make sure that there is enough free space in the database to rebuild clustered indexes. Another approach is to use the Database Maintenance Wizard.

8.3 Helping the Query Optimizer

Ensure that the UPDATE STATISTICS statement is run regularly.

The query optimizer uses information held in the *sysindexes* system table. Keep it up to date with DBCC CHECKTABLE or DBCC UPDATE-USAGE.

Check to see if what you think is a search argument is considered to be a search argument by the query optimizer. Use traceflag 302 to check.

Keep a look out for showplan output that reveals that a reformatting strategy is being used. This is the query optimizer crying for help. If the query is likely to be run regularly indexes should be created to support the join.

Always test query performance on representative data. Data distributions that do not reflect live data in the production database and tables that are smaller than those in the production database could result in query plans that are different from those used when the application goes live.

Make sure that join conditions are not omitted. Always check in the case of joins involving many tables that N tables must have a minimum of $N - 1$ join conditions.

Try and establish a standard such that program documentation includes an attached showplan output. This has a number of advantages. First, it forces the SQL developer to actually run the query and obtain a showplan output which otherwise may not have happened. Second, it allows the person responsible for database performance to quickly scan the showplan output for obvious problems. Third, if the query performance suddenly degrades in the future it is easy to check if the query optimizer has adopted a new query plan. Attaching statistics IO output is also recommended.

Only use query optimizer hints if it is absolutely necessary. Revisit them to check if the plan they force is still the most efficient.

Ensure that stored procedures are not being passed a range of parameters such that a highly inefficient query plan is being used for some values.

The use of *order by, distinct* and *union* in a query usually results in a worktable being created and SQL Server having to do more work. If they can be avoided do so. It might be that you know that there are no duplicates or a sort may be performed elsewhere, perhaps on the client.

Care with updates. For your critical transactions make sure that you know how SQL Server is performing the update by using trace flag 323. It might be better to switch variable length datatypes for fixed length datatypes in some cases.

8.4 Avoiding Lock Contention

No matter how well the database is tuned to minimize disk I/O, all the database designer's efforts will be wasted if lock contention is prevalent in the database. SQL Server's locking mechanisms were described in Chapter 6 and we will now look at some general guidelines that should be followed when designing a database. Remember that in most multi-user systems that make changes to data some lock contention is unavoidable. The secret is to minimize both the locking hot spots and the length of time for which locks are held.

Rule 1: Keep transactions as short as possible.

If a transaction has placed an exclusive lock on a page or table it will keep that lock until it ends with a commit or rollback. This is also true with shared locks if the HOLDLOCK keyword is used or the repeatable read or serializable isolation level is used. The longer the lock is held, the more chance there will be that the lock blocks another user. This has a cascade effect with the blocked user blocking other users. Minimize the time the locks are held for. Do not perform work inside a transaction that can be performed outside of it.

Rule 2: Do not hold locks across user interactions.

This follows from Rule 1. Unless special considerations apply, you have a real need to and you know what you are doing, this rule should be adhered to at all costs in a multi-user environment. What does this mean? It means that transactions should be completed before control is passed back to the user and the transaction should not be *active* while the user is staring at the screen.

The reasons are obvious. The computer may process a transaction's workload in less than a second and if that transaction then completes another transaction will only have waited a fraction of a second before it acquired its locks. If, however, a transaction places locks on pages or tables and the transaction is left active while the application returns to the user, it will keep its locks while the user stares at the screen, scratches his or her head, chats to a colleague, or worse still, goes to lunch!

This could, and usually is, disastrous for system throughput and it is more commonplace than one might imagine! I know of instances where businesses have stopped trading for critical periods of time because a user went to lunch while a screen prompt sat on their workstation. This is not the user's fault. Blame resides with the application designer.

If it becomes necessary to browse data in the database it is usually far better to choose an option where locks are not held on database objects and an *optimistic locking* approach is taken, that is, the retrieved rows are not locked and, when updates are eventually performed, a check is made in the application to see if another user has changed the data since it was read. SQL Server provides various means of doing this, such as the timestamp datatype and the TSEQUAL function.

Rule 3: Try not to interleave updates and reads.

If a transaction changes data when it starts it will hold exclusive locks until it finishes. Try not to change data and then spend time reading data. If possible read the data, save all of the updates until the end of the transaction and then issue them in one short burst. This minimizes the length of time that exclusive locks are held.

Rule 4: Help the query optimizer to choose indexed access.

The query optimizer chooses whether a table scan or index is used to retrieve data. Judicious use of indexes and care when writing Transact-SQL statements will help the query optimizer to choose an indexed access. From a locking contention viewpoint this is preferable to a table scan as a table scan will lock at the table level if HOLDLOCK is used.

Rule 5: Choose indexes carefully.

We have already seen how clustered indexes can help to remove hot spots in a database table when multiple users are inserting rows. Also consider the columns chosen when creating nonclustered indexes. If, for example, a chronological key is used for the index key such as an order date and for any given day that order date will be the same for all users entering orders, contention in the index is likely to occur. This is also true if the application generates a monotonically increasing key for the order number and there is an index defined on order number. Use of insert row level locking will help in this situation.

Rule 6: Only lock as strictly as is necessary to meet your integrity requirements.

For example, only use HOLDLOCK if you require that the row you have read must not be changed by anyone else before your transaction ends.

Rule 7: Update tables in the same order throughout the application.

If one program updates table *A* and then updates table *B* and another program updates table *B* and then updates table *A* there is potential for deadlock. It is better to settle on some simple application development standard such as always updating tables in alphabetic order wherever possible. In this case, the first program will cause the second program to wait cleanly and avoid the potential deadlock scenario.

Rule 8: Perform multi-user testing before the application goes live.

This is often forgotten or left to the last minute. Whether you use sophisticated multi-user testing products or you persuade your users to stay late in the evening—do it!

We could add more rules but we have found that, if the above eight are adhered to, lock contention should be minimized.

8.5 Database Integrity

Integrity is the natural enemy of performance. The greater the data consistency requirements the more the impact on performance.

Do not implement your data integrity checks at the last minute before you go live. It does not matter whether you have used triggers or constraints, your performance is likely to suddenly drop.

Remember that, if you do not index your foreign key column(s) you are likely to experience bad performance if you delete a row from the referenced table as a table scan will probably be performed on the child table.

A table that has many foreign key constraints defined on it will have degraded insert performance as many look-ups will be performed against the referenced tables.

8.6 Database Administration Activities

Avoid running DBCC statements, UPDATE STATISTICS and backups during periods of high user activity.

Consider creating a reporting database to off-load reporting and ad hoc querying.

When loading a table using BCP try to use fast BCP to avoid logging. Consider using table backup and restore instead if moving data between servers.

Try and run BCP on the same server as the database and data file to avoid network traffic.

Creating indexes will usually impact performance on the server so it is better to perform index rebuilds during a quiet period.

Creating a nonclustered index has less impact than creating a clustered index. Clustered index creation uses an exclusive table lock whereas nonclustered index creation uses a shared table lock.

Use the *sorted_data* and *sorted_data_reorg* options if at all possible to speed up clustered index creation. The *sorted_data* option will avoid the rebuilding of nonclustered indexes.

The DBCC statements CHECKTABLE, CHECKDB and NEWALLOC can be run using the *no_index* option. SQL Server will then only check the consistency of the data pages and clustered index pages for each user table, not the nonclustered index pages.

8.7 Archiving Data

This is a requirement that usually gets left until the last minute to specify, if at all. The fact remains, however, that the larger a database gets, the more performance is likely to degrade. Many database administration tasks will also take longer such as database dumps, the update of statistics, DBCC checks and index builds.

The reasons that performance degrades include the following:

▶ Larger tables mean longer table scans.

▶ Larger tables mean deeper indexes hence more I/O to reach the table row.

▶ Longer table scans and index traversals means locks may be held for longer.

Ensure that there is an archiving strategy in place before the database gets too large.

8.8 Read Only Report Databases

If we consider a typical OLTP production system perhaps comprising many users we would probably expect to find that the system comprised of many short transactions that updated the tables in the database in real time. In reality, we would also find that there was a requirement to run long and perhaps complex reports against portions of the database. The fast response time requirements of the lightweight online transactions and the data hungry requirements of the heavyweight report transactions often do not mix well. The report transactions may often severely impact the response times of the online transactions in the production system and in the worst case may cause lock conflict.

One option is to separate these two different workloads into their own databases on their own server. This can never, in reality, be completely done as there is usually no clear break between the requirements of the two systems, but there is a case for off-loading as much reporting work as possible to another database. This also means that there will be a natural *frozen* cut-off point. If the report database is only updated overnight then it will hold the close of day position all the following day which can be a useful asset.

A separate report database can also have extra indexes added to it that would have been unacceptable in the production database for performance reasons.

Updating information in the report database could be a simple matter of restoring it from last night's backup of the OLTP database or the replication capabilities present in SQL Server could be used. Whatever the method, consider the approach of separating the different workloads as it can greatly help performance and increase flexibility.

If the report database is created from last night's backup there are also two more added bonuses. First, the fact that you are restoring your backup means that you can feel confident that your backup/restore scripts work. Second, as the database is identical to the OLTP database, those lengthy DBCC integrity checks can be run on the report database instead of the OLTP database.

8.9 Denormalization

Before considering denormalization a fully normalized database design should be your starting point. A fully normalized database design helps to avoid data redundancy and possible update anomalies but it usually results in a design that requires tables to be joined frequently.

Possible approaches to denormalization include the duplication of columns from one or more tables into another to avoid the join in a critical query. For columns that are volatile this can make updates more complex.

Another denormalization technique is to store derived data in the database. Transactions that change data can, usually by means of triggers, modify the derived data column. This can save query time as the work has already been done calculating the derived column. The downside is that the modifying transactions have additional work to do.

At the beginning of this book I said that I really enjoy tuning databases and taking an elusive performance problem, tracking it down, and fixing it. I hope that after reading this book you begin to track down your own performance bottlenecks and derive the same pleasure. May I wish you happy hunting!

Index

Related Digital Press Titles

Microsoft Exchange Server
Planning, Design, and Implementation
Tony Redmond

1996   450pp   1-55558-162-5   pb   DEC Part No: EY-U042E-DP $34.95

Migrating to the Intranet and Microsoft Exchange
Randall J. Covill

1997   250pp   1-55558-172-2   pb   DEC Part No: EY-V420E-DP $29.95

TCP/IP Explained
Philip Miller

1997   450pp   1-55558-166-8   pb   DEC Part No: EY-V416E-DP $39.95

Essential Linux
Steve Heath

1997   250pp   1-55558-177-3   pb(+ CD-ROM)   DEC Part No: EY-V446E-DP $39.95

Strategic IS/IT Planning
Ed Tozer

1995   530pp   0-7506-9666-4   pb   DEC Part No: EY-T887E-DP $51.95

Detailed information on these and all other Digital Press titles may be found in the Digital Press Catalog (Item #400). To request a copy, call 1-800-366-2665. You can also visit our web site at: http://www.bh.com/digitalpress

These books are available from all good bookstores or in case of difficulty call: 1-800-366-2665 in the U.S. or +44-1865-310366 in Europe.

E-Mail Mailing List
An e-mail mailing list giving information on latest releases, special promotions/ offers and other news relating to Digital Press titles is available. To subscribe, send an e-mail message to majordomo@world.std.com. Include in message body (not in subject line) subscribe digital-press

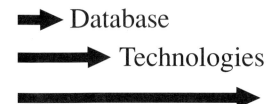 Database Technologies

Authorized by Microsoft

SQL Server 6.5 Consulting and Training

Consulting Services

⇒ Microsoft SQL Server Database Design

⇒ Microsoft SQL Server Performance and Tuning

⇒ Microsoft SQL Server Database Health Check

Training Courses

⇒ Microsoft SQL Server 6.5 Overview and Concepts (1 day)

⇒ Microsoft SQL Server 6.5 Performance and Tuning (3 days)

⇒ Microsoft SQL Server 6.5 Data Replication (2 days)

⇒ Microsoft SQL Server 6.5 Fast Track (Administration and Implementation) (5 days)

Database Technologies Limited
Nortons Farm
Kent Street,
Sedlescombe, Battle
East Sussex, United Kingdom
TN33 0SG

Voice: (44) 1424 870077
Fax: (44) 1424 870101

Email: 100114.166@compuserve.com
          KenEngland@msn.com